EMPOWERED Women

STORIES AND STUDIES OF WOMEN IN THE EARLY CHURCH

BY JANET BURTON

Tate Publishing & *Enterprises*

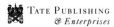 Tate Publishing
& *Enterprises*

Tate Publishing is committed to excellence in the publishing industry. Our staff of highly trained professionals, including editors, graphic designers, and marketing personnel, work together to produce the very finest books available. The company reflects the philosophy established by the founders, based on Psalms 68:11,

"The Lord Gave The Word And Great Was The Company Of Those Who Published It."

If you would like further information, please contact us:
1.888.361.9473 | www.tatepublishing.com
Tate Publishing & *Enterprises*, LLC | 127 E. Trade Center Terrace
Mustang, Oklahoma 73064 USA

Empowered Women: Stories and Studies of Women in the Early Church
Copyright © 2007 by Janet Burton. All rights reserved.

This title is also available as a Tate Out Loud product.
Visit www.tatepublishing.com for more information

No part of this publication may be reproduced, stored in a retrieval system or transmitted in any way by any means, electronic, mechanical, photocopy, recording or otherwise without the prior permission of the author except as provided by USA copyright law.

Unless otherwise noted, all Scriptures are taken from The Holy Bible, New International Version, Copyright 1973, 1978, 1984, by the International Bible Society. Use by permission of Zondervan Publishing House. The "NIV" and "New International Version" trademarks are registered in the United States Patent and Trademark Office by International Bible Society.

Scripture quotations marked "KJV" are taken from the *Holy Bible, King James Version*, Cambridge, 1769. Used by permission. All rights reserved.

The opinions expressed by the author are not necessarily those of Tate Publishing, LLC.

Book design copyright © 2007 by Tate Publishing, LLC. All rights reserved.
Cover design & interior design by Janae J. Glass
Published in the United States of America

ISBN: 978-1-6024707-5-X
07.01.23

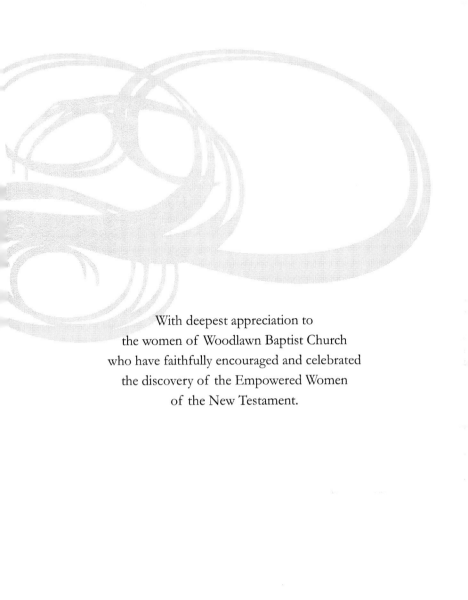

With deepest appreciation to
the women of Woodlawn Baptist Church
who have faithfully encouraged and celebrated
the discovery of the Empowered Women
of the New Testament.

TABLE OF CONTENTS

A Letter to Readers, By Way of Introduction 10

PART I: WOMEN IN THE PENTECOST ERA

Chapter 1 18
  EMPOWERED: The Women of Pentecost
  Mary Magdalene, Joanna, Salome, Sapphira, and others serve at the house of Mary in Jerusalem during the days following Pentecost (Acts 2 through 5).

Chapter 2 38
  NEW FRIENDS, NEW CHALLENGES: Choosing the Seven to Serve Widows
  The Jerusalem church women minister to needy widows as the church continues to grow and diversify (Acts 6 and 7).

PART II: WOMEN HELP TO MOVE THE GOSPEL FORWARD

Chapter 3 58
  A FRIEND IN NEED: Tabitha, Raised from the Dead
  Friends intervene to bring Tabitha (Dorcas) back to her life of ministry (Acts 9:32–43).

Chapter 4 80
  BREAKTHROUGH IN CAESAREA: Cornelius' Family Welcomes Peter
  Cornelius' wife and daughter help bridge the way for the Gospel to come into the Gentile world in Joppa (Acts 10 and 11).

Chapter 5 97
  ANGEL AT THE GATES: Rhoda Answers Peter's Knock
  Mary and Rhoda provide refuge for the church in their home, as persecution intensifies (Acts 12:1–19).

PART III: WOMEN OF THE ASIA EXPANSION

Chapter 6 .... .114
  LETTERS TO MARY: John Mark Writes Home
  Mary and Rhoda receive reports from John Mark about Paul and Barnabas' mission to Cyprus (Acts 12:25–13:13).

Chapter 7 .... .133
  A LEGACY AND A PROMISE: Lois and Eunice Prepare Timothy
  The faith of a mother and grandmother play a key role in the rebuilding of Paul's mission team (Acts 14:8–20 and 2 Timothy 1:5–7).

PART IV: WOMEN OF MACEDONIA AND GREECE

Chapter 8 .... .155
  EARTH-SHAKING EVENTS: Lydia Hosts the Mission Team
  Lydia's openness of heart and home helps Paul to begin a strong church in Philippi (Acts 16:11–40).

Chapter 9 .... .170
  GETTING TO KNOW GOD: Damaris Believes
  Among the pagan altars of Athens, a few find the Unknown God, and choose to believe the truth (Acts 17).

Chapter 10 .... .188
  PARTNERS IN MINISTRY: Priscilla Joins Paul's Mission
  In Corinth and later in Ephesus, Paul finds strength and partnership with Priscilla and Aquila (Acts 18 and 19).

Chapter 11 .... **208**
   SISTER, SERVANT, SAINT: Phoebe Carries the Letter to Rome
   Amid the struggles of the church to survive against persecution, Phoebe helps preserve God's Word for the Romans (Acts 20:1–5 and Romans 16:1–2).

PART V: WOMEN OF THE PRISON YEARS

Chapter 12 .... **228**
   FOUR GIRLS WHO PROPHECIED: Philip's Family Hosts the Travelers
   Philip's daughters manifest gifts of the Spirit, including the gift of prophecy (Acts 21:1–14).

Chapter 13 .... **246**
   LOYALTY AND ROYALTY: Philip's Daughters Witness Paul's Courage
   During Paul's Caesarean imprisonment, and his witness before royalty, Philip's family ministers to his needs (Acts 21–26).

Chapter 14 .... **262**
   LETTERS FROM PRISON: Apphia, Empowered to Forgive
   Paul's team nurtures a runaway slave and sends him home to find forgiveness (Acts 28:11–31 and Philemon).

A LETTER TO READERS
By Way of Introduction

Sequels carry certain "givens." *Empowered Women: Stories and Studies of Women in the Early Church*, is somewhat a continuation of my earlier book, *A Touch of Jesus: Stories and Studies of Women in the Life of Jesus*. As such, it picks up the Bible's story as told in the Gospels, and carries it through the narrative of Acts. *A Touch of Jesus* followed the life and ministry of Jesus: how he established his Kingdom and commissioned his Disciples to continue the work. *Empowered Women* begins with the coming of the Holy Spirit—the Spirit of Jesus—at Pentecost, and follows his work through the women and the leaders of the Early Church. Both books tell the story through the experiences of the women in Scripture. *A Touch of Jesus* is a telling of the Gospel from a woman's view, and *Empowered Women* is the story of Acts from a woman's view.

We call them *empowered women* for a good reason, so we should begin by defining *empowerment* as it is used in this book. Women today are encouraged to seek empowerment. Some see empowerment as equality in the workplace: breaking the "glass ceiling," being as dynamic as their male counterparts. Others look for empowerment within themselves: realization of their full potential through better self-understanding. Another view of female empowerment holds that financial freedom through smart investing will arm women for success. Yet others pursue advanced professional degrees to achieve status and value in society. Some seek empowerment quietly, while others crusade for it. Empowerment wears many faces, and boasts many gurus and devotees. Many such pursuits are worthy, but these are not the kind of empowerment we espouse in this book. We speak here of *spiritual empowerment: that adventure of being filled with God's Spirit, and gifted to serve him in his Kingdom.*

In all of the Gospels and in Acts, the women are in the background; but always they are vital to the story and to the work of the Kingdom. Women have always been—and will always be—critical to the story in the Bible. Who were the *empowered women* of Acts? We have picked up with those who were there at Jesus' resurrection: Mary Magdalene, Salome, Joanna. But quickly we were introduced to some newcomers, like Sapphira. As the narrative developed with the choosing of the Seven, and Peter's early missions to the Greek-speaking Jews and some Gentiles, we became good friends with Tabitha, and Cornelius' wife and daughter (we think he must have had them).

Before long, the story returned to Mary's house at Jerusalem, her servant girl, Rhoda, and her son, John Mark. That gave us the bridge to Paul's missions to Cyprus and Asia Minor, where we met Eunice and Lois. When Paul moved into Macedonia, we stayed a while with Lydia and her friends; and when he ventured southward into Greece, we encountered Damaris, Priscilla, and then Phoebe. As circumstances became more difficult, and Paul experienced imprisonment in Jerusalem, Caesarea, and Rome, we included Philip's four daughters; and finally met Apphia, to whom Paul wrote from his Roman house arrest. Fourteen encounters in all, each with a fascinating story behind it, and each full of insights and truths for women today.

As you read the lists above you may have found a few less familiar names. It is our hope that those will become real to you, as they have to us, through *Empowered Women*. As with *A Touch of Jesus,* we have created a story—a fiction vignette—for each chapter, which is designed to bring those women to life and point you more deeply into the Bible background for their lives. *The goal of Empowered Women is to help today's women better identify with the mission of Christ and his church, through studying the role of our sisters in the Early Church.* Readers who are familiar with *A Touch of Jesus* will find this book similar in the format, with carefully researched fiction vignettes, followed by deeper study of the Bible passages on which they are based.

But *Empowered Women* differs from the first book because Acts is different than the Gospels in significant ways. In Acts the story moves very quickly. The dynamics are sometimes breathtaking, and almost unbelievable. We encounter angel visits, stonings, riots, threats, plots, shipwreck—all the drama of Peter's and Paul's missions. Also Peter and Paul are different personalities than Jesus, so some of the gentleness is lost in this book. Another contrast: the women in the gospels often came out of brokenness, seeking healing. Acts as we know, is a book of action, and the women therein are generally strong women of action. And finally, whereas the Gospels focus mostly on the three short years of Jesus' ministry lived in one small country, Acts ranges over thirty years and much of the northern Mediterranean world. In *Empowered Women* we are dealing with multiple cultures, and an advancing and changing empire.

Researching this was often challenging. We have relied on

many sources to become familiar with the lives of women in First Century Greek and Roman society. Our first source is always the Bible, and we are heavily indebted to *The New International Version Study Bible*, which is rich in footnotes. It sent us searching through cross-references and related passages. One cannot adequately study Paul's journeys without studying also his letters to the churches. Understanding the stories often required our formulating a mosaic of many Bible passages. Another dependable source for us was the *Zondervan Pictorial Bible Dictionary*. What a wealth of help! Each location named in *Acts,* each church, each person, each vocation, and all the related facts, directed us to articles in that volume.

Beyond those we leaned heavily on the credibility of Dr. Frank Stagg's *The Book of Acts: The Early Struggle for an Unhindered Gospel,* and on our old friend Dr. William Barclay and his commentary, *The Acts of the Apostles.* We dabbled some in Dr. Merrill C. Tenny's *New Testament Times,* an old acquaintance from college and seminary days, and several other background books and commentaries. To familiarize our minds with Greece and Rome we researched extensively from both *The Cambridge History of Ancient Greece* and *The Oxford Illustrated History of Greece and the Hellenistic World.* Finally *Life in Ancient Rome* by F. R. Crowell helped to bring that city to life for us. Even the *National Geographic* articles on Rome helped. From all of this we hope that our stories are credible, historical fiction, and our Bible background true and reliable.

The process of writing a book of this nature begins with Bible study and research, but it goes on from there into intuition and inspiration. We strive always to work out of a prayerful mind, continually asking the Lord to guide us into insights and truths. These women had to become my friends—they had to speak to me—before I could interpret them to you, the readers. Fifty years in ministry with Jack came into play in every chapter. One cannot study the women of Acts without seeing our sisters in the churches of today. I have taken personal privilege in sharing some precious relationships from our ministry with you throughout this book. As you discover those, make your own parallels to the women in your own life—the *empowered women* of today.

No author is an island. I am so indebted to my pastor husband Jack for his encouragement, his sharp mind, and critical eye. One funny story will illustrate. In developing Priscilla's vignette, I was at a loss to build an early morning setting in her kitchen. It seemed logical to me that she would drink hot coffee on a cold Corinthian morning, and serve it to her houseguests. Jack was highly amused. "Janet!" he admonished, "coffee was unknown to them! It wasn't well known until after the 1600s." That sent me quickly to the encyclopedia, to discover that he was absolutely correct (as usual). Nor did they have hot tea yet, poor creatures. Whatever did they drink to warm up on a winter morning? We *do know* that most Mediterranean homes relied heavily on a brew of wheat porridge as a main part of their diet; so, embarrassed at my naivety, I quickly revised the story. That is just one of so many times that Jack rescued me from my fantasies. He is my truest friend and supporter and the only reason these books ever see a publisher.

Another great help to this book has been our son, John Burton, who is always one of my technical advisors. For us "grandmas" who came up in the age new to automatic washing machines and television, the world of computers will always hold great mysteries. While we have a working knowledge, the processes of creating a master document, and adding necessary headers and footers, always requires some coaching. John is a writer himself, and always willing to advise and explain. Countless phone calls and encouragements, and a trip in from Phoenix, went into the assisting. I thank these two especially, but many others also, including Wayne Shipp, a true friend who handled many tricky technical details—often on an emergency basis! The enthusiastic readers of *A Touch of Jesus* spurred me on to do this second book. (Several bought copies for every woman on their Christmas list!) My women friends at Woodlawn Baptist Church convinced me that this sequel book had value. Heartfelt thanks to every one of these mentioned.

My most-favorite verse from the book of Acts must be Acts 17:27–28, a part of Paul's address to the Areopagus on the character of God. *"He is not far from each one of us. For in him we live and move and have our being."* It is my prayer that, as you read the stories and studies in *Empowered Women,* you will find God that near to you. I ask him to walk with you and talk with you through his Spirit as you study. I pray that, in the reading, you, too, will find yourself *empowered* for his work.

Blessings,
Janet Burton

A Note about Group Study

Empowered Women lends itself very well to a group study situation. Warm inspiration can grow as women hear the fiction stories and then delve into their Bibles for deeper understanding. Valuable sharing and insights come from discussion and note-taking together. Life changing decisions and personal growth often result. An *Empowered Women Study Guide,* complete with interactive lesson plans for leaders and worksheets which may be duplicated for each attendee, is available from the author's web site: www.burtonministries.org. *Visit us there!*

PART I

Women In The Pentecost Era

Chapter 1
EMPOWERED: The Women of Pentecost

Chapter 2
NEW FRIENDS, NEW CHALLENGES:
Choosing the Seven to Serve Widows

EMPOWERED
The Women of Pentecost

Acts 2:38–5:11

The three old friends were going through familiar motions in Mary's kitchen, scraping bowls, storing leftovers, washing vessels. Only this time the chore was unbelievably larger than before. Newcomers were hurrying to be helpful, snatching up drying cloths, bringing dishes from the upstairs tables, asking necessary questions, trying hard to catch on to the systems of a new kitchen.

"However do you ladies keep up with all this work?" wailed Jessicah, wiping her sweaty forehead with the sleeve of her wilted tunic. "I never saw so many mouths to feed in one place! And so many dirty dishes!"

"Catch that pot of warm water from the hearth and switch with me," Salome called over the noise. "We've never had this big a crowd before, Jessicah. We're all struggling to keep up!" She turned to help her new friend with the very heavy container. "Careful! I'm not as strong as I used to be, and I don't want to spill on anyone."

"The dinner crowds have tripled since Pentecost," Mary Magdalene explained with wide eyes and a gentle shake of her head. "We're all thrilled, but it surely has made a difference in our women's work! Salome and Joanna and I are very glad for your help—all of you who have pitched in with us today." Her eyes scanned the room with a grateful smile as she reached for one last stack of dirty serving bowls.

"We need to ask Mary what we should do to get ready

for tonight's late supper," Joanna ventured. "We've just about eaten her and her family out of house and home here, and the crowds just keep coming. In another five hours we'll need to have the next meal on the tables, and some of the food is running low."

The Magdalene nodded toward Rhoda, the family's cheerful servant girl. "Honey, would you find your mistress and ask what plans she might suggest for this evening's supper?" Then, looking at the exhausted faces around her she continued apologetically, "I wonder if a couple of you would mind stepping out into the courtyard and grinding another couple of measures of grain so we can bake again. I'll see if one of the men will restart the oven. It goes without saying that we will need another supply of flatbread by night."

"Let me help with that," Naomi volunteered quickly. "I'm new, and I don't know all the places to put these clean dishes, but I sure know how to grind flour and make bread. Where does Mary store the grain?"

"Thanks, Naomi—it's kind of you to offer," Mary Magdalene responded with a tired smile. "Her grain is stored in that shed behind the acacia tree, and the mill should be standing beside it. Maybe you can find some shade and a little breeze for the work. But cinch the bags up tightly to keep out the varmints." Turning back to the others she suggested, "Let's all sit down a while, maybe get a drink of cool milk or water, and put up our feet. Can we take a break, Salome?" she asked her trusted friend who nodded agreeably.

"I'll go help Naomi," Judith chimed in, and was quickly out the door, with Jessicah right on her heels—both glad for the fresh air.

"Do I need to be doing something?" It was Sapphira, just coming in with an unexpected load of wine cups on a platter. "I found this one more batch of stuff upstairs—it needs washing."

"Help yourself, my friend," Joanna replied, motioning her toward the fresh washing pot. "And thank you so much for pitching in with the chores."

"Oh, I don't mind," Sapphira reassured. "But next time I think I'll bring along a couple of my servant girls to help us. And maybe Ananias will let us bring a lamb for the spit. This is just a huge crowd of people to cook for!"

"Things have really grown fast since Pentecost," Mary Magdalene said again. "I think the church has multiplied twenty—maybe twenty-five—times over! We had no idea what Jesus meant when he promised us Power from on high."

"Actually, Mary, we've multiplied about forty times over!" Joanna explained. "Cuza was just figuring it on the abacus last night. He and Matthew have been trying to make some sense of it all. With this last influx of people after Peter and John healed the crippled man at the Beautiful Gate, we now have over five thousand believers."

"Five thousand!" Joanna repeated, almost not believing it. "Well, thank goodness they don't all eat here at Mary's house! Whatever would we do?" she wailed in mock dismay.

"Five thousand," the Magdalene echoed in amazement. "No one can doubt the Power has come. And those Twelve—it's nice to have twelve again, isn't it?—have turned from hunted criminals to almost celebrities overnight! It just boggles the mind."

"Well, Sapphira," Salome picked up the earlier conversation and addressed her new friend, "we are very glad to have you and the other new believers to help us with this workload. We could not make it otherwise."

Sapphira shook water off the last of the cups. "It's the very least we can do. You all have been so kind to take us in and accept us. Tell me, has Peter always been such a good preacher?"

Joanna, Salome, and Mary Magdalene cut their eyes to each other and burst out laughing. "Oh, how funny!" Joanna answered. "No, Sapphira. Peter is a changed man since Pentecost. We are all so amazed—and so very pleased—with the way God is using him. He just seems to know exactly what to say and when to say it—and that's quite a change for him," and she laughed again at the memories.

"Some day we'll fill you in on all that," Mary Magdalene promised.

"Some day when we don't have a hundred mouths to feed!" added Joanna. "Peter is a wonderful man, but to see the transformation that has taken place in him these last few days just thrills us all. If we can't have Jesus with us, then Peter is the next best thing, I'd say."

"Ananias and I were so sorry to have missed the big Pentecost excitement," Sapphira complained. "We were at the farm taking care of some business that came up. We usually try to make all the important feasts, but it just didn't work out for us. So we missed the whole experience—the fire falling, and the baptizing of the three thousand. Everyone was telling us about it when we got back into town that night. But we did get in on the second great event a few days ago, when Peter and John healed the cripple at Beautiful Gate. That convinced us, and we became believers right away. Ananias said, 'Anything that touches that many people must be from God. Wife, we've *got* to join them!' So we did—that very day!"

"So many came, but we are very glad to have all of you," Joanna assured her.

"This Barnabas," Sapphira ventured, "is he also new to the group?"

"Not actually," Mary Magdalene explained. "He's a relative of our house mistress, Mary. They are cousins, I think. He is from Cyprus, so has not lived here all his life. But we really do like him."

"Ananias and I were so surprised at the large gift he gave," Sapphira pressed the conversation. "It must have been a large piece of land that he sold. And—did I hear right—he gave the *entire amount* to the offering? Didn't keep back even enough for a rainy day?" She waved her drying rag in emphasis as she asked.

"That's what we hear, Sapphira," Joanna answered with enthusiasm. "I think it may be the largest gift given to date. Others have given what they could in food and money—all of us have, in fact—and a few others have sold land. But Barnabas surprised us all with such a large gift. He gave it just to help this struggling new group. I guess he felt that God was telling him to do it."

"Well, it was generous, I agree," Sapphira responded. "But Ananias and I could not believe he didn't even put away some for a rainy day."

"Did I hear my name?" The deep male voice startled

them out of their kitchen talk, as Ananias opened the courtyard door. "Is that my chatty wife I hear talking a-furlong-a-minute in there?"

Hearing him Sapphira called, "Yes, Husband, it's me—talking as usual. What brings you to the kitchen? I know you aren't looking for dirty dishes to wash," she mocked with a saucy grin.

"Let's get going, Sapphira. I have a man to meet at the farm before sundown, and it's getting late. If we are going to make it we will have to leave now," and he motioned her to hurry.

"Well, ladies, I guess I'm done here," Sapphira responded. "Sorry I can't be here to help with the supper meal, but we'll be back—probably tomorrow," and she hurried out the door.

"Thanks again for your help," they chorused as she left, and then all found a place to sit down.

"She seems nice," Joanna said, pouring herself a cup curds. "Sapphira, I mean. She tries to fit in and do her share of the chores."

Mary nodded and Salome agreed. "Her husband seems to be fitting in well with the men also. He has a lot business experience, and that should help us. So much is happening so fast, all our heads are spinning."

"And they seem to be people of some means," Joanna observed with a little caution. "They talk about their business matters, and she mentioned her servant girls."

"Well, we can certainly use some more people of means," Salome mumbled under her breath. "All these mouths to feed are not cheap. Barnabas' gift should keep us going for a while longer." Looking around she asked, "Did Rhoda ever come back with Mary's plans for supper? I can't believe we have to fix another meal before night!"

"And three more tomorrow—and three more the next day—and . . ." Mary Magdalene was showing the stress of the week. "But," she added quickly, "this is how Jesus wants it. He sent the Power, and he began the Kingdom. And if it means extra dishes to do—we can handle that until he returns."

"Funny thing," mused Joanna.

"What's that?" asked her friends.

"Jesus told us to go into the world with the message—into Jerusalem, and all the towns of Judea, and even to our unfriendly neighbors in Samaria, and beyond to places where we've never been. But on Pentecost it seemed the whole world just came to us!"

"And they were all hungry!" Mary quipped. "I wonder where it will all go from here. I wonder what will happen next?"

The door creaked and Rhoda's youthful form bounded in from the courtyard. "Shalom, ladies," she began, catching a deep breath. "My mistress says she'll have the servants put two more lambs on the spits for tomorrow; and she wonders if you would mind beginning two big pots of leeks, barley, and lentils with the leftovers of lamb from dinner for this evening's savory stew. Miss Mary says we just got two bushels of fresh oranges from Zacchaeus in Jericho—his servant brought them for our supper—and she thinks Joseph will bring extra wine and olives from his place when he comes. Now me and Dinah are off to the well for fresh water. And my mistress told John Mark to milk the nannies for supper." With all that said, she bowed and was gone again in just a blink.

The three old friends caught hands and began to pull each other up from their benches. "So much for the break," sighed Salome. "I guess we'd better get back at it. It will be time for afternoon prayers in just a little while." She reached up on the wall for two bunches of dried onions, and began chopping them for stew. "Praise be to Jehovah who keeps the rains coming and vegetables growing!"

BEHIND THE SCENE
A Study of Acts 2:38–5:11

Pentecost from a Woman's View

What fun to think into the world of women who lived the Pentecost experience: empowered, involved, excited, exhausted. Whatever would it be like to experience a church that grew from 120 believers to 3,000 in just one incredible day! And on to 5,000 in just a few more weeks? Acts 2:44–47 gives us precious clues.

> "All the believers were together and had everything in common. Selling their possessions and goods, they gave to anyone as he had need. Everyday they continued to meet together in the temple courts. They broke bread in their homes and ate together with glad and sincere hearts, praising God and enjoying the favor of all the people. And the Lord added to their number daily those who were being saved."

Someone had to have been on the kitchen crew! We suspect it was the same group of gals we met in the Gospel stories—the ones who followed to the cross and the burial, and discovered the empty tomb—who were present at Pentecost. That would be Jesus' mother, her sister Salome, Mary Magdalene, Joanna, the *"other Mary,"* and probably a few more whose names we do not have. But along with them we can visualize some newcomers—women with gifts of helping and hospitality, also unnamed. So we have chosen a few probable names: Jessicah, Naomi, Judith. One day we will know them—our foremothers on the Kitchen Committee. And, if there are church dinners in heaven, we'll grab up drying towels and join them in their tasks!

And someone's home had to be opened for the occasion. It is commonly held that it was the home of Mary, mother of John Mark, as told in Acts 12:12. Actually, many such homes were made available among the believers, but we know Mary's to be one of the first. All these Marys! It's hard to keep them straight. Five are most often mentioned:

- Mary, mother of Jesus, from Nazareth;
- Mary Magdalene, the prominent leader of women;
- The "other Mary," also thought to be mother of James and Joses, and the wife of Cleopas;
- Mary of Bethany, sister of Lazarus and Martha; and
- Mary, mother of John Mark, in whose home the disciples and early believers often gathered.

Where did the food come from? Who grew it? Who gave it? Who cooked it? Who cleaned up the mess? We've made some educated guesses, but there are no certain answers. We just know it happened. Where crowds of believers gather there are bound to be meals and messes. But . . .

Not Just In the Kitchen!

Let's not leave the impression that the women were only involved behind the scenes, cooking, serving, cleaning, and running the households—as vital as that was to the times. Peter went far out of his way in his Pentecost sermon to explain that the coming of the Holy Spirit in power was not just a male phenomenon. Listen to Acts 2:17–18, where he quotes from the Prophet Joel:

> "'In the last days,' God says, 'I will pour out my Spirit on all people. Your sons and daughters will prophesy, your young men will see visions, your old men will dream dreams. Even on my servants, both men and women, I will pour out my Spirit in those days, and they will prophesy.'"

God nowhere indicates that any of his spiritual gifts and power is given only to men. Paul in his later listings of the gifts never designates them as gender specific. (Check out Romans 12:5–6 and following, and 1 Corinthians 12:27 and following.) The gifts of helping, teaching, and hospitality are placed right along side of the gifts of prophecy, administration, and tongues. And in each place Paul carefully states that *we all* have been given gifts, and *we all* are parts of the same functioning body of believers.

Does this present a dilemma for us? If the women were free to receive and use the power of the Holy Spirit—even to prophesy or preach—why do we show them still in the kitchen in our story? Maybe part of the answer lies in a look at our congregations today. Gender roles still apply in modern church life. One hour we find the women teaching, serving on committees, leading groups, even preaching. But in the very next they are bringing covered dishes, keeping the babies, fixing the altar flowers, cleaning up the kitchen. In real life, women blend their spiritual gifts with the functions of life—very smoothly, very admirably. And so it has been from the beginning. As we travel through our study of Acts, we will encounter Lydia, a business woman who was a church starter. After her, Priscilla, who partnered with her husband in church leadership and teaching. Then Phoebe, a deaconess whom Paul trusted to carry his letter to Rome. And, later still, the four daughters of Philip who were prophets. We see that the gifting and the chores blended gently and naturally, and that is how it still should be today.

The filling of God's Holy Spirit does not come to us to take us out of our work-a-day lives, but rather to *empower* us to live and witness in them. Women have always blended the spiritual and the routine. Picture primitive women—way before the First Century—back even to Native American culture. The men dug their kivas, and retreated to dream their visions, and talk their wisdom. Women, by contrast, could not get free of the babies, the grinding, the weaving, the cooking. No such respite was provided for them. So women have grown up multi-tasking, working at their work in the office, the school, the home, while blending it with their spiritual service. *Empowerment comes within the toil, the doing, the living of life responsibly; not separate from it.*

A few women may choose to withdraw, and take the

vows of the convent. Most live by managing the tension of serving God within the pressures of life. Jesus prayed for women when he said, *"My prayer is not that you take them out of the world but that you protect them from the evil one . . . Sanctify them by the truth; your word is truth."* (That is part of his John 17 prayer, verses 15–16.) And so we live in the world, and use our spiritual gifts in very practical ways. We pray with dish towels in our hands. We witness in the coffee break room at work. We minister to a troubled friend by cell phone as we watch our children at soccer practice, or fold the clothes. It is the *Presence,* not the absence that matters. The *submission—*the *availability—*when an unexpected opportunity happens. That is how *empowerment* looks for the woman who walks with God.

So while we enjoy thinking about the First Century gals on kitchen duty, let's also remember that they left their drying rags at the appropriate times and joined into the witnessing, the sharing of Good News, the prayers, and all phases of the life of the church. And we can look forward to the later stories in this book which will highlight women using their leadership gifts also.

Who Told Their Story?

We come back to revisit our good friend, Dr. Luke. After all the pros and cons are trotted out, most everyone believes that Paul's physician, Luke, the Greek who traveled on the second, third, and last missions, was the historian who penned this book. And from his first volume (Luke 1:3–4) we can know something of how he did it.

"Therefore, since I myself have carefully investigated everything from the beginning, it seemed good also to me to write an orderly account for you, most excellent Theopholus, so that you may know the certainty of the things you have been taught."

Luke was a scientist, and he investigated the facts before writing. It is curious that he did not live in Judea during these early days of the church—he joined up about fifteen years later. The stories of Paul's journeys likely came from Luke's travel diary. But how did he know in vivid detail the early events of Acts 1 to 15 which preceded his time? Most scholars believe he learned by interviewing others who remembered or had kept written accounts. Think about men like Matthew, who was a bookkeeper; and Cuza the husband of Joanna, who was Herod's accountant and manager. God has his ways of preserving the record for us. Luke was an important person in that process.

And Luke had a personal stake in the story. The main thrust of Acts is foretold in Acts 1:8: *"But you will receive power when the Holy Spirit comes on you; and you will be my witnesses in Jerusalem, and in all Judea and Samaria, and to the ends of the earth."* The church was empowered for this purpose: to carry the Good News of salvation through Jesus to all people groups. Much of the value of the book of Acts comes in the story of how Christianity freed itself from Judaism's legalistic ownership, and became the Gospel for all people. Luke, being a Greek and not a Jew, was one who received the Good News and believed. It is no wonder that he felt the telling to be such a sacred trust, and paid the price of authorship.

Writing takes time, though—especially when it is done

by hand with quills and homemade inks, on imported papyrus or skin scrolls. Luke probably found that time on the long ship journeys with Paul, and in the days of waiting while Paul was imprisoned for four years in Caesarea and Rome. Paul found time to write, and Luke probably joined him in his efforts. It was too important—too exciting—to ignore. And he was inspired.

The Deeper Messages

Interesting as the kitchen scenes would be, we must move on, looking for the deeper messages of the book of Acts. While our purpose is to highlight the empowered women from the exciting Acts narratives—reading between the lines and using intuition to enhance the facts which Luke recorded—women's stories are not why the book was written. What are we meant to discover and learn from these earliest, purest views of the fledgling church? Two things stand out in bold face: **how the believers responded to the Power;** and **what their message was in their world.**

We love the details of Early Church life. (Take time here to read Acts 2:41–47 to refresh your mind of the facts.) Faced with this huge influx of uninitiated believers, all on different levels of knowledge and experience with their faith, the emphasis was on *the Apostles' teaching*. Everyone had to be brought up to speed. Some had known and followed Jesus. Some witnessed the crucifixion and knew of the resurrection. It was the talk of the town, much as the authorities tried to squelch the story. A few had experienced personal miracles. Visualize the blind man from the Pool of Siloam, the leper from Samaria, the blind beggar of Jericho, and a host of others. Some had been fed when Jesus broke the five loaves and two fishes in Galilee. Others had listened to the Sermon on the Mount. But many had little or no background. The Twelve (now that Matthias had been selected by lot to replace Judas) were kept busy just retelling the stories, preaching the truths, explaining the Old Testament prophecies. Teaching was the priority of those days.

A close second, however, was *fellowship*. Imagine trying to learn all those names, become familiar with everyone's story, make new friends, and keep up with the old ones (with no computers or cell phones)! It was all so new, nobody wanted to go home. They planned and ate many of their meals together—the first covered dish events which we all still imitate. Homes were opened, upper rooms and rooftops made available. And the Temple courts and porches were utilized. Daily they gathered on Solomon's Porch, and held open air gospel meetings. What exciting days and nights!

Not a lot of thought was being given to the future. Their belief was that Jesus would return quickly, so . . . they began to sell out, and to give what they could for the astronomical costs of feeding and clothing these thousands who were continuing to come.

But in all of this the Apostles worked hard to see that the congregation did not lose sight of who they were: Believers in Jesus Christ. *Worship, prayer, praise*—these are mentioned again and again. They could not turn to the physical Jesus, but they continually went to him in prayer. It was as though he was still there—a Reality and a Presence that we also yearn to know. They talked to him, sang to him, thanked him, blessed him, remembered him in the bread and the

wine. Those were precious days of growth in every realm.

And, when they preached, what did they preach? We have actual sermons—these first ones mostly from Peter. (Check out Acts 2:22–24 and 32–33.) Somebody was taking notes! *Always the message, though adapted to the occasion, centered on Jesus—who he was and what he had done.* His life of good works, his sacrificial death for our sin, his undeniable resurrection and return to glory, his promise to return—these were the heart of the Good News, and they preached it over and over, every day and at every opportunity. And we still preach it today.

The invitation was the same, too: *Repent and be baptized in the name of Jesus, and you will be forgiven and receive the Holy Spirit as we have.* Do you take comfort in knowing that the message and the call are clearly preserved in any evangelical church today? That's how you and I came to faith, and we can thank the Early Church for being faithful in keeping the message pure.

Genuine and Counterfeit Faith

It never takes long. Satan just can't stand it when Christians are *empowered,* and excited, and growing in their faith. He's the master at finding a willing victim who will look for a shortcut to glory—a path to personal power within the family of believers. And he found it in Ananias and Sapphira, newcomers who wanted to belong. Their sad tale actually begins in Acts 4:36–37, when Joseph (nicknamed Barnabas, or Encourager) sold a plot of land and brought the money for the Apostles to use on church expenses.

Barnabas calls to mind Mary of Bethany, who broke her

expensive vial of nard to perfume the head and feet of Jesus at supper. Barnabas' extravagance leaves us breathless and asking, *"Could I make a sacrifice like that?"* Most of us are not millionaires, or Michael Dells—we just make do. A few of us have extra and give extra. But for "regular folks" to cash in our retirement funds, or sell our investment properties, and give the cash outright to the church!? Few have the faith and abandon to do that kind of generous giving.

Everyone was impressed—and blessed. Ananias and Sapphira were right there, impressed—but also jealous for the glory. And so they imitated Barnabas, only in a counterfeit sort of way. (Read Acts 5:1–11 with fear and trembling.) They, too, sold their plot of land, and brought the money to the Apostles. But, wanting the glory without the full sacrifice, they told a whopping lie. They pretended to be giving the entire amount, but actually held back some for themselves. It wasn't the holding back that was bad: it was their money, after all, and they could decide how much of it they would give. A tithe would have been good. The problem was the lie, the deceit, the greed for glory and power. Peter put it bluntly: *"How is it that Satan has so filled your heart that you have lied to the Holy Spirit . . . ?"*

Just like David had done generations before, Peter hit the nail on the head. *"Against you, and you only, I have sinned and done what is evil in your sight"* (Psalm 51:4). And God was justified in his judgment, because the church was so new and vulnerable, and such deception could not be allowed to go unpunished. It was a severe tragedy, long to be remembered. Ananias and Sapphira taught the church a great and costly lesson that day: God is not to be mocked. Honesty is required. Integrity is valued. It is the only way believers can live together in trust and work together on the vital mission we have been assigned: taking the Good News to a lost world.

What Kept Them On Task?

It wasn't just the Ananias and Sapphira calamity that upset things among these new believers. We have already alluded to the earlier story of Peter and John healing the crippled man at the Beautiful Gate of the Temple. (Find it in Acts 3:1–10.) Right under the noses of the priests and temple guards, loudly calling on the name and power of Jesus Christ of Nazareth, these two brave men fixed a problem others had been walking past day after day. They healed a man who could not walk. It stirred up no little excitement. And coming right on the heels of the Pentecost revival a few days before, caused great concern in the halls of traditional Judaism.

Seeing the gathered, admiring crowd around them, Peter again seized on the opportunity to preach Jesus to the people (Acts 3:12 and following). With his usual blunt approach he laid out the situation clearly.

> "You handed him over to be killed, and you disowned him before Pilate, though he had decided to let him go. You disowned the Holy and Righteous One and asked that a murderer be released to you. You killed the author of life, but God raised him from the dead. We are witnesses of this."

He didn't hold anything back, did he? Is it any wonder that a second revival broke out, and by the end of that occasion, the believers had grown to number about 5,000? Peter and

John paid for their boldness—they spent the night in jail. They were called to account before the rulers (where, by the way, Peter again took the opportunity to preach!) and they were threatened and warned soundly not to speak of this Jesus person again in public. Scary stuff, considering that this was the very counsel that had killed their Lord and Savior just a few weeks before. These were no paper tigers they were facing. Their lives were at stake here. So what did they do?

They ran home. But did they hide and keep quiet? Read Acts 4:23–31, and let your heart be thrilled in an unusual way. They ran home to report to the church and to fall before God in prayer. Surely they prayed for safety, we say? Surely they asked God to remove the threats and make the way easier? Look again. They asked not for these things, but that God would make them bold and fearless in the face of these very real risks. All the church joined to pray—men and women together—and God's response was immediate. He did not say, "Go to bed, and tomorrow things will look brighter." His Holy Spirit fell on them afresh, and the house shook with the fall of it, and they went back out into the streets to speak boldly—that very same day!

It takes our breath away! The source of their great courage was the renewed empowerment that came when God again filled their spirits with his Spirit. What a lesson they learned that day—a lesson that would carry them into *Jerusalem, all Judea and Samaria, and to the ends of the earth*. When troubles come, run to God, ask for boldness, and open your arms wide to the power of his Spirit.

The troubles and the blessings, the struggles and the

victories, were just beginning for these brave saints. Like Mary Magdalene, we wonder what is ahead for this gangly group of adolescent Christians. We wish them well, and look forward to more chapters of the drama. And more stories of *empowered women*. Chapter 2 will find them back in the kitchen—but look! The men will be joining them there!

NEW FRIENDS, NEW CHALLENGES
Choosing the Seven to Serve Widows

Acts 6–7

"How are you coming with that basket, Joanna?" Mary Clopas asked as she stuffed another bundle of bread into the corner of her own. Friday afternoons the two friends always worked together in the alms distribution, and it was quite a task to get all the baskets ready and delivered before Sabbath began at sundown.

"I'm almost finished," Joanna answered without looking up. "I need to get on to Anna's house so she'll have food for her supper. And, if I can get there in time, I'll be able to tidy up a bit for her. It has become almost impossible for her to do even the simple chores with her blindness as bad as it is." She reached for a towel and spread it over the bulging load, tucking the corners in as she talked. "I've known Anna most all my life—we used to play in her yard as children—and it is so hard to watch her growing feeble and helpless this way. I wish she had a daughter to check on her every day."

"It's that way with Sarai, too," Mary sympathized. "It's so sad to see her alone and neglected. Last time I was there her dress was stained, and I talked her into letting me help her change so I could wash it. She has so little, and I think her no-good nephew is stealing what she has when she isn't looking. The neighbor told me she had taken extra oil over for her lamp, but it was gone by the next day. It makes me angry to think she is being taken advantage of."

"Anna is alone most of the time, too," Joanna responded sadly, leaning back against the table. "Her only son works as a shepherd for his uncle who lives outside Bethlehem, and he seldom gets home long enough to care for her at this time of the year. The house needs repairs badly—the roof leaked in last week's rain, and the cistern is cracking. She's really being neglected by her family."

"Can't her grandson, or maybe her son's wife, help her with those things?" Mary asked. "Families are supposed to do that!"

Joanna shrugged. "Her son's wife died several years ago. And Seth, the grandson, just can't seem to be bothered. I'd like to give him a good thrashing! If he were mine, I'd have done it long ago!"

"Sarai never had children, so she doesn't have anyone left who lives near enough to help—except that nephew." Mary covered her basket, and then looked up. "Her sister used to live with her, and they tried to helped each other; but her sister died a year or so ago. What hurts my heart is that, when she was younger and able, she was so faithful to help others. She loved the babies so, and was always offering to care for them, always sewing for them. She cooked for her neighbors. And prayed! My, how she could pray! But I don't think she can do much of that any more. Her memory is so poor."

"I guess we need to get going," Joanna said, swinging her basket up to balance it on one shoulder. Then seeing one of the Greek-speaking women still working at the back of the room she called, "Helena, you seem to be struggling with two satchels at once. Do you need some help?"

Helena looked up appreciatively, and shook her head. "No, I'll manage. You two probably need to get on your way if you are going to make evening prayers."

"Why do you have two sacks to fill?" Mary pursued. "Will you be delivering both of them? Because we can try to find someone to help you."

Helena paused from her chore of wrapping some small, dried smelt in a cloth. "I always take a basket to my friend's mother, Anya," she explained, "because I promised to care for her when her daughter—my friend—died last winter. But she has a next-door neighbor who is also a believer and alone, and nobody is caring for her; so I thought I'd try to get a basket to each of them this week. It seems like someone should care." And she continued packing the two knapsacks, filling the remaining spaces with some nearly-ripe figs and a couple of small squashes.

"This job just keeps getting bigger and bigger by the week," Joanna said, resting her basket back on the table. "It's wonderful that so many are believing and joining with us in Temple services and at home gatherings. But as more come, and as the old ones grow feeble, our list of believing widows just grows and grows. We need more people to help with this Friday afternoon alms ministry."

"You know," Mary said carefully, "so many of them do not speak Aramaic as I do, and I don't really know very much Greek. Helena, you are so fortunate to be able to use both languages; but I think some of our people don't volunteer because they are not fluent in Greek. It's hard to go to strangers' homes—it feels awkward. Who is this neighbor of Anya's that needs help?"

"I think her name is Athena, but I'm not sure. I've just met her one time. She isn't really very old—maybe 75 or so—but she is so crippled she can barely come to open the door." Helena cinched up the two satchels as she spoke. "Anya says she came to Jerusalem with her husband for Pentecost on the year of the great revival, and they stayed here to be part of the new group. Now he has died, and her family is all back in Tarsus, so she is alone. But she can't get out of the house now—can't come to prayers any more, or to fellowship meals. She's just skin and bones—I'm surprised she hasn't starved."

"That's really sad," Mary responded.

Joanna agreed. "I guess it's harder for those who haven't lived in Judea all their lives. We seem to have a lot of them, but I don't know them, because they go to the Greek-speaking synagogues, and to other house meetings. We've just gotten so big!" Joanna shook her head, trying to grasp this new reality. "Some days I wish for the little group we used to have—when we could all know each other and be close friends."

"But," Mary reminded, "Jesus told us he came to seek and save all the world—not just Judea—not just Israel. And 'all the world' is way too many to fit into any house or even any synagogue I ever saw!" They laughed a little to ease the tension.

The door opened and a friendly face caught everyone's eye. "Stephen!" they chorused, almost in unison.

"We were just about to leave to deliver these alms to our older widows who cannot attend," Mary volunteered. "But you know, now that you are here, we need to talk to you."

"Oh, oh!" the younger man hedged with mock remorse.

"What have I done this time?"

"Not enough! That's just the problem," Mary quipped. "But—do you know our new friend Helena?"

"Oh yes!" he assured her. "Helena and I attend the same Grecian synagogue, and we've been friends several months. So, is Helena in trouble?" He was still playful.

"Silly! No!" Joanna responded. "But we were all talking about how many of the widows need our help every Friday, and how few of us there are to take their supplies. We know of more who need food and care, but there just aren't enough of us to get the job done right. And Helena thinks maybe it's even worse among the Greek-speaking believers."

Helena nodded in agreement, and Mary continued. "We think we need some kind of a better system, because things are just so much bigger than they were. And it's very sad to see the older ones neglected."

"Strange you should mention it," Stephen said, swatting at a bug on the doorpost. "This is the third time it's been brought up to me in the past two days. And some of the others were not nearly as polite about it as you have been. In fact, I had a discussion with some of the men of my synagogue just this morning, and we think the problem is worth bringing to the Twelve. You are certainly right—we've gotten so much bigger."

"Stephen, I think we who have lived here in Judea just haven't realized how hard it can be for those Jews who came in later; and left behind their families and lands and all the things that should comfort them in their old age." Joanna spoke, but the other two women nodded in agreement. "We just must do something before there is a real tragedy, and someone gets sick and dies from neglect. We need to find out who needs food and money . . ."

" . . . and fuel for lamps, and warm clothing, and firewood," Helena added. "The basic, simple stuff of life can be very hard when you are blind, or crippled, or forgetful, or ill. We just have to care more and do more. There has to be a way."

"Ladies, you are absolutely right," Stephen agreed, stepping back to open the door wider for them. "I'll talk with my friends, and we'll speak to the Twelve and get something done—and soon!" Then noticing Helena's double load he added, "So now, Miss Helena—where are we going with these two heavy bags? Lead the way, and I'll be right behind you. Sabbath prayers are almost ready to begin!"

BEHIND THE SCENE
A Study of Acts 6 and 7

Distribution to the Widows

Among the world's peoples the Jews are known for their compassion for the poor and vulnerable in their midst. Care for widows, orphans, and the needy, is part of the structure of their social and religious lives. So it was natural that, when the Christian church was young, the Jewish believers immediately included the widows in their ministry.

Researchers tell us that First Century synagogues made a basket collection, going door-to-door and to businesses, each Friday. Then in the afternoon the commodities and money collected were divided and distributed to those in poverty. Needy persons received enough for fourteen meals—two each day in the coming week. On a daily basis, urgent needs were met with extra house-to-house contributions. Acts 6:1 indicates that the believers were following a plan similar to this. So many church ministries just rise up out of the need, without much organization or official status; but later, when they outgrow themselves and begin to falter, folks begin to call for more structure and financial support. Sometimes the situation has to become almost dire before action is taken. That seems to be the story of the ministry to widows in the Early Church.

The group of believers had mushroomed beyond any expectation. In Acts 4:4 we hear they have neared 5,000; and in the next chapter (Acts 5:14) we read that, in spite of quite severe persecution, *"more and more men and women believed in the Lord and were added to their number."* Among them were many widows. Now, try to imagine our own society minus health insurance, social security, telephones, public transportation, prescription drugs, cataract surgery, elevators, Meals on Wheels, wheelchairs, and nursing homes. How would that affect the frail elderly among us? How would they function in day-to-day life? Who would be there for them? The Bible's answers are: first the family, and then the church. Timothy deals with this extensively in his first letter. (See 1Timothy 5:3–16.)

Compassionate ministries remain vital to the life and

witness of our churches today. God gifts some of us especially with mercy, kindness, and compassion. If we are true to our charge, we search our church rolls for persons who are unable to attend because of health, age, or transportation concerns. Then we tailor a ministry to meet their needs. We may run carpools or van service, put hearing devices into the pews, or send a visitor to check on them and share Scripture and prayer monthly or more often. We have one lady in our ministry who loves to design computer cards, and she sends each of our homebound members a birthday card from our church as the special day approaches. At our church-wide Christmas dinner, we take a kind of "meals on wheels" to many elderly. Children make tray favors for that occasion. Regularly we mail to them, call them, pray for them; for, even with all the social safety nets in place, the one-on-one touch of a Christian brother or sister is keenly needed and appreciated. And deserved, we may add.

The "In As Much" Ministries

Let me talk just a little more about the importance of the compassionate ministries in our churches. As Jack and I served together on our church ministry team—he as senior pastor, and I as minister of education—a priority for us in an aging congregation was to support and develop ministries to the vulnerable. Christians with great hearts were led of God to adopt these ministries as their own, and many have continued in them for half an adult lifetime. I call them today's *empowered* "Heroes of the Faith." I think of Reed and Dot, who began going to a nursing home facility every Sunday morning more than thirty years ago, and are faithful still at the writing of this book. Sunday in and Sunday out they take music to brighten lives in that place, sharing an hour of joy and praise with the residents. Lovingly they visit the bed sides to listen, read Scripture, and pray with those too fragile to come into the gathering. They are the hands and heart of Jesus in that place. *"Great is your reward in heaven."*

Let me tell you about Wayne and Charles, deacons who adopted a ranch for mentally challenged men as their place of ministry. For more than twenty years they have gone every Sunday at the Bible teaching hour to hold classes there. Because they care about excellence, they have taken training workshops on teaching adult mentally handicapped, and worked in retreats for them. At holiday times they take parties and gifts to these men whom they have come to love so deeply. We count them both as heroes and brothers. *"In as much as you have done this for the least of these, my brothers, you have done it for me."*

Annie is too dear to forget here. With a heart of compassion she has spent her life caring for the babies in our church. Not just on Sundays and midweek services, but also on Mother's Days Out, in Vacation Bible School, and more. Along the way she extended her nurturing to include our elderly homebound, and for many years directed that home-visitation extension of our church. She was the "Homebound Angel" who visited my own mother in her last years, so my appreciation for her loving ways is a very personal thing. Now ninety years old herself, Annie still cares for infants and their parents, and still drives to a nursing facility to carry literature and love to friends whose health is failing. Her kindness and stamina in the work of the Lord are a witness to us all. *"And let us not be weary in well doing . . ."* even when we are ninety! Bless you, Annie!

The Problems of Diversity and Inclusiveness

Now back to Jerusalem. Bible scholars indicate that there was a significant time lapse between Acts 5:42 and Acts 6:1—perhaps four years. At this stage of the church's development the believers were almost entirely Jewish. They were still attending synagogue worship, along with gatherings on Solomon's Porch at the Temple, and meetings in homes. Although many priests believed and would soon join with them (see Acts 6:7), and even though they believed Jesus was the sacrifice for our sins, still they had not abandoned the sacrificial systems and priestly authority totally—that would come later.

What the rapidly increasing growth did bring into the church was an influx of Jews who had been born outside the country of Israel. These are referred to as the *Grecian Jews,* or *Hellenists.* Their native language was the universal Greek, and their thinking and customs were more global than those of the Judean-born, Aramaic-speaking believers. Some of the many (hundreds) of Jerusalem synagogues were basically Greek-speaking institutions, so a natural division occurred as the thousands of believers found their way into local worship places which suited their individual needs and backgrounds. All this was intensified by their history: the locally-born Jews always believed themselves to be purer and somewhat superior to those raised in outlying Jewish settlements. Fertile ground for misunderstandings.

Think back to Pentecost, and the many pilgrims who experienced that day (Acts 2:5–11). This passage reflects the Jewish settlements—some very large ones—all around the Mediterranean. The one in Alexandria, Egypt, was considered to be the largest settlement of Jews in that world. Historians believe that some of these pilgrims who had come in from all over the empire, on hearing and believing the Good News, had elected to remain in Jerusalem area. Others continued to come in for reasons of commerce, family, and celebrations of the major Jewish feasts.

Choosing "The Seven"

Of course, these foreign-born Jews brought with them older women and widows, some of whom needed the church's care. And that brings us to the story in Acts 6:1–7. It was time for some structure and system for this important ministry. Until now the Twelve had handled most of the teaching, preaching, administrating, and worship gatherings. Now it was time to share leadership. And it is interesting how they chose to do that.

We now call it "the congregational form of church government," but little did they know they were establishing a pattern that would be in use almost 2000 years later. Rather than hold a closed-door meeting of the higher-ups, they put the responsibility and privilege of decision-making onto the believers. *"They gathered all the disciples together,"* and trusted them to be led of the Holy Spirit in their choices. It showed a great heart in the Twelve Apostles—a managing of personal egos—a humility.

In so doing they also set some important priorities for the future of the New Testament church. *"It would not be right for us to neglect the ministry of the Word of God . . ."* These who had been carefully trained by the Master needed to do what they were prepared and gifted to do: the work of preaching, teaching and leading worship. The ministry of distributing the goods from the benevolence tables could be done by others, and should be. And so we have the priority of the Word in our churches, with the very vital social ministries also being done, but not necessarily by our trained leadership. In the body, many others also are gifted and can serve, and are blessed when trusted to do so.

Third, but equally notable, they established some qualifications for leadership that remain important to us today. They instructed: *"Choose seven men from among you who are known to be full of the Spirit and wisdom."* Regardless of the office, those are still the two most important things we look for in a church leader. Skill and experience count, but they cannot replace the inner, demonstrated, life of one who *walks in the guidance of the Holy Spirit.* People skills and charisma are desirable, but they do not substitute for being *full of wisdom* which grows out of knowledge of the Scriptures and time spent in prayer. In all our churches, Jack has looked for and sought out men of wisdom and spiritual depth to be his personal friends and advisors. We work through elected leaders and committees, task forces and staff meetings; but nothing matches the help he has received from one-on-one consultation with the wise and deep members of the church.

Were these *Seven* the first deacons? We hear it pro and con, but at the very least they were the prototypes for church leadership. Later deacons took many of the same responsibilities, and had similar qualifications. Many of us are comfortable with calling them deacons, although Acts 6 does not so designate them. We see no indication that they were seeking a title or an office. But they were important to the life of the church, and everyone recognized it by the laying on of hands of blessing and authority for the task. Notice also that they all had Greek names: Stephen, Philip, and the others. Six were Jewish born, and one was a Jewish convert, but they had been raised in the Hellenist communities, so were well-suited to quell the feelings of neglect that had arisen. Doesn't God work things out wonderfully well when we allow his Spirit to lead the process? There is room for all of us in the family of God!

Women, Involved and Ministering

We have chosen to put the women into the picture, packing baskets at the tables of distribution. Admittedly we have read between the lines in that, but it isn't really much of a stretch, is it? Women care for women's needs—a universal fact of life. Daughters and daughters-in-law care for aging mothers, and neighbor ladies notice and meet the needs of those near by. We selected Joanna and Mary Clopas for the fiction vignette because of their probable connections to Jerusalem four or five years after Pentecost. Whereas Mary Magdalene, Mary the mother of Jesus, and Salome would very likely have returned to their homes and families in Galilee at some point, Joanna's husband worked for Herod, and would have lived in and out of Jerusalem as occasion demanded. Mary Clopas could have been the wife of "Cleopas" mentioned in Luke 24:18, a resident of the Jerusalem area. If these two were not among those behind the scenes in Acts 6:1–7, there were other compassionate women involved in the ministry.

True that none of these first chosen *Seven* were women— it was First Century Israel, not modern America, where women have different status. But later we will meet Phoebe, who was described as a *deaconess*—proof that women did share in this ministry with the blessing of God. Women are nurturers. Women have ministering hearts, and where would we be without them? Over the years Jack and I have found our dearest friends among the deacons and their wives. Indulge me as I tell you about three who are in our personal "Hall of Fame."

Winston and Leona Forrest served the church at Blum, Texas, our first full-time church during seminary years. How many, many important lessons God taught us in those almost three years, and Winston and Leona helped Him on an almost-daily basis. How we loved them! Funds were scarce (the church could only pay fifty dollars per week, plus a house). We had a new baby and Jack's school commuting costs to cover. Winston offered Jack a job driving a milk truck for his dairy business on the regular drivers' days off—two days' pay each week that kept us afloat financially. Leona loved our baby boy, and would spend hours with him. In fact, he learned to count to ten collecting eggs with her in her hay barn. Precious memories of precious people! Winston was a godly man, and a wise leader, who kept the church on track in decisions month in and month out. We owe our good beginnings to men like him.

Clayborn and Alice Wayne picked up the mentoring role when we moved west to Hatch, New Mexico. Another baby was soon on the way, and the one-hundred dollar per week salary could not stretch to cover the budget. Pastoral visits to hospitals were seventy or one-hundred-and-fifty mile round trips. Church and family business over those desert caliche roads beat our tires to shreds. Car expenses consumed a full fourth of our income. Those were earlier days in southern New Mexico, before the highways were improved. We loved our work, but for those four years I did not buy one new dress, and we could not afford one piece of furniture. We just marked time, keeping our babies fed and clothed. When emergencies arose, Clayborn and Alice would always be there with an extra check to cover the need. Bless them for that, but even more for their quiet leadership in all the decisions of the church. Clayborn was such a man of integrity that the congregation never took their eyes off him, and he always led them well.

Forrest and Neta Dickerson came into our lives and ministry several years later. By then we probably had outgrown the need for mentoring, but we never would outgrow the need for trusted friends. Our children were about the same ages, and we shared so much with them: youth leadership at the church, mission trips and ministries, fellowship, teaching. They were always at our side—or perhaps a step or two ahead of us. We often say that Neta and Forrest have been every pastor's best friend at First Baptist Church, Carlsbad. Forgiving, understanding, loving, helping, blessing—priceless friends and partners in the faith. So wise—so encouraging. Thank God for their influence in our lives, and the lives of our sons!

Empowered lay leadership—both men and women of God who serve in a spirit of good faith and deep dedication—is the very heartbeat of the work. Acts 6 illustrates in such a beautiful way Paul's later words in Galatians 3:26–28:

> "You are all sons of God through faith in Christ Jesus, for all of you who were baptized into Christ have clothed yourselves with Christ. There is neither Jew nor Greek, slave nor free, male nor female, for you are all one in Christ Jesus."

Filled, Empowered, Gifted

It may be wise to stop and define some terms that keep cropping up in these pages. We speak of being *filled* with the Spirit, being *empowered* by the Spirit, and being *gifted* by the Spirit. Are these synonyms, or should we distinguish differences in meaning, or perhaps a progression of process? I use them somewhat interchangeably, but actually believe they express three steps in the process of our being useful to the Spirit of God in building the Kingdom.

Believers are *filled with the Spirit* when we receive Jesus into our lives as Savior and Lord. *"If anyone does not have the Spirit of Christ, he does not belong to Christ,"* Paul tells us in Romans 8:9. The Spirit of Christ is the same as the Holy Spirit of God. At salvation he comes to dwell within, although often a new believer is not fully aware of all this can mean in her life. As we grow in the faith, we welcome the presence of the Spirit within, and learn to listen to his leading, feel his urging, and depend on his praying to God on our behalf. We call this *walking in the Spirit*.

It is possible to have the Spirit within, but not be fully *empowered* by him. God is always respectful of the free will which he placed in each person. He waits on us to allow the Holy Spirit to control and to work through us. We have the ability to stifle the Spirit's leadings, to grieve him by our sinfulness, to wrest control and take it into our own hands. The

Spirit will not *empower* a believer unless that person willingly gives him permission to do so. It is a daily, hourly—perhaps moment-by-moment process. Our wills are so strong, that we must continually give them over in submission to the Spirit's wiser counsel. When we allow him, he will *empower* our thoughts and actions. When we ask, he can control circumstances, and work in the hearts of those around us. We call this *empowered living*.

The *gifts of the Spirit* are the special abilities he gives us by which we help him build the Kingdom. Every believer is given spiritual gifts. *"All these [gifts] are the work of one and the same Spirit, and he gives them to each one, just as he determines."* (You can read more about the spiritual gifts in 1 Corinthians 12:1–11.) Whereas we all come to salvation in the same way, through belief in the sacrificial death of Christ, and we all receive the Spirit in that same experience of faith, our *spiritual gifts* are unique. The Spirit designates to each individual the gifts which best suit her or his abilities and personality. Paul lists some of the gifts in the passage just mentioned. We recognize our *spiritual gifts* through serving God, and discovering what brings us joy and fulfillment. There is a sense of "oneness with God" which comes when we serve him through our spiritual gifts. An awareness that his power is working through us as we teach, or minister, or administrate. We cannot take credit for the results, because we recognize that God has *empowered us through his Spirit to use our gifts for his glory*. And that is how the process is completed.

Celebrating the Life of Stephen

The story of the choosing of the *Seven* is followed by some thrilling stories of the ministry of two of them: Stephen and Philip. Chapters 7 and 8 of Acts are definitely exciting reading. The transfer of leadership from the Apostles to the Seven went smoothly; and as these new, Grecian Jews took their places among the Christians, God did surprising things. Spiritual abilities (gifts) began to surface in them that may not have been seen before. They could preach and witness very effectively, and *"signs and wonders"* happened at their hands. God was using them, probably to a greater degree than the Apostles could have predicted. God has a way of developing new leaders before our eyes; and if we are working with him, we will take hands off, and pray and encourage them through the growth period, so they and the congregation can see what God's Spirit is doing.

In Stephen we have a picture of the *filling, empowering, gifting* process just discussed. With the others, Stephen was filled with the Spirit in a fresh way in the Pentecost experience. He was one of those *"known to be full of the Spirit,"* as described in Acts 6:3. We can determine that he allowed the Spirit to *empower* him, because he was also known for his wisdom, and recognized as a potential leader. Once he had been prayed for and set apart to the ministry of a deacon, we can see the Spirit's *gifts* manifested in his ability to do *"wonders and miracles"* (Acts 6:8) and preach with power.

Stephen's life was cut tragically short by the avarice of self-important leaders in the synagogue. Men, recently released from slavery in these outlying areas, called *"freedmen,"* seized power and strong-armed his arrest, conviction, and execution. It was a sobering day for the young church family. One of their brightest and best was lost—the first known Christian martyr. But the excellence of the choice of

Stephen is brilliantly illustrated in the way he died. He kept his sweet spirit *("his face was like the face of an angel")*. And he kept his head as he took the opportunity to witness clearly, both to his Jewish-ness, and his new faith in Jesus. His last words were words of forgiveness, and then he died.

Stephen's death was not without value. It was a sacrifice play which brought out the next major player in the field *"white unto harvest."* Young Saul, swelled with his traditional education, sure of his rigid, fundamentalist theology, mentored by the powerful, was watching with approval. And the picture of Stephen's brave witness and death was seared into his memory in a way he could not escape. It was the stirring of a new era, soon to be born in the Early Church. The believers, who had come from local Judaism to diversity within Judaism, now would begin to scatter from Jerusalem and Judea into *"Samaria, and to the ends of the world."* Pack a bag! We're going to begin traveling with them in the next chapter!

Part II

Women Help to Move the Gospel Forward

Chapter 3:
A FRIEND IN NEED Tabitha, Raised from the Dead

Chapter 4:
BREAKTHROUGH IN CAESAREA
Cornelius' Family Welcomes Peter

Chapter 5:
ANGEL AT THE GATES
Rhoda Answers Peter's Knock

A FRIEND IN NEED
Tabitha, Raised From the Dead

Acts 9:32–43

"Auntie Esther! Auntie Esther! Come quickly! Someone is sick!"

Without looking out the shuttered window, Esther knew the voice. It was young Rachel, probably sent by her mother. Abigail would not be sending for her unless it was urgent. Before the child stopped knocking, Esther had grabbed her herb bag from the shelf beside the door, and was following the child up the steep path.

"Who is it, Rachel? Who is so ill that we must hurry this way?" Esther was already winded trying to keep up with the ten-year-old ahead of her.

"It's Tabitha, Auntie," she called back over her shoulder, not slowing her pace. "Mama said to hurry, because she may be dying. Mama just found her, and she can't wake her up. She said to go for you, because you are the best healer we know."

"Tabitha!?" Esther was amazed. "But she is still—young and healthy." Her words came between gasps as she struggled on the uphill climb. "Why on earth—would she be—so ill—so quickly?"

The little head before her shook in bewilderment, dark curls flying in the breeze as she ran. "She was not at the gathering of believers last night, but we thought she was just busy with her sewing and all. But now we guess she was sick and didn't call for anyone to help her." The distance between the girl and her older follower was widening.

"Slow down—just a bit, Child," Esther called. "I'm not so—young anymore. This is too—fast for me." Then, thinking again, she said, "No, just—run on ahead—and tell them—I'm coming. I'll get there—just as soon—as I can."

Rachel sped on like a scared goat, pebbles scattering as she dug into the hillside path. Esther slowed to a brisk walk. She knew the way. Everyone knew where Tabitha lived—rich and poor alike. Wealthier women made their way up the hill to her cottage when they had clothes to be mended, or needed a fine new cloak for a festival. Tabitha was a seamstress without compare in Joppa. Penniless and modest women climbed her path when in need, knowing she would have a new or reworked garment for them at little or no cost. In Joppa, the poor often dressed as well as the rich, thanks to Tabitha's skills with the loom and the needle. And few people went coatless against the cold.

Breezes blew in from the sea below, boosting Esther along as she climbed the steep path to the cottage door. Inside she found Abigail on her knees beside Tabitha's pale form, wringing towels in cool water to bathe the fevered body. Esther opened her bag and picked through the herbs, quickly selecting some to brew into a tea. "Is she any better?" she asked as she worked.

"No better, Esther. I am so glad you are here! I've stirred and fanned the coals and begun the water for you. The cottage was completely cold and dark. I think she has been this way for hours. I barely found a spark to start the fire." Abigail continued wringing the cloths as she explained anxiously. "At first she felt hot—quite hot—but now she seems to be cooler." Abigail moved away to make room for the healer to work. As Esther stirred the herb tea, Abigail began massaging her friend's still legs, hoping to stimulate some response—some sign of life.

Drop by drop, Esther spooned the healing tea into closed lips, stroking Tabitha's throat, talking to her in quiet tones. "Take a little of this, Dear. It will make you better. Come now—just a little—swallow, Tabitha—it will do you good." But the eyes remained closed, and there was no response.

Rachel stood by, fidgeting and fearful. "The tea is dripping out of her mouth, Auntie," she sobbed. "Is she going to get better? She promised to make my new dress for me soon. And look . . ." pointing to a project lying on the floor by Tabitha's chair, "I think this is my dress, because I asked her for purple, and that's what she is sewing."

"The dress can wait, Rachel," her mother gently chided. "We can make the dress another way. Right now we must worry over Tabitha, and not ourselves." For a minute she waited and watched, hoping for a sign that simply was not there. Esther shook her head sadly, even as she continued urging the tea on their silent friend.

"Rachel, go call your brother. I need him to come and run an errand for me right now." As the girl started out the door her mother added, "And tell him I said *right now*, and not a minute later!"

The two friends sat back on their heels in silence. "She is either gone, or nearly so," Esther said sadly. "Whatever could have overtaken her so fast?" They looked around the small room with its stacks of robes and tunics in varying stages of progress. The one beside the chair still had a needle in the seam. "It looks like Rachel was right—she was working on her dress when something happened."

Abigail moved to pick up the garment, fold it and lay it on the chair; then went to the lamp stand and checked out the vessel. "It's cold, and the oil has run dry, so it must have happened in the evening or night hours—last night probably—or even the night before. I think it was sudden, don't you?"

The healer nodded thoughtfully. "It may have been a seizure of some kind, although I don't remember hearing that she has had them before. I see she seems to have vomited on her dress—or choked." Pressing her cheek to Tabitha's still face, she listened for a long moment. "I think she may be gone, Abby. I can't feel her breathing. I don't know what else we can do."

Abigail caught her breath and covered her mouth with her hand. "Oh, I hope not, Esther," she whispered. "I sent Rachel for Thad because we need some of the men to come and help us decide what to do next. I'm thinking we might call for Simon Peter to come and look at her. If she isn't dead, then he is the best healer in the area, and Lydda isn't very far away. The men can make it in an hour on a swift horse. We heard at the meeting last night how Peter healed a man in Lydda just last week. Miracles do happen, and surely our Tabitha is worth a miracle!"

"I wonder if Peter would come for a woman," Esther mused aloud. "But if we impress on him that she is not just *any* woman, but a doer of good works among the believers, maybe he will come."

"I think we must ask the men to go for us," Abigail answered. "He would listen better to the men. And they can ride faster than we can." The two agreed on their plan just as Rachel returned with her older brother on her heels.

"Good, Thad!" their mother began. "Now I need you to run down to the docks and find your Uncle Mathias and tell him we must send to Lydda for Simon Peter. Tabitha is sick unto death, and we have tried all we know to do. Ask him to drop everything and come, and to bring another of the brothers with him. We must do it now, or it will be too late. We dare not wait until the morning." As the children started for the door Abigail shouted to her daughter, "Rachel, not you! You must not go to the docks. It isn't safe for you to be among all the men and boys down there. Uncle Mathias expected ships in from Lebanon and Egypt today, and we don't know those people. Let your brother go alone. It's a man's world down there."

Seeing her daughter's disappointment, and not wanting to answer further questions on the matter, Abigail continued. "Besides, I have another very important job for you that a girl could do better. I need you to find clean linens in that chest in the corner," she said, pointing, "and take them to Tabitha's upstairs guest room. Make up that bed in case we need it for company."

Rachel started for the chest, still frowning, found the linens and scuffed out the door and up the outside stairs. When she had gone, Abigail turned to her healer friend. "Do you think Tabitha could just be in a coma, or do you think she is actually dead?" she asked bluntly.

After a silence Esther responded, "I think she is dead."

"Then . . ." Abigail hesitated, "should we still send for Peter, or is it too late for such an effort?" The question had no answer.

"Let's let the men decide when they come," Esther

responded. "If Jehovah should so will, it may not be too late. I would rather try and fail than not try at all." Getting a nod from her friend she added, "We could use the warm water to bathe her, and put on a fresh dress while we wait. Tabitha would want to be in clean clothes if we are to call in strangers."

It seemed a way to put the time to good use as they waited for the men to come from the docks. Abigail brought the kettle from the hearth and began the task. "How will the poor folks of Joppa ever make do without our Tabitha?" she said sadly to her friend. And then they worked together in silence.

BEHIND THE SCENES
A Study of Acts 9:32–43

A Vignette of Friendship

You may have known her better by her Greek name, Dorcas. We think she was a Jewish lady who probably preferred to be called Tabitha among friends. Likely she was too young to be referred to as an older woman or a widow. Perhaps she was still active, like the graceful gazelle for which she was named. What is certain is she was very well loved and respected by the believers in Joppa, known for her kindness to others. And she would be missed by her friends, were she to die at so young an age.

Her Home Town

Have you lived in a small city? Not a village, but a bustling energetic, small city? Or perhaps you have lived by the sea, where you could watch the comings and goings of the large vessels in the ever-changing waterscape? The seacoast is a wonderful place to live. From day to day—even from morning to evening—the view changes as full ships arrive and empty ones go, and the skies meld from grays to cloudy blue. Gulls fly over, laughing and diving. The tide rolls in and out ceaselessly, and salt air permeates everything. Sunsets over the water can be breathtaking!

Joppa was such a place. Described as "more than a village," it was the major port for the inland city of Jerusalem. Just thirty-five miles northwest of Jerusalem on the Mediterranean Coast, Joppa had been a port city since Old Testament times. In fact, it was then the only port for Israel south of Mount Carmel. Ships easily reached it from Lebanon, Egypt, Africa, Greece, and beyond. Lest we think of global shipping as a recent business, it is good to remember that trade went as far north as England, and around the cape of Africa to India, in the First Century world.

The eastern Mediterranean has a long history of such trade, largely because of seagoing Phoenicians who lived just above Israel, and were excellent ship builders. In Solomon's day (about 1000 b.c.) they were active in bringing the timber from Lebanon for building the temple. It is thought that they discovered the trade route around the cape of Africa while searching for expanded markets and greater wealth. Joppa, situated south on the coastal plane, was in the area inhabited by Philistines in those early days. Remember Dagon, the "fish god," whose temple was destroyed by Samson in his final burst of brute strength? (See Judges 16:23 ff.) This is some of the history of Tabitha's home town.

Although the port of Joppa sits on a coastal plane, cliffs over 100 feet high surround the harbor. Pictures of the city show it high on the gentle coastal hills above. Tabitha could look out from the hillsides of Joppa and see merchant vessels from all over, coming to bring goods vital to Jerusalem and southern Judea; and to purchase the grain and oils, olives, and other products of Israel in return. With them came slave ships, and Roman warships. In the open sea beyond, pirates plied the waves—and a few years later overran Joppa itself! It would have been an active, interesting place to live. Stop a minute to feel the sea breeze on your cheeks. Joppa was home to Tabitha.

Peter's Prominence in Those Days

In the early chapters of Acts, Paul had not yet surfaced as the most colorful and charismatic leader of the young church. The Twelve Apostles and new deacons ("The Seven") still had center stage. We read of Peter, John, James, Stephen, Philip—each a thrilling tale of courage, struggle, and growth.

Peter emerged shining at Pentecost, when he seized the moment and stood to bear witness before thousands. It was from his sermon in the Temple area, in a city crowded with holiday pilgrims, that the first great ingathering began. With John, Peter continued to preach, heal, and witness, in and out of prison and court, until the church grew from 120 believers to 3,000, and then to over 5,000 or larger. And many, including Jewish priests and leaders, believed and joined the fellowship. It was an exciting time. No building could hold them. They met in the huge colonnade of the Temple daily, and miracles were commonplace. (Acts 4:4 and 5:12–16 give details.) In fact, the Sadducees and the court of Jewish priests and leaders were so disturbed they held daily debates on what to do about this fast-growing sect (Acts 5:33–6:2).

After the death of Stephen, a great persecution broke out against the believers in Jerusalem, and most of them scattered to outlying areas. Of course, as they went they carried the Good News with them, so the Word of God spread throughout Judea and Samaria and northward. One of the exciting stories coming out of this persecution is that of Philip the deacon, who traveled into Samaria. There he confronted a sorcerer named Simon who became a vociferous believer. A great revival broke out and many believed. Now, these were not Jewish believers, or even Greek-speaking Jews, but Samaritans—people of mixed race—whom the Jews did not claim as relatives. When word got back to the Apostles in Jerusalem that non-Jews were believing, it created quite a stir. They sent Peter and John to investigate, and—sure enough—they found it to be the authentic work of the Holy Spirit! This new faith no longer belonged just to Jews and Jewish converts—it was going global. (This exciting story is found in Acts 8: 1–17.)

As Philip went on about his mission in Samaria, Peter also began to travel. We pick him up again in Acts 9:32, as he went to visit the scattered believers who were now in Lydda, a city northwest of Jerusalem on the road toward the port of Joppa. There he healed a man who had been bedridden for eight years, and another great revival broke out. It was while he was there that the saints at Joppa called him to come and heal their friend, Tabitha, who had fallen ill and died.

Her Gifts of Hands and Heart

We are told only three things about Tabitha for certain. First, she was *"a disciple,"* a believer in the Lord Jesus. Second, she was *"always doing good."* Third, she was known for *"helping the poor."* What a great epitaph for a tombstone:

> Here Lies Tabitha
> A believer in Jesus
> Who did good works
> And helped the poor

From Acts 9:39 we guess that her kindnesses were mostly about sewing garments for those in need. In our story we assumed that she made her living by sewing for the rich, so that she could then give freely to the needy. But the works of her hands drew a picture of her heart. She was a woman of kindness and generosity, sensitive to the needs of others, and always busy about doing good. Wonderful legacy! Wonderful role model for us!

As Christian theology evolved, and early believers put into practice the *"love your neighbor as yourself"* teachings of Jesus, some of these qualities—helping and mercy—were recognized to be gifts of the Spirit within us. Paul includes love, kindness, goodness, and gentleness in his list of fruits of the Spirit in Galatians 5:22–23. Tabitha would have fit well into those lists. These are characteristics that should set groups of Christians apart from secular associations—not to say that others cannot show these positive attributes. But Christians should *always* show them toward each other, and outwardly to the neighborhood.

My life as pastor's wife, teacher, and writer is lived very much within the Christian community. So it happened that, as I sat one evening in an angry neighborhood association meeting, I was scalded by the rancor, the acidic remarks, the self-serving half truths, directed toward those they opposed. I thought, *"Where I live we don't treat each other this way."* Christianity should make that difference. The community should see us as they did Tabitha.

And she was a servant. Perhaps she had heard of Jesus' teachings, *"I came not to be served, but to serve." "Those who would be first among you must be the servant of all."* No sense of self importance denied her the freedom to see another's need and move to help. She was not caught playing "Queen of the Mountain" with the sisters of her fellowship. Tabitha must have been at peace with herself and others, mature enough to resist selfish competing, and able to focus beyond her own desires. She busied herself *"doing good and helping the poor."*

Their Gifts of Concern and Intervention

Well, we haven't read the rest of the story, have we? Stop now and read it all in Acts 9:36–43, and be thrilled! Tabitha's friends didn't let nature take its course. They did not just sit and hold a prayer meeting over the corpse. Instead they took immediate action which gave her back her life. And note that the women sent men on this mission; and the fact that the men agreed to go indicates that Tabitha's respect was not just a "girl thing." The men also saw and appreciated her gifts of hands and heart. All could see that her death was a great loss. So the men made a quick trip the fifteen or so miles from Joppa to Lydda, and brought Peter back with them. *"Please come at once!"*

We call that *intervention*. It means taking some action to try to prevent a catastrophe. It could be talking for hours with a depressed friend who is hinting at self destruction. Or, keeping small children so a mom can get help. Helping a friend see her options and work her way out of a jam. Walking with a new widow through the first, dark days of grief. Taking hot meals to the elderly so they can stay in their own homes. Giving Christmas to a family down on their luck. Helping build a new home with Habitat for Humanity. Getting involved in some constructive way to save someone's life! Tabitha's friends did that—they called Peter—they made the trip.

Peter knew what to do, because he had watched Jesus do it at Jairus' house some years before. He went into the room. He exercised privacy, prayer, expectant faith, and action. And Tabitha's eyes came open. Put yourself on her couch for a moment—sleeping the sleep of death. You hear your name called. You open your eyes, and there kneels the lead Apostle beside your bed! What do you do? Tabitha sat up—startled, no doubt—accepted his hand of assistance, and stood smiling beside him as he opened the door and presented her back to her friends alive again! Bathed and in her best dress!

Well—no surprise—it was front-page news in Joppa that day: APOSTLE RAISES LOCAL SEAMSTRESS FROM DEATH. *"This became known all over Joppa, and many people believed in the Lord."* Oh, there were scoffers—there always are. But to Tabitha and her friends there was no doubt. She was raised back to life to do more good works and deeds of kindness, especially for those in need. It would be a warm winter in Joppa that year.

Friends—Vital to Life!

Tabitha's story is a story about friends. When were friends not important in your life? Our moms were inviting friends over when we were still in our playpens. (Probably it was an extension of their own need for company more challenging than a toddler's!) Friends took on new importance when we started to Preschool—when we left home and the security of our mothers. We needed to know that someone thought we were special. We needed a partner on the playground. We played "house' to re-create the home we were leaving, practicing the skills vital to becoming women one day. Little boys have friends, too, but they do it differently. Boys play ball and vie on the monkey bars. Little girls hold hands and tell secrets.

Friends saved the day for us. Friends saw that we had someone to talk to at lunch, and that we were not left out when teams were chosen. By middle school, friends were life or death. We saw them all day in class, and talked to them all evening on the phone. We had sleepovers on weekends, and sat together in church. To be without a friend was to die! All the raging physiological changes, our sexual identities, our social skills, were screaming for understanding and support. Moms were basic, but friends were our life! And by high school it was a matter of structure. Belonging to a group, being liked, being popular, having an identity—it all demanded friends. Learning was secondary to the sub-culture of our teen world. Friends cued us about what music to like, what movies to see, what clothes were hip, and what the buzz words were. More importantly, they whispered who had a crush on us. (Today they text message!)

Finally, by college days, without the structure of school and home to shape our choices, we were on our own to find friends—both male and female. Then we truly began to discover who we were, alone in the dark. To be sure, we brought with us all the influences that had gone before. But, in the end, we had to make it alone in the world, to choose our adult friends based on the values and goals we were trying to live out. And it remains that way today.

For married women, couple friends are important; but women need women friends. A husband may be—if we are married, should be—our best friend, but we are surprised at how much pours out when we sit down with a secure woman friend to share one-on-one. Men have fishing buddies, golfing foursomes, gym and business associates; but women *talk* over lunch and cell phones. Friends are very important to our well-being—and will become more so as we grow older. When life comes full circle, and mates and kids are gone, friends may again become the major support system in our lives. So let's talk about loving a friend, keeping a friend, being a friend.

What Is A Friend?

Someone observed, "Friends are the family you choose for yourself." As true as that is, we might add, "Friends are God's special gift to your life." That surely has been the case for me! One of the nicest things about reaching God's *threescore years and ten* is the perspective that one gets with age. The landscape of life flows backward over so many wonderful friendships, some of which have weathered and warmed through the years.

Friends come into our lives in many different ways. Some are just *everyday friends*—people who live in the neighborhood, work in the office, and are part of us on a daily basis. Here and there a woman will rise over the others, like cream coming to the top of grandma's milk jar; and we love having them in our lives. Carmen was that kind of friend to me. For several years we partnered at work, and when Jack and I retired from the church, I was careful not to retire from Carmen. Her lack of pretense, her ability to read people, her concern for my needs, her excellent advice, her loyalty—these are gifts from her heart that I treasure.

Others are *church or club friends*—women with whom we share a common interest. We see them on a weekly basis, or maybe oftener, as we sit together in the choir, teach together in Sunday School, or work out side-by-side at the spa. Our homes may not be near each other, but some common value keeps bringing us together, and we seek one another out at those times. Sue is one of those special people in my life. Over many years we have walked through good times and hard times, shared laughter and tears over lunch, built a quiet understanding. Her unexpected phone calls come just at the minute I most need encouraging. We try to be there for each other.

Then there are the *old friends*—the ones we grew up with, went to school with, or raised our babies with in early years. Time and distance diminish most of those relationships from common heritage, but a few become dearer as life moves on. Carol is one of those for me. We met on the school playground in fourth grade, attended the same church, had sleepovers, dated the same boys. Not coming from a church-going family myself, I watched intently how her Christian family lived. Her mother became a mentor to me in very formative years. Now sixty years down the road, Carol and I still talk over the miles, pray for each other, and catch overnight visits as vacations allow.

But in more recent times I have come to treasure *short-term friendships.* Life is fluid, ever-changing, and we must all learn to "bloom where we are planted," as the adage goes. Since retiring, God has led Jack into several interim pastorates which have lasted a year or more each. Commuting from our home to temporary, apartment living has many challenges, not the least of which is leaving behind friends and comforts. Few people, encountering a temporary pastor and his wife, can see value in investing themselves deeply in a transitory friendship. Younger members feel little in common with a new "grandma" who comes into their lives for one short year. Linda was one who seemed to feel differently. God touched her heart to feel my need for a friend in a new place. Busy and established as she was, she made time to pick me up for coffee, take me to a favorite boutique, introduce me to a cozy restaurant, share a new recipe. It is amazing how bonded we became in just a few, short months. I still seek her out for late-night chats and weekend get-aways. It's a friendship worth keeping.

Some of these friends—the everyday friends, the church friends, the childhood friends, the short-term friends—some become what I like to call *"forever friends."* They are chosen sisters who live and remain at the center of our lives, and become deeply a part of us. On my wall I have a calligraphy which reads: "We never really leave a place we love: part of it we take with us, leaving a part of ourselves behind." The tapestry of my life is rich with the friends God has given me—precious treasures to my life. Emilie Barnes in her darling book, *The Twelve Teas of Friendship,* said, "A friendship is one of the greatest gifts you've ever had. Cherish it and invest in it."

How to Love a Friend

If time, distance, and neglect are three of the worst enemies of friendship, email and cell phones are surely the best things that have happened to it in recent years. What a boost to intimate communication, just to sit down after a weary day and jot off quick notes to several people we value. However did we live before email? But that is not to say that the hand-written, personal note, the unexpected call, the surprise done up in a cute and frilly bag, is not needed. These are the special touches that keep a relationship alive and growing. Let's go on to mention a few other good friends of friendship—things that help us love our friends wisely and well.

One is *freedom.* Our friends are not just like us—nor should they be. We have commonalities and similarities, but we are unique and individual. We grow at different rates and in different ways, as God works with us in the circumstances of our lives. Vital to a healthy friendship is allowing the other woman to make her own decisions, set her own values, without passing judgment. To try to make her like us is to stifle her—like turning a pot over a growing flower—she withers without the freedom to breathe and grow at her own pace. Encouragement and respect are the stuff of a healthy relationship.

Another gift to give a friend is *discretion*. The closer we become, the more we may share. But there are things we should not share—things that are more a hindrance than a help to know. It is a kindness not to overburden a friend with confidences she must then try to keep. There are professionals to carry those details. This is not to say we cannot bear one another's burdens, pray for each other's concerns. It is rather a plea for using good judgment in how much we share. Conversely, when we receive intimate information, we treat it with *confidence*. Confidences should be broken only when life or death matters are involved, and then carefully.

Joy is a third component of friendship. Friends are drawn to each other because the time shared is enjoyable. Make time for fun, for play, for a little splurging. Take in a movie your husbands do not want to see. Window shop, scrapbook, join a spa, meet for early morning walks. Friendship should add joy to life—most of the time, at least. Then, when the hard times come, as they always do, we can share them in a healthy context.

Friends *grow together*. Libby, one of my younger friends, says her friendship motto is Psalm 34:3 (KJV): *"O magnify the Lord with me, and let us exalt his name together."* Isn't that a wonderful foundation for friendship? We grow so much from hearing the bits of wisdom and insight God gives our friends. We are strengthened by friends who chide us when we want to gossip or be critical. We are helped when a Christian friend shares a book, or invites us to a seminar or retreat. Life can be so hard, we need to lift each other up.

When a Friend Is In Need

The hard times do come. As life goes on, they seem to intensify. This is what Tabitha's story was about. Family crises, health issues, disappointments, and losses come to us all. Much as we wish not to burden our friends with them, when the hard times come, friends are God's ministering angels. And we, in turn, minister to them.

On a daily basis the most important component of friendship is *prayer*. Jack and I keep an on-going, ever-changing, prayer list in the Bible on our dining nook buffet. Each morning after breakfast we read together, and then pray for our friends. It is a special privilege to have time to commit to this in retirement. We claim God's promise that where two people gather in Christ's name he is there, and he hears and answers. Friends and acquaintances know this and call or mention needs that are heavy on their hearts. We try to stay in touch and follow up. *"Carry each other's burdens, and in this way you will fulfill the law of Christ"* (to love each other as ourselves).

But when the world really tumbles in, it is important to *be there for a friend*. Be there in person, to listen, to hold, and to hug. To be heard is to be validated, and there is no greater need for a hurting heart than to know someone cares. We don't have to have all the answers—we may not have an answer at all. If God wants us to speak, he will give us a thought to share. It's probably more important to ask a few questions, and to give encouragement and hope. Even if we feel the situation is of her own making, chiding and fussing do not help a hurting heart. But the presence of a friend does comfort. *Find ways to help:* do the dishes, care for the children, make needed phone calls, activate the prayer list, bring in a meal, spend the night at the hospital—whatever needs to be done is what you should do. A broken heart is like a broken leg: we just need some support for a while until healing can take place. Be there in the dark hours.

Sometimes *long-term help* is needed. We can be the ones to draw in a support group of friends, share a helpful book, have coffee or lunch together once or twice a month to lend a listening ear. Deep hurts take a while to mend. Researchers tell us the human brain is actually damaged by trauma. After the loss of a child or a mate, it may take nine-to-twelve months for brain synapses to repair themselves. We cannot rush people back to "normal," much as we long to see them return to life.

Walk the walk of friendship. Be part of the healing team. Tabitha's friends took time to ride to Lydda, find Peter, convince him to pack his bags, and bring him back. Look what a great thing God did to reward their loving efforts! Be a good friend this week. God surely works through friends.

Tabitha's "Bonus Years"

While writing this book we lost a young friend, Annie Jane, to cancer complications. She was only fifty-six, and it has been a sad loss for her family and for us, her friends. Annie had been a teenager in our Carlsbad youth group, always bright, gifted, musically talented. After graduating *cum laude* from college, she married John, and they settled into careers and into a church where they were faithful members for years. In her thirties, Annie won a battle with Hodgkin's Disease and lived another twenty-two years with us. John called those twenty-two years her "bonus years." It was her second chance at life, and she lived those years well—incredibly well.

Annie lived to raise their two beautiful, loving daughters, and care for them with devotion. She was a soccer mom, a T-ball mom, a horse show mom, and sponsor of countless church youth trips. She was president of her girls' choral group Boosters, and accompanied the school choir. Annie served as Music Director of her church. She involved herself in Bible studies and prayer groups, mentoring young moms and teenagers, and went on a mission to Mexico. She was deeply into the "Emmaus Walks" as a leader. With John she founded the musical ensemble "Soul'd Out" and was its pianist and vocalist. All this, as she bravely battled the after-effects of her cancer treatments, had multiple surgeries, lost a kidney, and developed breast cancer. She made her life full—full of good works for her Lord and her family. She was a Tabitha, a disciple *"who was always doing good and helping. . . ."*

Annie's story has caused us to wonder how Tabitha lived her "bonus years." Few are allowed to come back from death and live again as she was. Did Tabitha continue her ministry of kindness, sewing for the poor? Perhaps she witnessed to the power of the Lord in her life and told of her "out of body experiences." How did she thank the friends who had intervened to save her life? It must have been an unusual opportunity for *empowered living,* for it was the very power of Christ which resurrected her back to life. The intervention of friends, and the mercy of God brought her back, and surely now she lived her (second) life for his glory!

You and I, my friend, are also alive by the design of God. We probably have not died and come back in a physical sense, but we have known the *rebirth* into a new life in Christ—no less a miracle! We live by his grace and his power, so let us live these "bonus years" well. We are sisters of Tabitha!

BREAKTHROUGH IN CAESAREA
Cornelius' Family Welcomes Peter

Acts 10–11

"Father? Father, are you all right?" Julia worried as she came to the top of the stairway. "You've been at your prayers an extra long time, and I was concerned about you."

Cornelius shook off his thoughts and turned towards his daughter, a little distracted. "Yes, Dear, I'm all right—at least I think I am. It was such a strange thing—I'm still not sure what happened just now."

"What do you mean, Papa? Are you feeling ill? Shall I call Mother?" Julia turned to start down just as her brother came up.

"Is something wrong up here?" he asked. "Father, is everything all right?"

"Father seems ill, I think. Go and call Mother to come up and see about him," Julia instructed. "Something has happened."

"Now, children, don't overreact and alarm your mother—I'm all right," Cornelius assured his two worriers. "But, do get your mother, Justus. I think we may all need to have a talk. I've just seen an angel."

"An angel?!" they chorused.

"Uh—yes Sir, I'll go get mother—right away!" the son mumbled, and rushed back down the outside stairs calling, "*Mama!* Mama where *are* you?"

Porcia, hearing tension in her son's voice, broke off her

conversation and quickly stepped out the door. "What is it, Son?" she asked.

"It's Father," he warned gently. "He was on the rooftop at prayers, and Julia found him. He's talking out of his head about seeing an angel. We thought you should come."

"An *angel?*" she repeated. "He thinks he saw an angel? Did he hit his head—or maybe have a sunstroke? He's been up there in the hot sun for quite a while." Porcia was hurrying up the stairs behind her son as she spoke.

She found Cornelius and Julia sitting on his prayer mat, talking quietly. Julia moved to make room for her mother. "He seems better, Mama. But you need to hear his story," the girl explained.

"What happened, Dear?" she asked, as she knelt to feel her husband's brow with her wrist. "Did you get too much sun?" Then, turning to the children she said, "One of you run down and get your father a cool drink."

"No, wait!" Cornelius intervened. "I want you all to hear this. I know it sounds a little crazy, but don't think me mad—it *did* happen just as I am saying. I was at prayers in the usual way, when I distinctly saw a man in shining clothes—I think he was an angel—and he spoke to me—he called me by name."

"And what did he say, Papa?" Julia asked softly.

"He said, 'Cornelius, God has heard your prayers, and he has seen the offerings you have given to the poor, and has accepted them.' And then he told me to send men to Joppa and find a man called Simon Peter, and bring him here."

"The God of the Jews, Father?" Justus asked, amazed. "The true God of Israel that we hear of at the synagogue?"

"That God, Justus. He has been watching."

"Joppa is a big place, Husband. How will you locate a man with such a common name? How will you ever know it is the right person?" Porcia persisted.

"The angel said he was lodging with Simon the tanner, who lives by the sea. I think we can find it by that description."

"Or by the smell," Justus added. "Whew! Those tanneries really have an odor you never forget!"

"Will you be going right away?" Porcia asked with concern. "Are you sure you feel well enough to travel? Maybe you should wait until morning, when it is cooler."

"Actually, I don't think I can go at all right now," Cornelius responded with concern. "The military ship for Rome sails in the morning, and I must finish my reports to send with them. So I think I'll have to send some others—a couple of the troops, or maybe some servants—in my place."

"Will this Simon Peter believe and come with them?" Porcia asked. "It may not be easy to get a Jew to come to our home—they don't mix with the Gentiles, you know—and especially if only a servant asks him."

Julia nodded agreement. "My friends at synagogue are not allowed to come home with me, Father. They have such different customs, and their Law does not permit mingling. He may not want to come."

"I know that's true," Cornelius agreed, "but I feel that, if Jehovah sent an angel to me, then he will send some sort of sign to Simon Peter also. Can you spare a couple of the servants for this trip?" he asked his wife.

"Yes, of course!" she assured him. "We could send

Hamid and Nouri, I think. But—I agree with Julia—I wonder if Simon Peter would come just for servants. The soldiers might be a better idea. What do you think?"

Cornelius stood and walked to the roof abutment, his eyes searching the dockside scene below. "Justus, would you go for Julius, please, Son? I think you will find him in the barracks at this time of day, or maybe in the stables. I'll talk with Julius and see what he thinks."

"Good choice, Father. Julius is a sharp guy, and also a God-fearer. He would stand well in your place for this mission. I'll be on my way," and he started down the outside stairs, but then turned back. "Father? Could I go with Julius on the trip? I would like to meet this Simon Peter and bring him back," he asked hopefully.

"Son, I know you would," Cornelius sympathized, "and you are responsible enough to go; but your tutor will be here for lessons in the morning, and you need to complete your studies if you are to make it in the ranks as a soldier in the Emperor's army. I think you had better stay here and tend to business."

Porcia saw her son's disappointment and added, "You can meet Simon Peter when he comes, Son. In fact, you can be his official aide, if you like."

As Justus turned and disappeared, Julia questioned, "But Mother, surely you don't think Simon will stay overnight with us? The Jews do not even come into Gentile homes, and surely do not stay the night! He will probably want to lodge with one of the synagogue families."

Porcia looked at her daughter fondly, so lovely and bright, and growing up so fast. "You do have a point, Julia," she responded admiringly, "but we shall make every preparation, and invite him. If he should, by some miracle, choose to break tradition, we will be ready and happy to have him."

"But what would we feed him, Mother?" Julia persisted. "The Jewish people do not eat like we do. My friends tell me they have strict rules from the Torah to follow. They even have special dishes to eat from. They don't eat any pork, and some kinds of fish are not allowed. We don't know about all that."

"Well, we'll just have to find out, Girl," her mother responded with a smile. "Things like that can be learned. I'll send Tirah to the Jewish market, and she can get the right kind of fish. And I'll have Nouri put a lamb on the spit before he leaves—I know they eat lamb."

"But don't fix it with milk! Sarah tells me they can't cook any meat with milk—something about not fixing it in its mother's milk," Julia warned.

"All right, we won't fix it with milk, Dear. But don't worry, we'll get it right. We'll just have enough choices that Simon Peter can find something he likes to eat. Now, I think I'll talk to Tirah and get her started on preparations."

"Julia, you help your mother," Cornelius admonished. "I need to get to headquarters and get on with the paper work, so I can be free when he arrives."

"Will you send Julius on horseback, or by foot?" Porcia asked. "It makes a day or more difference in when they will arrive, and I can plan meals better if I know."

"I'll send Julius and the servants on horses, but they may return by foot. I'd say it will be late tomorrow, or possibly the day after, when they come back. It will depend on Peter's reply."

"And who would you like to have here to meet him when he comes?" she pursued. "Just our family, or do you want to include any of our friends from synagogue or the headquarters?"

Porcia's question was well taken, and Cornelius thought for a moment before responding. "I think—that's a good question, Porcia—I think we should include Julius' family and the other God-fearers from synagogue. We could also ask some of our Jewish neighbors, but I'm not sure they will come."

"What about the household servants, and my sister and her family? Should I ask them in also?" Porcia was mentally counting the number, wondering how many could fit into their great room comfortably. "We could use the courtyard—it's a little larger," she suggested.

"Yes, invite them all," he responded. "Jehovah will send who he will send. Tell them to be here early on the day after tomorrow. And I guess we should have some extra wine and fruits, maybe some side dishes, in case he is delayed. It should be an interesting time," he said, kissing her and turning to go down the stairs. "I'll see you for supper."

Porcia and Julia exchanged knowing glances, shaking their heads. "How do we get into these situations, Julia?" the mother asked, laughing. "Being married to a centurion certainly has its challenges!"

Janet Burton

BEHIND THE SCENES
A Study of Acts 10:1–11:18

Momentum for Change

The Good News of Jesus was beginning to move like a tidal wave outward from the epicenter, Jerusalem. When persecution came to that city, believers scattered, carrying with them the stories of Jesus. Their prayers for boldness in the Spirit (see Acts 4:23–24, 29–30) had been answered, and were moving them forward on this swelling tide. Philip went north into Samaria preaching, and a revival happened. Shortly afterwards, Peter began preaching westward, toward the Mediterranean coast. We met him last week in Lydda and then Joppa, and there he stayed a few more days.

Peter was waiting on God. No doubt the believers were somewhat unsettled with this persecution, and the waves of revival surging into strange territories. The Gospel had found its way into the hearts of believers who were Greek-speaking Jews—foreign born, but Jews, none the less. Then on to some Samaritans, who were mixed race citizens, not accepted by the Jews as brothers, but accepted as believers. Philip had even baptized an African man from Ethiopia. Where would the Message find a home next? Peter was catching his breath in Joppa, waiting on God to lead him on in this great *"Go Ye"* adventure.

Roman Beginnings

We will leave Peter on R&R at Joppa, and trek northward on the coast about thirty miles to Caesarea, headquarters of the Roman army and government in Israel. Pilate had lived there, as would other Roman governors appointed by the Emperor. The governors made frequent trips to the Jewish center at Jerusalem, but chose to command their civil work from Caesarea, a port city. Herod the Great had rebuilt the port just before the birth of Christ, and it afforded easily accessible transportation "back home" to Rome.

At Caesarea we find an interesting Roman named Cornelius, a centurion who had become a believer in Israel's True God. They called these people *"God-fearers:"* non-Jews who had become disenchanted with the pagan gods of the Greeks and Romans, and now accepted the monotheistic concept of One True Creator God. As God-fearers, the Jews allowed them to worship and participate to some degree in local synagogues. Cornelius and his family did not just attend and believe, they also gave alms to the poor and participated in regular prayers. They did not convert to Judaism by observing circumcision and all of the laws of Moses, but they were seekers. And the Jewish community of Caesarea respected Cornelius and his family for their acceptance of, and participation in, the faith.

A centurion was an important man, comparable to a captain in our military, commanding one hundred troops. Centurions were chosen for their leadership abilities and steadfastness. A centurion would stay in a fight and die at his post. There were only six centurions in every regiment (cohort) of 600 men, so Cornelius stood tall among his peers. It is interesting to note that, while we think of the Romans as an occupying force, often despised by their Jewish subjects, all the pictures we have of centurions in the New Testament show that they were rather sympathetic to

Christians. Recall the one at Caesarea who came to Jesus requesting that his valued servant be healed? (Find him in Luke 7:1–10.) He is the one who told Jesus not to bother coming into his (Gentile) home, but just to speak the word, and his servant would be well. Jesus said of him, *"I tell you, I have not found such great faith even in Israel."* We are told that the Roman officer had built the Jewish synagogue!

Even the centurion, who oversaw the execution detail which crucified Jesus, although he allowed the terrible atrocities that preceded Christ's death, did later admit, *"Surely this was a righteous man"* or *"a Son of God."* And toward the end of Acts we will come upon the centurion, Julius, who was charged with taking Paul safely to Rome as a prisoner. He showed several favors and kindnesses to Paul. It's fair to say that these were quality men, open minded and, at times, used by God to further the Gospel. Cornelius and his family were some of these.

Angelic Intervention

God's angel messengers were kept busy in the days of the Early Church. In Acts 5:19 we find one of them letting Peter and John out of jail in the middle of the night. One of the questions we might ask in our next life could be: *What circumstances prompted God to ask an angel to become visibly involved, so that earthlings could identify them for what they were?* Angels may be all around us, watching and helping, but generally we do not know they are there. In this case, Cornelius was quite sure of what he saw. (Read that exciting story now in Acts 10:1–8.)

Rarely, but on occasion, we hear stories from missionaries about devout seekers in unevangelized places who want to know God, but have no one to bring the truth to them. God sends them a vision or a dream, instructing them where to go to find help. One of the exciting things about Cornelius' vision is what the angel told him: *"Your prayers and gifts for the poor have come up as a memorial offering before God."* How encouraging to realize that our prayers and good deeds are known to God, even when we may feel too insignificant to be noticed. Cornelius must have felt very affirmed to know that his efforts toward establishing a relationship with this "borrowed" Jewish God had been accepted, and now God wanted a relationship with him! Our God is a seeking God, and he rewards those who, in turn, seek him.

This was no vague, oblique, cloudy vision—it was filled with specifics. God not only knew Cornelius, *he knew his family*—his wife and children—his household servants! And, *he knew them by name!* He even gave him Peter's address in Joppa—his borrowed, temporary address. Never again doubt that God knows who you are and where you are at any given moment. God keeps his hand on his faithful, and keeps account of his resources. He was about to connect some dots here.

The Counterpart Revelation

Well, Peter didn't see an angel, but he did get a trance—a sleep-level revelation from God. (Find his story in Acts 10:9–16.) It could make a good comedy routine: sleepy-headed Peter, seeing a sail-like sheeting lowered, full of animals, when he was hungry enough to eat a bear. But bears, like camels, pigs, dogs and cats, frogs and other creepy things, were definitely off limits to a good Jew. Leviticus 11 lists, in Technicolor, all the disgusting things a good Jew could not eat. Those laws were reasonable—they protected the Jewish people from plague-carrying rodents, and parasite-carrying mammals, and other diseases borne by varmints. Peter would rather have starved than eat any of those things. *No thank you, Lord, I'll wait on the cook.* Even a bad cook's fare would be better than the stuff in that tarp.

It took three times, but God finally began to get his point across to Peter. We have to recall the three times Jesus had to ask, *"Peter, Do you love me?"* Peter wasn't an easy sell, was he? It was not that God wanted Peter to eat a pig, but he wanted to make a point: that God can change the rules when he chooses to, and God was choosing at this very moment to extend the Good News into the Roman community. Jews were still thinking that the Messiah was mainly for the Jews, but God was illustrating to Peter the new day ahead.

Peter was still rubbing his eyes and scratching his head when Cornelius' entourage arrived at the door of his host, Simon the tanner. (Look now at Acts 10:19–23.) Still not fully aware of the implications of his vision, Peter met these Gentile emissaries at the door, graciously heard them out, and invited them in. In fact, they spent the night in that Jewish home. The rules were already changing.

The Crucial Meeting

It was too late in the day to begin the walking trip back to Caesarea, but the dark hours allowed Peter to pack his bags and make preparations. Early the next morning he set out with Cornelius' messengers, taking with him six trusted, Jewish brothers from the Joppa community. Peter had slept on the vision, and he now understood what he was to do. His heart was listening and learning. He must have stepped lively on the way.

Peter and Cornelius met as equals. (This part of the story begins in Acts 10:24.) Without hesitation Peter entered this Gentile home, and found that Cornelius and his family had gathered a large group in to listen to him. Imagine the scene: his wife and children, their trusted household servants and their families, perhaps some God-fearing military families, close neighbors and friends, other relatives, even some slaves. With his recent, eye-opening vision as a backdrop, Peter began to do what Peter did well by now: he preached about Jesus.

He included all the important things: the plan of God that all people might believe; the importance of the life, teachings, and death of Jesus; his victorious resurrection; and the commission to preach. But, before he could even give the invitation, down came the gift of the Holy Spirit on the gathered crowd. The meeting turned into a praise service, each speaking in his native—or a new—heart language. It must have been a joyful bedlam, and finally Peter turned to his Jewish, Joppa companions and asked, *"Can we deny these people baptism? They have received the same Holy Spirit as we have."* A new group of believers was born into the church that day at Caesarea.

Searching for the Women Folk

None of them are named. We only have the Bible's implication that women were part of this experience. Cornelius' family, *"all his family,"* was listed, with *"his relatives and close friends."* Acts 2:17–18 assures us that these Holy Spirit outpourings included both men and women, young and old; so we wrote into our story a wife and daughter for this godly centurion. It isn't much of a reach to assume other wives and daughters were also part of the event. Often the Good News is carried through relationships and hospitality, as it was in this case. And, although "Porcia" is not named in Scripture, she was a likely partner in this very significant, turning-point event: the coming of the Gospel to Romans.

Our churches are full of Porcias—quiet women who work to create an atmosphere of warmth and welcome in which the story of Jesus is heard and received. The gifts of the Spirit are evident in this: hospitality, kindness, helping, sharing. Sometimes the quiet women among us feel that they are overshadowed by those who have more recognized, "up front" abilities. The ladies who can sing on the praise team or play the piano, those who teach a class, lead the children's sermon, chair the ladies' retreat ministry—these are the ones whose names get printed in the weekly church mail out. But behind the scene are the many who are rocking our babies, washing our dishes, sewing for the poor, stuffing the office mailings, cataloging library resources, emptying trash. They are no less *empowered* for the *"Go Ye"* adventure.

Fifty-plus years ago my sister and brother-in-law, Barbara and Joseph Grimes, were appointed by Wycliffe to be Bible translators for a little-known people group in Western Mexico. As a new bride Barbara moved with Joe out to a remote village in the mountains, where they settled in to become part of the Huichol culture and life. There were just two believers, Roman and his wife, Vicenta, and for the next ten or so years they lived beside them, translating the New Testament, teaching the people to read. In the course of it, three babies were born to them (in a Mexico City hospital), and raised out in that far-away, secluded tribe. They lived as the people lived, without electricity or running water, learning the language and the lore, and becoming fast friends. The family forded rivers on horseback going to and from their adobe home. The community of believers grew, and God blessed their work.

One of their crucial goals was to teach the people to read and write so that they could study the Bible for themselves. After generations of having only an oral language, many—especially the women—could not find motivation for becoming educated in this way. Barbara searched for ways to interest her Huichol women friends in literacy. Noticing that they liked some of her recipes—especially the cakes she made for festivals—she began adapting her ingredients to available commodities. From their simple cornmeal she developed a cake recipe, and wrote it down. When she offered to teach the women to read the recipe they saw the advantage of learning. In time many of the Huichols became literate, heard the Gospel, and helped each other come to faith in Jesus Christ. What a homespun illustration of how women reach women with the gospel through gentle friendship and hospitality. These are the wings on which the Good News is carried across cultural and economic barriers, from person to person. Never underestimate the quiet ways of *empowered women* who love the Lord!

JANET BURTON

Breakthrough in God's Time

God's timing was perfect, and his choices superb. He selected Peter, the lead Apostle, to be the one to break this new ground into the Roman community, knowing the other church leaders would follow his lead. He chose a God-fearing Roman, already accepted by the Jewish community in Caesarea, to host the meeting. Read how quickly the church fathers in Jerusalem agreed with Peter's "breaking the rules" to enter a Gentile home and share Jesus with them (Acts 11:17–19). When it is God's will, he makes a way.

Change is at crisis levels in many of today's churches. Jack and I have been amazed as we watched our own church family in recent times morph from an almost-all-Anglo congregation toward more diversity. Change came mostly through the momentum of our youth ministry, as teens brought their friends, and neighborhood gangs were reached and welcomed. Our youth minister, youth parents, and youth workers helped lead the way. Mission trips into other cities' ghettos showed us a broader view of life. We looked outside our "Jerusalem," and discovered a new vision for who we could become. During our thirty-plus years at Woodlawn, the church has transitioned from being a neighborhood church to a regional one which includes many economic areas of our city. And as the congregation changed to reflect our community, our worship services also began to change.

Admittedly the worship style changes have been far more traumatic to deal with than the racial and social diversity was. Because of our great desire to reach our neighbors, and to attract younger, unchurched families, we have been forced confront new ways to sing, to dress, to use media, and to preach. Traditions sacred to us older Christians were not known or valued by the newer members. Just one example: the pulpit, always central to our emphasis on preaching the Word, is now gone (but the preaching has not gone). Change has a way of forcing us to rethink our beliefs, and weigh what can and cannot be tossed or lost. Self-examination of motives and attitudes, prayerful soul-searching, must under gird the process of learning to love those who were not raised up in our traditions,

In our minds we see parallels between Woodlawn's changes and this giant step forward, when Peter took the Gospel into a Roman home. In the weeks, months, and years ahead, the Early Church would confront the painful process of change. There were things that had been accepted by the Jewish Christians for generations. Take, for example, the matter of circumcision: the sacred sign that a man belonged to God's people. Jews had insisted on it for nearly eighteen-hundred years, since God commanded the rite of Abraham's family. With the influx of Gentile Christians, that most-valued tradition—actually a command from God—was compromised, but not without great debate and division in the ranks. It remained a divisive matter for years to come, as we shall see while tracing the missions of Paul in later chapters of this book.

Change comes, and we must ask searching questions: *Is what I am holding onto a vital doctrine of the faith, or is it an old tradition, which I need to let go? Is God trying to work a new thing for his Kingdom in this? Can we learn to honor God in this new way?* Only by the grace of God can we change with the times in healthy ways. Look up! Maybe God has sent a vision—like a sheet full of pigs and bears—down onto our rooftops to help us learn the lessons!

ANGEL AT THE GATES
Rhoda Answers Peter's Knock

Acts 12:1–25

Barnabas and Mary sat quietly in the cooking area downstairs from the prayer gathering. Food and drink were on the table near them, but neither could eat for the urgency of the moment.

"I cannot keep from thinking of how Peter must be feeling," Mary ventured. "Alone in that prison, guarded, chained, knowing that tomorrow he faces trial before a demented, power-mad king. It must feel very hopeless."

"Yes, no doubt it does," her cousin agreed. "But Peter is a guy who rises up with courage in the face of danger. Think about his attacking Caiaphas' servant in the garden, and standing tall at the Pentecost outpouring. He, more than most of us, I believe, will stand true, even to—even if it means death," he finished, tears glistening, mouth trembling.

"He has been amazing these ten years," Mary agreed solemnly. "I sent John Mark with a servant to take him food this afternoon, and they found him in reasonable spirits. But, it was sad for Mark to see him in chains. And you know how things seem worse in the dark hours. Just having lost one of his closest friends, the reality of a bloody execution cannot help being on his mind. I just pray God will strengthen him. He must be having a sleepless night in Herod's jail."

"This is the worst persecution we've had in a while, Mary," Barnabas spoke the obvious. "It was bad before, when the leaders attacked us just after Pentecost; and Peter caught the brunt of it then. After Stephen's death we all felt the danger was so close to home, and so many fled to the countryside. But always before God protected his own special Twelve—the ones Jesus so carefully discipled and sent out. But now, with the loss of our James, I guess we all have had to confront the possibility that Herod could kill the very pillars of our faith. It's a frightening reality." Barnabas' eyes betrayed the depth of his concern and grief. "James was such a good man—such a strong and trusted leader. He leaves a very big hole in our young church."

"Has John gone back to Galilee to comfort his parents? With both of the brothers gone from Jerusalem, and Peter in prison, who will *lead* us through this dangerous time?" Mary's voice was filled with fear.

"God will provide," Barnabas assured, reaching out to pat her arm. "He always has. Others will come forward. Andrew is still among us, and Matthew is back from Ethiopia. Thomas is also home from Arabia. God will bring us the leaders we need, because Jerusalem is the center of things. And—who knows? Perhaps he has others, outside the Twelve, like Philip and Nicolas and . . ."

" . . . and yourself?" Mary finished the thought just as her servant girl, Rhoda, came rushing through to grab a honey cake and head out the courtyard door. "Rhoda," Mary called, "who wants the honey cake at this hour of the night?"

"Oh, Miss Mary," the girl answered with a breathless bow, "it's for John Mark. He is so upset about this trouble with Mr. Peter, I thought a cake might comfort him. You know how he loves them."

Mary smiled weakly, shaking her head as mothers will do. "All right, Rhoda, take him a cake, but I think you are spoiling him."

"He probably needs a little spoiling tonight," Barnabas defended. "Take him two cakes, Rhoda." And they all laughed quietly as she bounded out the door. Mary got up to rescue the remaining cakes, and wrap them carefully in a towel.

Finding John Mark still moping in the courtyard, Rhoda offered him the sweet treat. "Look, John Mark—your mama sent you this honey cake you like so much. Cousin Barnabas said to bring you two of them, but I thought one was plenty this late before bed."

"How could I eat a cake when my best friend is about to be killed?" John Mark retorted, angrily. "Those bloody Herods! I can't understand why God allows them to stay in power, committing all these atrocities. They are an evil family—*ruthless! Selfish!* Why doesn't God just wipe them out with a plague or something?"

Rhoda drew back at his outburst, wanting to help but not knowing how. "I don't know, John Mark," she answered weakly. "It's all too hard for me. I just don't know. I just thought the cake might make you feel better."

"Nothing will make me feel better," he said, dropping his head into his hands, fighting back his tears. "Seeing Peter like that today, all chained up to those Roman guards—*both* hands chained!—it just made me feel so bad, and so angry. I couldn't do anything to help him. All I could do was leave the food basket and tell him that the brothers were going to pray through the day and night that God would save him."

"And what did he say—or did he say anything?" Rhoda sympathized.

"Not too much. The guards were just inches away, so it wasn't much of a time for talking. But he told me he was all right, and not to worry overmuch, and thanked me for the food and the prayers. Then he offered to share the food with the guards! I wanted to shout, *No!! That food isn't for the Roman dogs!* But then I remembered that Jesus taught us, *'Feed your enemies. Do good to those who despitefully treat you and persecute you.'* And Peter was doing just that. He is an amazing man, Rhoda. I wish I could be just like him—but I probably never will be."

"Sure you will be, Mark," she encouraged him. "You have watched him so carefully, followed him like a puppy since you were a child, listened to all his stories. I think you just may grow up to be very much like Peter."

John Mark reached over, took the treat from her hands, and tasted one corner. In just a minute he had devoured it. The two sat a while in silence, listening to the night sounds. Delilah, the pet nanny, roused herself and came to lick his fingers, hoping for a bite, and eyeing him accusingly. Mark tousled her ears and rubbed her forehead, remembering how he had raised her from a kid when her mother took ill. "Go back to bed, Lolly," he chided with a playful shove. "It's way past your bedtime."

"Do you think Peter will be set free again?" Rhoda asked him hopefully. "God sent him an angel once before—a few years back. He could do it again, couldn't he?"

"Could—yes," Mark answered skeptically, "but realistically, Rhoda, *would he?* I mean, he didn't send one for James last week, and James was just as important as Peter is. Realistically . . ." Mark groped for an honest answer, not liking any that came to mind. "Realistically, I think we have to be ready to hear the worst, and to give him up if God does not choose to do another miracle."

"Oh, Mark! Let's not talk that way—not yet. There is still time."

"I just will be so lost without him," Mark grieved. "He has been the one who took time with me, especially after my father died. He told me the stories of Jesus, and took me with him when he could."

"But you will still have Cousin Barnabas," Rhoda reasoned vainly. "He'll be there for you."

"And Cousin Barnabas is a good man also, but he wasn't one of the Twelve. He didn't see Jesus in action those three years, and he doesn't know the stories as well as Peter does."

John Mark stood and walked to the acacia tree beside the shed, shoulders bent. Rhoda knew he didn't want her to see his tears. For a minute she sat quietly watching him, wanting to go to him and hold him close, but not daring. *Maybe another honey cake would help,* she thought, and slipped back inside the house quietly.

"What's happening out there?" Mary asked, seeing her come in. "You two have been talking quite a while."

"I just thought maybe that second honey cake was a good idea," Rhoda answered, apologetically. "John Mark just can't seem to get peace in his heart tonight."

"Well, he's a growing boy," Barnabas observed. "Another cake will not hurt him a bit. Take him two, Rhoda."

"*No!*" his mother objected. "Not two at this hour. But do take him one more, and tell him it's time for him to be getting settled for bed. We don't know what tomorrow will bring."

Rhoda found the cake wrapped in a towel, and hurried back outside. "Those two are certainly together a lot these days," Mary observed. "He is so lost without Peter, and she is such a giddy little thing. They make a funny pair."

"She'll grow up, Mary," Barnabas answered sagely. "I remember what a pitiful little thing she was when you got her a few years ago. She has come a long way."

"Yes—she's a favorite, even if she doesn't always have her head on straight. She was kind of pitiful, wasn't she?" Mary remembered. "Losing her mama at birth, and then her daddy just a few years later—she just didn't have much of anyone. Her uncle tried to raise her, but he made such a difference between her and his own youngsters, she was mostly just angry and neglected. I was happy to take her. We needed a helper for Jacintha, who had been with us for so long but was ailing. I think Jacintha has taught her well. But, I imagine our days with Rhoda are numbered. Her uncle will be marrying her off before long."

"Was that a knock?" Barnabas asked, listening toward the front of the house.

"I didn't hear it. Why would someone not ring the bell?" Mary wondered. They both listened in silence, and—sure enough—it sounded as if someone was outside the bolted gate. "Rhoda!" Mary called toward the courtyard. "Run check the front gate for me, please. Someone is out there wanting in, and the bolt is thrown." Rhoda hurried through the room, and Mark followed her in the door. "Who could be coming at this late hour?" Mary asked.

"Probably some more of the believers who have just gotten off work," Mark suggested. "Maybe they didn't ring the bell so the neighbors would not be wakened."

"Or maybe they were worried that soldiers were following," Barnabas added. "Everyone is expecting the worst right now. I just hope we are all wrong about it."

"Maybe it is bad news about Peter," Mary worried. "It's after midnight, and good news never comes at this hour." And the three waited for Rhoda to return.

BEHIND THE SCENE
A Study of Acts 12:1–25

Ominous Times in Jerusalem

The Jewish leaders were angry and demanding. This sect of Nazarenes continued to grow. Ten years of opposition, threats, and imprisonments had not quieted them or stopped their advance. Not only had they corrupted Judaism with their insistence that Jesus was the promised Messiah, and that he was alive from the dead. Now they were accepting Greeks and Romans into their faith. Next they would be bringing them from the Court of Gentiles into the Temple proper! The very sacred courts of Judaism were threatened! They simply had to be stopped.

Conveniently, the Jewish leaders found a new ally in King

Herod Agrippa I, who came to power about 41 a.d. He was one of a dynasty of bloody Herods who wrecked havoc on God's people over several decades. His grandfather, Herod the Great, had killed the babies of Bethlehem following the birth of Jesus. His uncle, Herod Antipas, beheaded John the Baptist, and consented to the death of Jesus. Herod Agrippa's own father and mother had been murdered by his grandfather in jealous rage. It was a bloody family beyond our imagining.

His family heritage had marked Herod Agrippa I in another way also. Crowned king of the Jews by his cronies in Rome (he had been a classmate of both Caligula and Claudius, and helped them rise to power as emperors), Agrippa knew that his power was not well received. He was not a pure Jew himself, having been born to a Jewish father and an Edomite mother. So it was in his interest to garner favor with the Jewish leadership in Jerusalem, and strengthen his right to rule in that way. At some point it was made clear to him that the Jews would favor his executing of one of these pesky Christ-followers. So for reasons of personal power, not because of any fault or crime on the part of the believers, James the brother of John was seized and beheaded. And the Jewish leaders were pleased. (Find this part of the story in Acts 12:1–4.)

Seeing that his act was appreciated, and with a lively eye to future favors, Herod Agrippa then seized Peter, intending to do the same with him. But he was caught in his scheme by the Jewish calendar—it was Pentecost week. Executions were not allowed during Pentecost. The leaders would frown on that, and his "good deed" would surely backfire.

Herod had no choice but to hold Peter securely until the feast had passed. No doubt he remembered the debacle under his uncle, Herod Archelaus, when several Apostles had disappeared without explanation from prison in the middle of the night (see Acts 5:17–21), and were found preaching illegally in the temple at first light the following morning! Agrippa was not about to repeat that mistake. He would see to it that Peter was kept bound to two soldiers day and night, with two more posted as sentries at his cell door. Not even an angel of God could breach that kind of security—or so he thought.

Prayers of Fear and Faith

Acts 12:5 tells us how the believers reacted to this second great threat in just a few days. They banded together at the home of Mary, mother of John Mark—a place where they had gathered many times before. Some think this is where they had prayed for the Power to fall at Pentecost. Some even hold this to be the probable location of Jesus' last supper with his disciples on the night he was betrayed. Now, about ten years later, this was still the place they gathered to pray for Peter's safe release.

Persecution was not new to them. Following Pentecost, when the Jewish leaders saw thousands flocking to believe in Jesus as Messiah, the Apostles were repeatedly arrested, jailed, and threatened. At one point they were even flogged. They answered that threat by praying for boldness, and went back out on the streets the next day to continue witnessing.

A few years later opposition surfaced again, when Stephen was confronted by the Jews of Greek-speaking synagogues. Furious with Stephen's powerful and successful preaching, they seized him and had him stoned. Young Saul was one who consented to his death. Following that tragedy, Saul led a great persecution of believers, and most of them were forced to flee from Jerusalem into the countryside. We have followed some of their stories in Chapters 2, 3 and 4 of this book.

This third great wave of persecution took place about ten years after Jesus' death, and it shook the believers' faith badly. The Twelve had been coming and going from Jerusalem on missions into the world. We have little biblical record of these early ventures. We know of Philip the deacon's trips into Samaria, and Peter's visits into the coastal plane. Some interesting clues have been preserved outside the Bible, in the traditions of the church historians. Nathaniel (Bartholomew) is said to have gone south around the Mediterranean coast from Israel, to Ethiopia and Egypt. Matthew, also is reported to have gone to Ethiopia; Thomas to Babylon and on to India; Judas (Thaddaeus) to Armenia. Simon (the Zealot) was reported to have gone to several of the countries of the empire, ever zealous for his Lord. Andrew, James, and Peter worked mostly in Jerusalem and Judea. In later years, while Paul was traveling to Asia Minor, Greece and Rome, other Apostles are said to have gone as far as Spain and Britain.[1]

Since the Early Church expected Jesus' return to happen soon, and since the Apostles did not see themselves as heroes of the new faith, few records were kept of their lives after Pentecost. Whatever the facts, surely they were obedient to Jesus' command to *"go and make disciples of all nations."* And all of them faced persecution as they went.

So it was that the believers gathered to pray for Peter, chained in Herod's prison. Did they expect a miracle? Apparently not. They had not received one for James the week before, so it seemed likely that God would not intervene now. But, to their credit, they *did* gather and pray earnestly for Peter. Isn't it comforting that God rewards our prayers, even when they are not perfect—not prayed in perfect faith? Peter's miracle came just in the nick of time.

Peter's Profile of Courage

Peter was a man who showed great courage in the face of danger. In Gethsemane, as the others stood paralyzed with fear, Peter lunged forward, dagger in hand, and swiped at the neck of Caiaphas' servant, severing his ear (John 18:10–11). Later that same night, already identified as a close follower of the accused Jesus, Peter followed into the courtyard of the High Priest's house while Jesus was being tried inside (John 18:15–16). Surely he had in his mind to wait for Jesus, and rescue him if possible. He could have run like the others did. Two days later he was back with the disciples in the upper room when news of the empty tomb was brought by the women. He raced again into the face of danger—the guarded tomb—to check out the story (John 20:3–9).

At Pentecost, Peter stood tall, preaching to thousands about the resurrection of his beloved Lord. Arrested, threatened, jailed, flogged, still he preached at every opportunity, and thousands believed. Facing an angry council, which had the power to take his life as they had taken Jesus,' he said, *'Judge for yourselves whether it is right in God's sight to obey you rather than God. For we cannot help speaking about what we have seen and heard."* (See Acts 4:19–20.) Soon he was off to Lydda, and to Joppa where he raised Tabitha from the dead; and then on to Caesarea, where he was first to share the Good News with the Romans. Did he deny Jesus on that awful night of his arrest and trial? Yes—but he had more than redeemed himself. We speak too much of his failures, and not enough about his courage.

Now we find him in Herod's prison, with a trial looming the next day, and what is he doing? Pacing? Worrying? Praying for an escape? Acts 12:6 tells us he was so sound asleep the rescuing angel had to prod him awake! (Read that exciting part of the story in Acts 12:6–12.) Knowing it could be his final night on earth, Peter, chained between two soldiers, kicked off his sandals, threw his outer cloak over him, and slept like a baby! He was so sound asleep he could barely comprehend what the angel was doing! He had to get clear of the chains, the cell, the prison, and out into the cool night air before it fully dawned on him what had taken place. He was a free man! Shaking off his grogginess, he headed for the place he knew his friends to be—Mary's house.

The Angel Rescue

Skeptics have suggested that there was no angel rescue at all. That this was probably an "inside job" by a Christian sympathizer who snuck in and set Peter free. Surely no one besides the guards could have unlocked two sets of arm irons, opened a cell door, passed two more guards, and opened the main prison doors, without being detected. Even that would have been a miracle of God! Nor would the four soldiers have willingly allowed it, knowing they would face execution in his place for their failure to keep Herod's prisoner secure.

There will always be skeptics—people who cannot accept what they cannot explain or understand. As my young friend, Jason G. Carr points out in his book, *Faith and the Christian Life,* to believers faith and reason are compatible, but to non-believers they are contradictory. Christians wonder about angels, and look for reasons and proofs, but when reason plays out and proof cannot be found, we accept the working of God by faith. Many of us believe that angels are real, though unseen. That there is a whole world of cosmic reality out there—a warfare between Good and Evil—in which angels are part of the forces of God. For us there is great comfort in knowing that angels are about us, protecting and guiding, although we are unable to see them. At times we think we feel their presence, or see the evidence of their working. Peter was privileged to actually *see* his angel for a few moments in time that dark night in Herod's jail.

Faith—that is the issue here. Faith in God, that is. Funny, isn't it, how we live by faith in so many other ways? Some believe the "Big Bang" theory by faith. No one saw it. Science is still trying to prove it. Yet we teach it by faith to our school children. We turn on the light switch by faith. We cannot see the electricity, and do not understand how it works; but we see its power and use it hundreds of times each day. But when it comes to believing God, it is trendy in our day to play the skeptic. We want to bring God down to our size—to explain him, and predict him, and *control* him for our own uses. Always remember that a God who can be explained is no God at all—he is a concoction of the human mind—a creation, and not an omnipotent, eternal being.

Some cannot accept an angelic intervention. We think unlocked arm irons in an empty cell and an open prison door are evidence enough.

Now About Rhoda . . .

We have just a couple of mentions of Rhoda. She was no heroine of the faith—she was just Mary's servant girl. Where did we get her story? Most of our stories just come as we research the Bible background and history of the day. They are suggested to our thoughts as we try to bring the women off the Bible pages, from two dimensions to three. Rhoda's is a little different. Her story comes from a romantic tale in Jack's family history.

About 1830 a baby girl, Elizabeth, was born in Snow Hill, Maryland. Her mother died in childbirth. Her father died when she was just four years old. An uncle gave her to a family in Kentucky, but at age seventeen she ran away and crossed the river by ferry into Indiana. There she found work with the Burton family. She soon was married to their son, David Absalom, and they became the great-great-grandparents of my husband, Jack. So we picked that delightful tale right off of our family tree.

It is of interest that Rhoda was at Mary's house very late into the night, indicating that she was a live-in servant. And her reaction—her joy at seeing Peter alive and free—tells us she was likely also a believer. There are several clues that she was still quite young. Upon answering the outer gate, she became so flustered that she turned to run for help, leaving Peter standing at the entrance, vulnerable to passing guards and prying neighbors. Her credibility was not very high—the group did not believe what she told them. (Finish the story now in Acts 12:13–19.) Girls generally married by the age of fourteen or fifteen, so Rhoda could even have been younger than that.

Finally someone went to check out her story, and found Peter patiently knocking. A noisy, if joyful and very short, reunion followed. Peter sent word that he was safe to the Lord's brother, James, who was now left to lead the church; and quickly departed for parts unknown. We find him back in Jerusalem a few years later, but for the time being, he had to find a safer place. God had more work for him to do.

Leaders Change, But God Controls

Circumstances change often, powers may threaten, valued friends and trusted leaders will die, but God's mission to save the world supercedes all of that. God's plan to redeem the world moves onward, above it all. Rhoda, Mary and the others could not stop the opposition, but they were part of the exciting movement of the Spirit of God as the Gospel survived all that Satan could hurl against it.

Just today, as I was putting these thoughts on paper, an email came from our nephew and his wife who are Bible translators in Indonesia. It was an urgent request for prayer from a Christian on East Timor, caught in another uprising of terrorist militants bent on killing Christians. For days their friends on the island have watched as houses were burned, innocent citizens slaughtered, equipment stolen and trashed. My nephew and his family, safely in Australia, receive and relay daily reports, filled with anguished cries for prayer. Australian troops have come in to try to keep peace, but the tirades go on. One Indonesian Christian wrote in today's email (and I will respect his English):

> One of our youth who was involve in a martial art group told me that this guy was killed by another martial art group. He also feels that it's not safe for him to stay [here]. Some of his friends told him to be careful because the rest of the group will be the next target. He was very scare and asked me to pray with him. I read Psalm 91 for him and prayed. I was worry about him because he also gave me his will: "If I die tonight, there are some money in my bag. So please manage to send my body [home]." But I assured him that God's angel will protects him. He also said "I was praying this whole afternoon . . . and now I feel close to God why such things happen. I'm not scare to die but I just don't want to die for nothing."

Christians still suffer, persecutions still come, friends and leaders sometimes die; but prayers are effective, and they are our only real means of defense in many situations. Today we are praying for these who are hurting in Indonesia, and for the safety of my nephew's family as they go and come from there in their translation work. Tomorrow, prayers will need to focus there and elsewhere. As long as the Gospel moves forward, Satan will try to stop it by any means he can. The prayers of the faithful, focused on the immediate situation, are the best counter defense we can bring.

PART III

Women of The Asia Expansion

Chapter 6
LETTERS TO MARY
John Mark Writes Home

Chapter 7
A LEGACY AND A PROMISE
Lois and Eunice Prepare Timothy

LETTERS TO MARY
John Mark Writes Home

Acts 12:25–13:13

Rhoda came into the courtyard from milking the nannies and found Mary sitting on a bench by the cistern, holding the parchment again. Setting her two buckets carefully in the shade she asked, "You still trying to read John Mark's letter, Miss Mary? You must have it about set in your heart by now."

Mary stretched in the morning sun and managed a smile. "Peter read it to me again last night after the gathering. I just can't keep him from my mind, Rhoda."

"Tell me again what he said, Miss Mary. It will comfort our hearts to hear it."

Mary unrolled the small scroll and studied its beginning. "I wish I could read better, Rhoda," she apologized. "But you are right—I just about know it by heart." And she began to recite the familiar opening words.

> From your devoted son John Mark, to my beloved mother, Mary, and to all my household in Jerusalem, greetings! May the Lord's peace be with you.

"I like that 'household' part," Rhoda giggled. "I hope he remembers me once in a while, too. He's been gone so long already, what with the time in Antioch, and now in Cyprus. Tell the part about the boat trip. I like that part," Rhoda said, pointing with enthusiasm.

"Oh, I'm sure he thinks of us and misses us all, Rhoda,"

Mary responded quietly. "He says he does. But not like we miss him. When a mother just has one son, the house is pretty empty when he leaves home."

Rhoda could see the sadness in her eyes, and knew she was struggling with the separation. She settled herself on the cistern bench, glad for the rest from her morning chores. "Go on, Miss Mary, tell me the part about the boat trip to Cyprus. I've never been on a big boat. It must have been really exciting—and a bit scary at times."

Mary rolled the parchment further, searching for the part about the trip. "I think this is it," she said. "It goes something like this."

> The trip was not too bad. I found it inter—interest-ing and learned a lot about ship life. We were at sea just over two days. The winds were favorable most of the time, with just a few lulls when we did not make much progress, but even that was pleasant. The sea is very blue when the sun shines and sea birds followed us most of the first day, sometimes landing on the mast above. We carried cargo of wheat sacks and oil jars mostly. That seems to be what the Cyprus people want at this time of year.
>
> Most of the sailors were young like me, but there were some crusty, old salts aboard, also. I became friends with Nasaar, a sailor younger than me from Egypt, who has been at sea since he was ten years of age. He told me tales about working aboard a large fre-freighter from Alex-an-dria. He's been all the way to Rome already, and he is only about twenty! He hopes one day to go on to Spain or even Britain. I can't imagine wanting to go that far from home! I guess he doesn't really have any other home than that ship. His parents have both died. We talked sometimes about losing our fathers, and how much life has changed.

Mary stopped briefly to wipe her eyes on her sleeve. "I hope he doesn't go farther way, Rhoda. My heart wants him to come home much sooner than that. There is a little more," she continued.

> The tramp ship doesn't go to Rome. It only plies the waters of the eastern sea, making the smaller ports mostly. That suits me well, because I do not have dreams of visiting the distant parts of the world. But I think maybe Saul has those dreams. He speaks of taking the Good News much farther than Cyprus.

Mary lowered the parchment to her lap and rested her head against the cistern wall, eyes closed in thought. Rhoda shook her head in wonder. "I can't even imagine it in my wildest thoughts," the servant girl said softly. "I guess I'm just meant to be a home body."

"I can't either, Rhoda," Mary agreed. "And I could not have let my John go so far, except that I trust Cousin Barnabas to care for him well. I know it is good for him to see some of the world beyond Judea; but it frightens me for him to be so far away. Who knows what is out there on the roads of Cyprus?"

"But don't fret, Miss Mary. Cousin Barnabas knows the way, because that's his home territory, and he can keep them safe."

"Oh, I know, Rhoda. He has relatives and friends in the synagogues where they can spend nights. In John's first letter he told how Barnabas and Saul got themselves attached to a group of officials traveling from Antioch to Selucia, so that their overland start to the journey was quite secure. And

I'm sure Barnabas and Saul are both well-traveled enough to know how to find safe passage, either by land or on the seas. I guess I'm just a worrying mama," she ended, standing up and smoothing the wrinkles from her house dress.

After a minute she continued. "I should probably be very happy, really, that John is having this opportunity to see some of the world, and be in the company of such good men as he does it. I can't think of anyone I'd rather have him working with than Cousin Barnabas. And I think Saul is a good man, too. The church at Antioch vouches for him. They would not have entrusted the offering to him for travel if they had not thought him trustworthy." Mary was moving toward the house as she spoke.

Rhoda picked up her two buckets carefully and followed, stopping to wait as Mary opened the cooking room door for her. Inside she began to pour the warm, goats' milk into a large crock to cool. "That Antioch church," Rhoda began, "it's a different kind of gathering than we have here, isn't it, Miss Mary?"

"I think so, from what John said in his earlier letter. He talked about the leaders being from all over. Two were even from Africa! Can you imagine it? We are so used to being led by our Twelve, and all the people who grew up in these parts. It would be very strange indeed to have men from other countries come in and lead us." Mary began washing fresh garden squash and slicing it as she spoke, and Rhoda joined her in the task. "But I guess the Antioch community is different—made up of foreigners in for the Roman government and commerce—and they don't think much of it."

"Shall I start the pot boiling for today's stew, Miss Mary?"

the servant girl asked, knowing the answer. "How many do we expect for dinner today?"

"Oh, not too many today, I think," Mary answered, stopping to tighten her apron over her dress. "Since the scattering we haven't had so many for meals. Probably just the house servants, and perhaps a few drop-in guests. Peter said Andrew is back in town from Galilee, and he may come here to stay a few days. But let's fix plenty so there will be some for the evening meal also."

They were busy about their tasks for a few minutes before Rhoda spoke again. "When do you think John will come home, Miss Mary? Do you think there is a chance they will go on farther after they finish in Cyprus?"

"I don't know, Rhoda. I guess I hope they won't. This Cyprus trip will take them probably half a year, and he has been gone already several months, what with the time in Antioch before they left. But Saul is a very strong person, and he could talk Cousin Barnabas in to going further."

"I know the sharing of the Gospel is important," Rhoda continued, uncertainly betraying her deeper fears. "I know Jesus said to go into *all the world*—like Brother Peter tells us so often. But John will be gone *years* if they do that! And letters don't come very often."

"The letters are slow and far between," Mary agreed. The first one came quickly from Selucia, with a man from the synagogue who had business here. But this last one—the one from Cyprus—took weeks. "I guess they had to find someone coming to Jerusalem through Joppa—someone who did not mind bringing it."

Mary was thoughtful for a few moments, and then went

on. "I have thought a lot about this Saul," she began. "I think he is a good man, but he is so—so determined—so aggressive. He could take them *way* farther than Cyprus, and—you are right—it could be years before we have John home again. I can hardly bear to think of that. I could be an old woman—I could even die—and not see him again." Her mother's heart was troubled at the thought.

"Oh, no, Miss Mary!" Rhoda protested, dropping her squash to pat her mistress gently. "Surely he won't stay gone so long. His heart will turn toward home, and he'll come back. But for now, I'll be here with you. I keep telling my uncle not to marry me off, because I want to stay here and help you and the believers, and wait for John Mark to come home." Rhoda giggled, holding back a funny thought.

"What are you thinking?" Mary prompted. "Come on, Girl! I know you are hiding something from me."

"Oh, Miss Mary, I just was thinking maybe God will send another big light to zap that Saul as he travels, and stop him in his tracks. Then maybe he will tell him to come home to Jerusalem—or at least to Antioch—instead of going on to some strange and distant place."

Mary laughed with her at the thought. "I keep trying to say to myself that it is so very good for John Mark to have this opportunity to work with such good men as Cousin Barnabas and Saul, and to be part of the Gospel mission. He has been so fortunate, since his father passed, to have good men take an interest in helping him finish growing up. I don't know what we would have done without Peter and Andrew. They treat him as if he were their own son. And the others of the Twelve have been so good to include him. He is a better young man because of these strong friendships."

"I just wish . . ." Rhoda did not finish her thought, and Mary waited.

"Wish what, Girl?"

"I just wish John Mark could come home and work with Peter, and be closer to us. He could still be part of sharing the Good News here with the Judean Jews, couldn't he?" she asked, not looking up from her work.

Mary thought again before answering. "I guess he could, Rhoda. That is, he could if Jehovah leads him to do that. He feels so strongly that he has been led of God into this work, and it can't be our place to tell him where to go—much as I would like to. Times are changing, Rhoda. And we have to change with them. But it is sometimes hard," she finished.

"It sure is," the girl agreed, reaching for a batch of garden-fresh leeks. "Maybe another letter will come soon, and we can get some answers to our questions." And they went about the chores of another Jerusalem morning.

BEHIND THE SCENE
A Study of Acts 12:25–13:13

Big Steps Forward

The appointment of Barnabas and Saul as missionaries to the Gentile world outside of Israel was a huge turning point for the Early Church. It was about 46 a.d. when this landmark event took place in Antioch, Syria, three-hundred miles north of Jerusalem. That would put it fourteen or more years after the Pentecost birth of the Early Church.

Much had taken place in that time span. Let's take time for a quick summary. The church had grown rapidly in the first months, from just hundreds to over five thousand. The growth alarmed Jewish leaders, and caused three great waves of persecution, all of which had caused the believers to scatter over the countryside. Many now lived in towns of Judea and Samaria, but some had gone farther, to Antioch in Syria, and beyond.

Many Greek-speaking Jews had come to believe in Jesus as the church swelled from hundreds to thousands. The cultural and language barriers which resulted created a need for more leadership, some of it from the Greek-speaking part of the church. Seven new leaders were chosen to administrate the everyday business of the believers, while the Apostles continued in the preaching and teaching of the Word. Many of the Twelve went on preaching missions into the countryside, and Gentiles began to understand and accept Jesus also.

We skipped over the conversion of Saul in our earlier chapters of this book, because the focus of the first part of Acts was on Peter and the Twelve. Saul, a young and aggressive leader among the Pharisees, was one of those most angered by the spread of this new sect. In Acts 8:1–3 we have the story of his ruthless persecution of the saints. But Acts 9 begins with the amazing story of his conversion to the faith. He did not immediately come into leadership in the church. It took a while for him to re-order his theological thinking, and to be accepted by the believers. In God's good time all of that happened.

John Mark—A Bridge between Two Eras

John Mark was just a youth in the days when the Apostles and Jesus were in and out of Jerusalem. Many Bible students believe that John Mark was himself the young man he described in his Gospel (see Mark 14:51–52) who had followed the Twelve and Jesus to Gethsemane, and was almost caught by the arresting soldiers. No other Gospel writers told the story, giving rise to the thought that it was Mark's private memory of the event, which gave him credibility as an eye witness to Jesus' arrest. If that is so, it is even more likely that the upper room where Jesus ate his last meal with the Disciples was in the home of Mary, Mark's mother. (Compare this to Acts 12:12.) Mark may have been a good, young friend to the Apostles in the years which followed.

In the days of the Early Church at Jerusalem, Barnabas was a valued leader. He was also a cousin of Mark and related to his mother, Mary, so he was probably in and out of the house often. We know that Mark and Peter were also close—a relationship which deepened over the years—because Peter referred to him in his letter as being *"my son"* (1 Peter 5:13). Early church historians from as far back as Eusebius and Justin Martyr, tell us that Mark's Gospel is mostly based on Peter's preaching. "Peter's memoirs" they say.

John Mark, the youth who probably knew Jesus, who grew up among the Apostles, who witnessed the birth of the church in his mother's Jerusalem home, and was the "sidekick" of Cousin Barnabas—this John Mark was uniquely suited to step across into the new era and carry the Good News into the Gentile world. Even his name suited that charge: John being Jewish, and Mark being both Greek and Roman in origin.

Enter Saul: Soon To Be Paul

Saul's conversion took place about 35 a.d. by most accounts. At that time God clearly told him that his mission would be to take the gospel to the Gentile world. (See Acts 9:15–16.) Saul, the bright and rising star of Judaism, did a total "about face" at his conversion. The Christians were terrified of this man who had been throwing their friends into prison, and trying to stamp out their faith. But the Jewish leaders were even more upset with him than the believers. Their strongest young leader had turned against them—the ally was now the enemy. They, most of all, knew his capabilities, and how effective he could become against them in his new-found faith. Their determination to kill him became known, and the believers in Damascus secretly took him away to the coast, and sent him back to his home town of Tarsus.

We do not have a clear account of how Saul spent the next few years, but part of that time was taken up with a sojourn in Arabia. (Study Paul's testimony of this era in his later letter: Galatians 1:13–17.) Scholars think he was probably rethinking his Jewish theological education, studying the Old Testament prophecies, and listening to God's direction for the job ahead. Meanwhile, the church at Antioch, Syria, was growing into a major center of the faith.

The Church at Antioch

It was a different kind of church than what we saw in Jerusalem. None of the original Twelve were leaders at Antioch. Believers who scattered there after the death of Stephen were probably the nucleus. Antioch was the third largest city in the Roman Empire, after Rome and Alexandria, and filled with "transplanted" people from all over the Mediterranean basin. It was a Roman capital for Syria, estimated to have had about half-a-million residents at that time. The Greek language and culture influenced the Antioch church much more than it had the Jerusalem one. Leaders in this new church were men from all over: some from Asia Minor, Cyprus—even Africa! Their hearts were moved by the need of their countrymen to know and receive Christ as Savior and Lord.

It is no wonder, then, that the Holy Sprit chose that church to be the first to appoint men to carry the Gospel out to the nations. The Antioch church became the home base of the missionary movement. And because of the fervor of its members, the nickname "Christians" was born there, and sticks to us all proudly until this day.

Barnabas, the Encourager

At this time in the work, Barnabas was a stronger leader among the believers than Saul. He had more credibility, having been a leader longer. He did not have a "past" to live down, as Saul did. Barnabas was loved and respected for the way he encouraged and enabled people. Actually named Joseph, he hailed from Cyprus, but came into the Jerusalem church early in their beginnings. (Find him in Acts 4:36–37.) He led by example and by integrity.

After Saul was converted, as mentioned earlier, the church was fearful of trusting him and allowing him leadership. Saul knew he was genuinely changed, and God knew that he was; but the believers were not yet sure. It was Barnabas who saw his potential, believed in him, and vouched for him to the Jerusalem church (Acts 9:26–30).

When the church at Antioch began to grow and reach out to the Greek-speaking community, the Jerusalem church asked Barnabas to go and investigate the new work, to determine whether or not it was a work of the Spirit. (This was still in the early days, when most Jewish believers felt that Jesus was sent mainly to the Jews. Find this story in Acts 11:19–30.) Barnabas not only went to see, but he stayed to encourage. And as the number of believers continued to grow, he saw the need for more reliable leaders for the work. God brought Saul to his mind, and, seeing that Saul's gifts were a good match for the new situation, he made a trip to Tarsus to find him and bring him back. Barnabas and Saul stayed a whole year in Antioch of Syria, teaching in the fledgling church. God used them to lay a strong foundation.

The Call to Go Out

The missionary call was born from prayer, and worship, and fasting. Find this awesome story in Acts 13:1–3. The call came first to Barnabas and Saul: *"for the work to which I have [already] called them."* These two men, whom God had been preparing for many years, now felt a strong, inner urging to break out beyond the safe "box" of the work at Antioch, and carry the message into the world. They may have shared this sense of mission with others, for soon the entire church became involved. *"While they were worshiping the Lord and fasting, the Holy Spirit said, 'Set apart for me Barnabas and Saul. . .'"* It was a local church action, a Spirit-generated moving, a congregational awareness. There was no mission board or bishop to initiate it. It grew out of a congregation that was seeking God's heart for the world.

The church obeyed, and Barnabas and Saul also obeyed—and quickly. With hands of blessing, affirmation, designation, these two were set apart to a new spiritual calling: missions. In so doing, the church took on the obligation of support through continued prayer and financial aid. In years to come, the Antioch church would be the one to which Saul and Barnabas returned to report and rejoice in the workings of God among the Gentiles.

One of the great blessings of our church has been to own and furnish a missionary furlough home. We make it available to missionaries coming in for a few days, weeks, months, or even years. A caring committee tends it, and acts as hospitality group when a missionary family arrives. Over years probably twenty families have sheltered there, and have blessed our church in their sojourns. Some have lived quietly, healing and preparing for return to their fields. Others have come into the church family as long-lost brothers, preaching, teaching, and leading out in new projects with our Missions Committee. Our members have gone with them on mission trips overseas, and the entire mission vision of our church has been exceedingly deepened. Through it mission work has become very personal to our congregation. It is a ministry we value and treasure—one way that we share in the *"Go Ye"* of missions.

A Mother's Heart

Mary, John Mark's mother, was still clearly in the picture. (We read the story of Peter's release from prison, and his standing at her door, in Chapter 5 of this book.) We can only surmise her feelings as her twenty-something son left home to go the 300 miles north to Antioch. How her concern must have intensified as word came that he had gone on with Cousin Barnabas and Saul to Cyprus, and perhaps beyond. (Compare Acts 12:25 and 13:4–5.)

Almost always when missionaries are appointed to go afar there is a family left to miss them and deal with their absence. We watched last Sunday as our church commissioned one of our college women to spend the summer in the Ukraine. She stood with her parents before the congregation as we prayed for her and set her apart for the work. Her mom fought tears at the thought of her daughter's going to such a distant, unknown place. Mission work is very exciting, but it is also frightening to the family left to wait, pray, write, hope, and care.

Travel and communication in the First Century were difficult by our standards, although they were made somewhat better by the *"pax Romana."* Romans had paved most of the major trade routes so that their soldiers could travel more quickly and securely. Overland travelers often attached themselves to merchant caravans or military movements for greater safety. Only the rich and important could afford chariots for comfort and speed. Merchant ships sailed in and out of ports—not passenger ships at that time—and allowed individuals to pay passage as cargo space allowed. The only postal service was pretty much reserved for government use; so private correspondence was mostly carried by messengers or friends. It was not like today's mission work, where emails and cell phone calls may be generated from remote locations, and emergencies are only an airline flight from help. Mary knew she might not see or hear from her son for months or years.

"John Left Them."

John Mark and the team began their travels from Antioch to Selucia overland, and went by ship to the island of Cyprus. There they walked the 100-mile-length of the island, stopping at Jewish settlements and synagogues to peach. Many of us as Bible lands visitors today have cruised or flown into Paphos, Cyprus, driven the length, and sailed out of Salamis on the other end. Cyprus, strategically positioned in the northeast Mediterranean, has been fought over for millennia by the Greeks, the Turks, the Brits, the Egyptians, and others. It was home to many Jewish communities, one of which was Barnabas' home town. No doubt they found friends and relatives along the way for lodging and board.

We have to make some mental comparisons of their trip and ours. Our flight from Athens to Cyprus lasted just a few hours. We bussed across the island to our port in less than two hours. The ship cruised overnight on a leisurely pace to Egypt, where we docked at breakfast. The later cruise from Egypt to Israel's port at Haifa was another overnight experience. What took only hours for us required days for them. But what probably took weeks for them—the preaching tour across Cyprus—Luke recorded in just three verses: Acts 13:4–6.

There was one significant event recorded during their time on Cyprus. In the town of Paphos (see Acts 13:6 and following) Saul and Barnabas confronted an evil "philosopher" who made his living with potions, magic, and false predictions. He had some degree of influence with the deputy of the town, and tried to interfere with the missionaries' witness there. God, through Saul, shut him down with a temporary blindness. The deputy was impressed, though possibly not truly converted. The team left Cyprus knowing the work there was not finished.

Two significant developments emerge at this point. One is that Saul began using his Gentile name, Paul. Likely he saw it as necessary if he was to identify with the people he wanted to reach. The second is that the leadership role seems to have changed, and now the team is referred to as *"Paul and Barnabas."* (Find these in Acts 13:9 and 13.) Immediately after this we hear that, *"John left them and returned to Jerusalem."*

Many reasons have been ventured as to why John Mark returned home. His relationship to Paul may have factored in. Paul's strong personality, his assuming the lead role, his decision to go on from Cyprus into further, unknown territory—all these may have been more than Mark was ready to handle. We can imagine him aboard ship, sailing from Cyprus to Asia Minor, weighing his choices and deciding it was time to go home. We know that Paul was disappointed with his decision, and refused to allow him to go on the second mission a few years later. Others have suggested that Mark was ill, or homesick, that he had to return to other obligations at home, or that perhaps Peter needed him in Judea. All of these, or maybe several combined, could have influenced his decision.

Dr. Stagg points out that Mark showed courage in striking out alone on the trip home.[2] Did he return by ship? Did Cousin Barnabas pay the travel fare? Or did he attach to a group going overland through Asia Minor and down the Maritime highway through Israel's coastal plane? At any rate, he returned home to the caring arms of family and friends. He did keep on helping Peter in the Judean work, we are told. And Barnabas continued to believe in him, and took him along on his second trip to Cyprus (Acts 15:36–41). Much later—over twenty years later, in fact—Paul and Mark had mended their differences, and Paul asked for him while facing death in a Roman prison (see 2 Timothy 4:11). *"Get Mark and bring him with you, because he is helpful to me in my ministry."* Mark lived up to his promise, and Paul forgave him and valued him in the end.

Mentoring: A High Calling for Women Also

The story of Mary and John Mark is a story of mentoring. Mark was mentored over many years by the best: Peter, Barnabas, the other Apostles, Paul, and later even Timothy, Luke, and other great men such as Tychicus, and Aristarchus. We find Mark's name mentioned with theirs in Paul's letters. Mark responded to their encouragement, and became an important part of the story in God's Word. *Mentoring*—a term that has come into its own in recent years, both in and out of the church. Women do it well, because it fits seamlessly into our nurturing natures. But, very practically, what is mentoring?

Mentoring is modeling: living a life of integrity and living out the way in authentic steadfastness. Role playing will not substitute for mentoring, because it is pretense. A mentor shows the way by a life that is genuinely good and faithful, deeply rooted in a walk with Christ.

Mentoring is guiding: keeping a watchful eye on the novice believer, offering gentle advice at critical junctures. The wisdom that is needed grows out of faithful study of God's Word over years. Our charges will glean wisdom from many places along the way, but the wisdom from God is what we want to channel their way.

Mentoring is partnering: walking the path with, or close by, over time. The time could grow into months and years, and perhaps a lifetime. It gives confidence to a newer or weaker Christian to have another person share the pilgrimage, and *be there* over the course.

Mentoring is enabling: providing resources, clearing obstacles, convincing him or her to make the effort. It is creating opportunities, praying for the Power to infill and give success, turning loose when the time comes.

Mentoring is encouraging: noticing the small successes, discerning the spiritual abilities, believing in the potential, writing the letter of reference, and the note of appreciation.

Mentoring is forgiving: allowing for failures, giving a second chance, rebuilding broken self esteem.

And *Mentoring is caring:* doing all the above from desire, not from duty or obligation. A mentor *chooses* to get involved as a friend, to share from the heart, to be a co-learner.

Coming into high school, my husband, Jack, describes himself as a gangly teenager, interested mostly in baseball, struggling with his studies. After ninth grade, his first Latin course having met with disaster, his parents found a neighbor, Mrs. Lena Binford who was a retired teacher, to tutor him. All summer they studied Latin, and in his second year he was tutoring classmates. It went so well that Jack and Mrs. Binford went on to study Latin II together, and geometry. By the end of tenth grade Jack had learned how to study, and his bright mind carried him through college with good success.

Anticipating seminary after college graduation, Jack again looked up Mrs. Binford. She suggested that they spend the summer studying Greek to prepare him for his new school. Her quiet, Quaker ways, her loving concern for him, and deep interest in his future, gave him great confidence for the days ahead. During his first year of seminary in Chicago—far from home and with strangers—he aced first-year-Greek. To this day he credits Lena Binford with getting him on the road to scholarship and ministry. She was his mentor, long before the word was commonly understood. She was his Barnabas, and he was her John Mark.

A LEGACY AND A PROMISE
Lois and Eunice Prepare Timothy

Acts 14:8–20 and 2 Timothy 1:5–7

It should have been a normal morning in Galatia. Eunice headed for the market for the day's fresh supplies, her mother at her elbow, and young son trailing not far behind. Dodging the bright sun, they ducked under a vegetable merchant's canopy, studying his gourds and melons, dickering over the price.

"Where is Timothy?" Lois worried. "The crowds are thick, and I hate for him to get out of sight on market days. One never knows who might be looking for an able-bodied boy to snatch for the slave trade."

"Now, Mother," Eunice chided," Timothy is old enough to watch out for danger, and to call out if he thinks there is trouble. You worry too much. He isn't a little boy any more."

"But only twelve," the grandmother defended. "Not quite a man yet, though our Law would soon judge him such. He just thinks he is grown, but he is really quite frail."

"He can hold his own, Mother," Eunice insisted, picking up several yellow and green gourds to purchase. "These look fresh and tender, don't you think? Ari likes them fixed with onions and peppers, and they would go well with the weekend's fare."

Lois nodded approval, still focused on Timothy's condition. "It's good for the children to have fresh things, I think, and Timothy could use some more flesh on his bones. By the way," she asked cautiously, "has Ari said any more about a celebration? I know we don't have a Rabbi here in Lystra, but the one from Iconium will come for ceremonies when invited—if we pay him something for his trouble. I hate for Timothy to grow up without a proper celebration as a son of the Covenant."

Eunice gave her one of those *not-again-Mother* looks before answering. "I told you, Ari just does not see the purpose of those rituals which are meaningful to us Jews. He wants Timothy to be known as a Gentile. The ceremony is not going to happen, Mother." Then, knowing her words had been harsh, she added, "But we can have a birthday dinner—maybe for our family and a few Jewish friends—and let him know how important the day is for us. That would be all right with Ari, I think. He is very proud of his son—he loves him dearly."

Lois turned to look back for her lagging grandson, happily playing a game with another boy at the edge of the market pathway. "Timothy!" she called, and he looked up quickly. "Don't lag behind so far! We are about to start toward home."

As the boy caught up, Lois pressed two small coins into his hand. "Take these across to Asa, the cripple, as alms," she instructed. "We always help the poor and lame when we can—it pleases Jehovah." And she gave him a gentle shove toward the beggar.

Timothy hesitated a moment, but then stepped out, walking cautiously toward the man whom he had seen many times before. Approaching, he smiled timidly. The beggar was almost asleep it seemed, and Timothy was unsure if he should waken him. "Sir?" he asked quietly. "Sir?" and he dropped his coins into the man's basket, and started back across the way.

"Thank you, Son," came Asa's weak reply. "You are kind to a helpless old man."

Timothy returned the words with a smile, and continued walking. About the time he reached his grandmother's side, a commotion caused them all to look back toward the beggar's mat. Two strangers were standing there—one a tall man about forty, and his companion who was less imposing. The foreigners had stopped to talk to the cripple in trade language. Their conversation was animated, and Asa seemed agitated. Eunice reached forward for Timothy, drawing him closer to her by one arm, unsure of the motives of the intruders. Lystra was not so large that strangers could go unnoticed in the morning market.

As the three watched, the smaller man reached toward Asa, and in a rather loud voice commanded, "Stand up on your feet!"

"Well, I *never* . . . !" exclaimed Lois in disbelief. "Can't that foreigner see that Asa is a hopeless cripple? What does he mean, embarrassing him like that?"

"Mother!" Eunice cautioned sternly. And to their astonishment, Asa stood up—a sight never seen by them before. "I didn't know he could do that," Eunice whispered, amazed. "Has he been fooling us all this time?"

"No—I have known him for years," Lois answered. "He was broken in a terrible accident at the quarries when he was a young man. He has never walked since, his legs healed so badly. It must be . . ." Both hands went to her mouth—the words would not come out. Lois shook her head in disbelief.

"Then it must be a miracle," Eunice finished, amazed. "I think we have just seen a miracle by Jehovah."

"What on earth is happening?!" Ari had come up from his grain brokerage at the end of the street. "What is Asa doing on his feet?"

"Father!" Timothy began. "Mother thinks Jehovah has done a miracle, and Asa is healed!" The boy's eyes were wide and questioning.

"More like sorcery!" Ari retorted. "Who are those foreigners, and what are they doing here in Lystra?" he asked anyone within hearing distance. Everyone continued watching, unable to look away from the amazing scene on the other side of the street.

"I'm going for the temple priest!" a nearby man answered. "These must be the gods. We've never seen anything like this in Lystra before!" He was hustling through the onlookers toward the temple of Zeus as he spoke. "Whoever they are, we dare not offend them," he called back as he ran.

"Foolishness!" Ari scoffed. "Miracles don't happen in Lystra. I've lived around here all my life. If the gods wanted to do a miracle, they would go to Antioch, or Attalia—someplace important—not Lystra!" And he turned back toward his grain booth. "Timothy, you come with me. I don't want you influenced by this religious idiocy!" and he swung his arm over the boy's shoulders and pulled him along. "We'll see you at dinner," he called to his wife as he left.

"What do you think?" Eunice asked her mother, fearfully. "Could it be a miracle? Is Jehovah going to do something here in Lystra after all these years?"

Lois shook her head in silence, surveying the faces of those standing near her. "People seem confused," she finally responded. And the two turned towards home and the chores that waited.

It was a couple of hours before Ari and the boy returned for the midday meal. *"Mama! Grandma!"* Timothy shouted as he came in the door. "You would *not believe* the things that happened after you left the market! Father and I saw it from the booth. The priests came with oxen, and they declared the foreigners to be *gods!* They put garlands on them, and called them Zeus and Mercury! It was *awesome!*" The boy's eyes were wide with amazement.

Eunice and Lois traded worried looks before the mother answered. "You know, Son, that we don't believe Zeus and Mercury to be true gods . . . we only believe in the True Jehovah God of Israel. People may *think* them to be gods, but . . ."

"But who knows *who* is a god?!" Ari finished. "Or if there are *any* gods? All this god talk is not good for a boy's ears. Where is my dinner?" He was washing up at the bucket as he spoke. "Wash your hands, Boy," he directed. "The marketplace is dirty, and you have been playing in the dust with your friends."

"Well," Lois ventured. "Did the strangers go along with that charade? Did they pretend to be gods, Timothy?"

"No, Grandma!" Timothy answered. "The two strangers told the priests to *stop!* The smaller one said, 'We are just men like you—we are not gods.' And then he started to talk about the True Jehovah God of Israel."

"Enough god talk," Ari interrupted. "Let's eat. I have

to get back to the market by mid afternoon. A merchant is coming to sell his wheat, and if I am not there, he will sell it to someone else." The women finished setting dishes on the low table, and the family sat on floor cushions to eat. Ari was filling plates when Eunice intervened.

"Ari, wait, please," she said. "Mother will ask the Jewish blessing for us." Resigned, the father sat stoically while his mother-in-law recited the familiar words. Then the meal resumed.

"All this marketplace uproar is not good," Ari said, finishing his stew. "The Romans will think it is an uprising and come down on us and close the shops, and I will lose business!" He wiped his beard on his sleeve and began to get up. "I hope those strangers are gone when I get back."

"May I go back with you, Father?" Timothy asked. "I want to finish my game with Joseph—he said he would meet me after dinner—and I want to see if the oxen are still there."

"Come if your mother doesn't need you here," his father replied, looking to Eunice for a nod of approval. And the two disappeared out the door.

Two days passed before Eunice and her mother returned to the market to shop again, but nothing had quieted in the town. Lystra folks were still abuzz with talk of the Jewish strangers who had healed Asa, and preached about a strange God in the streets. Rounding the corner, Eunice looked toward the place where Asa usually sat begging on his mat. She did not speak the question which had been on her mind: *Would the beggar still be able to walk?* Soon she saw him standing by the sidewalk café with several old friends.

He was talking and laughing, moving around like he had been on his feet for years. *"Look!"* she whispered to her mother excitedly, "Asa is still able to walk! It was a miracle after all!"

"Jehovah be praised!" Lois responded with awe. "Jehovah be praised indeed!"

A crowd was gathering across the street, and the two Jewish strangers seemed to be the point of interest. Lois and Eunice stepped back into the shade to see what would happen next. The smaller man—the one who had healed the beggar two days before—stood on a bench, motioned for silence, and began to speak. "Men of Israel, and those of you Greeks who worship the True Jehovah God, listen to me. You have been taught foolish and worthless things about the gods of this world, which are no gods at all. The God who made heaven and earth, the sea and the sky, and all that is within them, this is the God I have come to tell you about today. You know him from all he has made—from the rain he sends on your crops and gardens. But I tell you that he has sent a greater witness. He sent the man Jesus, by whom this crippled man was healed two days ago."

"The people of Jerusalem did not believe him," the man went on, "and they killed him, but God showed his power by raising him from the dead." A gasp went up from the bystanders as the man spoke of resurrection from the dead. Some continued listening, but some shook their heads in disbelief and turned away to other things. Lois and Eunice looked at each other but stayed to hear more. The man hurried on to explain, "This Jesus is the Savior of the world. We tell you this Good News. What God has promised through the ages—a Savior for the world—has now come. The promises are fulfilled. And you can receive forgiveness for your sins, not through sacrifices of oxen to false gods, but through the blood of Jesus Christ, if you will believe."

"He is saying that our Messiah has come!" Lois exclaimed, grasping her daughter's arm with joy. "The Messiah has come—and we missed him!"

"I don't doubt it, living away off here in No Man's Land," Eunice retorted. "You would not expect a Jewish Messiah to be known in Galatia! How can you believe this so quickly, Mother?" she challenged. "We don't even know if these are reliable men." And she turned to begin her shopping.

"We can certainly see that Asa is up walking around, Eunice," her mother defended. "That should be proof enough for anyone. What more could we want?"

"I don't know, Mother," Eunice answered doubtfully. "I just don't know what to think about all this. But I need to finish up here and get home in time to get Timothy ready for his tutor in an hour or so. Let's hurry!" Eunice picked up the food she needed, and turned back toward home.

They had just rounded the corner when noise of shouting stopped them in their tracks. Frightened, the two started to run. "If there is going to be trouble, I don't want to be anywhere in the vicinity," Eunice panted, pulling her mother along. "Let's get back to the house."

It was dark and quiet when they arrived. "Timothy?" the mother called. "Timothy, come and get washed up. The tutor will be here in just a few minutes." Getting no response she moved toward the back door. "Timothy?" she called louder, thinking him out playing with friends. But there was no response.

"Could he have gone to the market with Ari?" her mother queried.

"I told him to stay close to the house, because he didn't want to go with us to the shops," Eunice answered, agitated. "I hope he didn't go out without permission."

"Maybe Ari came for him. Maybe he needed some help with a new grain shipment, or something," her mother ventured.

"Maybe," Eunice agreed uncertainly. "Timothy is usually pretty dependable. I hope he is all right." And she busied herself with putting away the food, and beginning the midday meal. Lois went to the wicker chest, found her mending and resumed patching her grandson's other tunic, which he had torn on a fence a few days before. They passed the next several minutes absorbed in their chores before they heard the boy running up the path toward the house.

"Mama! Grandma! There's a *stoning* happening! And I can't find Father to stop it! *Come and help!"* the boy gasped tearfully. "They are going to kill the foreigners! Hurry, Mama! *Hurry!"* and he turned to run back toward the market street.

"Timothy, *no!"* Eunice shouted after him, running to catch up. "You can't go back if there is trouble! You might get hurt, and we are not strong enough to help." Grabbing his tunic neck, she stopped him with a jerk. "Stay here—there is nothing we can do. The men will have to stop it."

"But, *Mama*," the boy protested, "those are *good men*. They healed Asa, and they preach about the True Jehovah God like you and Grandma believe. We can't just let them be *killed*."

"If they belong to Jehovah, he will have to help them,"

Eunice countered fearfully. "I guess we can only wait and see what Jehovah will do." And she pulled her son back toward the safety of their home.

Timothy trudged along, obedient but unwilling. "One day I will be bigger and stronger," he threatened. "Then I can stand up for what I think is right against mean men."

"One day that will be true, Son," his mother consoled. "And that day is not as far away as you think. You are almost a son of the Covenant now, and I am proud that you want to stand for right. Those men may be the true messengers of Jehovah, and if they are, he will protect them. By evening we will know the truth."

BEHIND THE SCENES
A Study of Acts 14:8–20 and 2 Timothy 1:5–7

Timothy's Family Legacy

Timothy was blessed with both a mother and grandmother who had strong faith in God, and passed that conviction on to him as a child. We have proof of that in Paul's second letter to him (2 Timothy 1:5) where he says: *"I have been reminded of your sincere faith, which first lived in your grandmother Lois and in your mother Eunice and, I am persuaded, now lives in you also."*

Eunice, the Jewish mother, lived in a mixed marriage with a Greek man whose name we do not have. (We dubbed him "Ari" in our story.) We do not have any history about how they met and married, but we know that his father had not permitted Eunice to have the baby boy circumcised, as was the custom in Jewish families. Paul requested this of him as a youth, before taking him as a team member on the second of his missionary trips (Acts 16:1–3). So the influence of the father was felt, but in the end Timothy chose the faith of his mother over the pagan gods of the Greeks and Romans.

This gives us reason to believe that Eunice was able to keep the strong, Jewish, family traditions in their home to some degree. They must have observed Sabbath prayers, remembered the feast days and their historical significances, and talked about the Law of Moses. There is no mention of a synagogue in their town of Lystra, so much of Timothy's early Jewish education probably came through his home life.

Mixed marriages—those where the partners do not share the same faith—are always risky for the one who is a believer. There is a balance to be found, respect to be developed, and often convictions to be compromised. That Eunice had found ways to stay true to her faith in this Greek-and-Jewish mix speaks of her inner strength. She must have done it so that her young son, growing up between two systems of belief and values, was able to sort out the differences and make a choice of his own. That would place Eunice, in our minds, in a list of other Bible mothers who passed on their faith to their children.

Mothers of Faith Remembered

I think of *Jochebed, mother of Moses,* who saw that her son was no ordinary child. She defied the order of mighty Pharaoh to kill all Israelite boy babies, hid him in a basket, and then floated him in the Nile where she knew the Pharaoh's daughter would find him. On receiving permission to nurse him until he was weaned, Jochebed spent those precious few years of his infancy instilling in him a sense of the True God. It was because of her that Moses was able to hear the voice of God calling him to lead Israel out of Egyptian slavery. (Find her story in Exodus 2:1–10, 6:20, and Hebrews 11:23–25.)

Remember *Hannah, mother of Samuel,* who prayed for years for a son? In her anguish and desperation she promised that, if given a son, she would give him back to God. She also had just a few years with her son of promise, but she must have used them well. For when Samuel was probably no more than five years of age, Hannah kept her vow, took him to the priest Eli at the tabernacle in Shiloh, and dedicated him to God's service for life. Samuel grew to become the last of the great judges of Israel, advisor to kings, leader of the nation in God's behalf. (Hannah's story is found in 1 Samuel 1.)

There are many other godly mothers included in our Bible, but we will mention just two more. First, *Mary, the mother of Jesus.* Mary was not looking for a child just yet, but God selected her, and asked her to be the mother of his only begotten Son—an awesome task for a peasant girl. Mary's willing spirit and her tenacity carried her through the many ups and downs of Jesus' life and ministry, to the crucifixion and resurrection, making her a hero in our book. Mary believed in Jesus when his siblings did not, when the Jewish leaders rejected him, when he was ridiculed and murdered as a criminal, and when he was dead. God rewarded her by letting her be part of the resurrection and the great Pentecost victory day. (Mary's story begins in Luke 1:26.)

Eunice, too, was blessed with a godly mother who was *Timothy's grandmother Lois.* We do not know if Lois lived in their home, but Paul tells us that her faith was not only part of Timothy's legacy, but that she was a believer in Christ *first,* before her daughter. In that same letter (2 Timothy 3:14–17) Paul reminds Timothy that he was taught the Holy Scriptures from infancy. How often grandmothers, if not the primary teachers, re-enforce the Christian teachings of the parents to their grandchildren. Eunice must have been that kind of grandma. What she had taught to her daughter, she now helped pass on to her grandson. Early on, these were the Jewish traditions and faith. Their introduction to Jesus came later, when Paul and Barnabas visited Lystra on their first missionary trip, as described in our fiction story.

Timothy is a witness to the importance of giving our children a strong beginning in the Lord. Oh, God can find other ways to touch a youth—as he did in my own case—but what a boost to faith to have a godly mother and/or grandmother to teach those early concepts in the home. Timothy went far on that foundation, as we shall now discover.

Picking Up the Story

We left the Acts narrative in Chapter 6 when John Mark deserted Paul and Barnabas early into the first missionary trip (Acts 13:13). The three had trekked through Cyprus, and sailed to the southern coast of Asia Minor (now called Turkey) where Mark left to return to Jerusalem. It was a bitter blow to these travelers, with the formidable Taurus

Mountains looming ahead. Mark could have helped greatly with the baggage, but now Paul and Barnabas had to find other means of managing the tough climb.

Their first preaching stop was another Antioch—not to be confused with Antioch of Syria, from where they originated. (There were sixteen cities named Antioch in the world in those days.) This was Antioch of Pisidia, about one-hundred miles inland, a bustling city of trade, and a Roman colony. The preachers began their work at the synagogue, speaking to the Jews and God-fearing Greeks about Jesus. The sermon in Acts 13:16–41 is the longest recorded sermon we have from Paul's preaching. It was a strong beginning. The team was invited back the next week, but their success riled the Jewish leaders who felt threatened. Paul and Barnabas turned then to the Gentiles, and many people received the Good News about Jesus. The opposition continued, though, and the city leaders (including many Greek women) stirred up such trouble that Paul and Barnabas moved quickly on to the next town.

At Iconium their work at the synagogue was so effective that many Jews and Greeks believed in Jesus. But Satan is persistent, and again opposition arose. Again the Jews incited the Gentiles to plot against Paul and Barnabas—even threatening to execute them by stoning. Again the team moved on. (These first two stops are detailed in Acts 13:14–14:7.)

Lystra, the next stop, was Timothy's home town. The story there is far more colorful, and we touched on much of it in our fiction vignette. No synagogue is mentioned, but the ministry began with a street healing and open-air preaching service. The crowd response was amazing. The citizens thought them to be reincarnations of the local deities, Jupiter and Mercury, and tried to worship them! Then, just about as quickly, the crowd was swayed by the Antioch and Iconium opposition, and the worship service turned into a lethal stoning. Paul was taken for dead and dragged out of town in a nasty outpouring of venom. But—amazingly—he revived and walked back to town on his own power!

In the morning Paul and Barnabas left, went on to the next town of Derbe, preached there, and then retraced their steps backward through Lystra, Iconium, Antioch and to the coast, where they sailed home to Syria. It must have been at some point in that little saga that Timothy's grandmother heard and understood the truth about Jesus. She, and then her daughter and grandson, became believers and grew in the faith. It would be about two years before Paul would see them again.

Two Crucial Decisions

Back home in Syria, Paul and Barnabas reported to their home church as good missionaries do, and stayed a while on furlough. Their success among the Gentiles, along with what God had been accomplishing in Judea, Samaria, and Syria, had caused quite a demographic shift within the church. No longer was Christianity an extension of the Jewish community. Many incoming Gentiles had not been brought up observing the Law of Moses, were not familiar with Jewish social customs, and had not circumcised their men. Some Judean Jews were disturbed and began to teach that unless persons became Jewish in all these ways they could not really be Christians. Christ had, they reasoned, come as a Jew. The first believers were all Jews. So, it seemed to them, one must be first a Jew, and then a Christian. Paul and Barnabas took issue with them, and so it was deemed necessary to hold a council of the Apostles and elders and decide the matter.

That Jerusalem Conference was held in 50 a.d., and the outcome was to set the future course for the church—and for us. It began with a general meeting of believers, in which the Apostles and elders reported all that God had been doing. Some Christians who had formerly been Pharisees then raised their objections to Gentiles becoming believers without circumcision and the keeping of the Old Testament Law. The Apostles and elders held a lengthy discussion, during which Peter spoke on behalf of the Gentiles. Peter, we remember, had gone to Cornelius' house and experienced the giving of the Holy Spirit to Gentiles without these extra requirements. He carefully made the point that salvation comes through faith in Jesus Christ alone, and not by keeping the Law.

The general assembly was respectful of Peter. There followed reports by Barnabas and Paul of their recent work in Cyprus and Asia Minor. Finally James, the half brother of Jesus and leader of the Jerusalem church, stood to give the summary verdict. He explained that it had been God's intent all along to include the Gentiles in his plan of salvation. *"It is my judgment, therefore, that we should not make it difficult for the Gentiles who are turning to God."* (Find this very important story in Acts 15:1–21.) They drafted some letters, chose representatives of both viewpoints to carry them, and sent word of the decision to the churches. A few social requirements were tacked on, but for the most part, the churches were free to receive people by faith in Jesus alone.

Paul and Barnabas were getting restless to revisit the believers who had been won on their first mission to Cyprus and Asia Minor. This led to the second crucial decision. Barnabas felt that John Mark, now about three years older and wiser, should be given a second chance. Paul was not ready to forget his failure and risk on him again. Their disagreement was so severe they could not reconcile it. Barnabas set off with John Mark to revisit Cyprus. Paul chose Silas to accompany him back to Asia Minor. Did they part as friends? We hope so. But where there had been only one strong team, now there were two. The story of Acts follows Paul's team.

Building the New Team

Paul and Silas traveled overland to Asia Minor this second time, rather than by sea as before. This changed the route, as they approached from the east, rather than the south. They came first to Derbe, and then proceeded to Lystra, Timothy's home town. There they were pleased to find that Lois, Eunice, and Timothy were a strong family of faith. (Find this in Acts 16:1–5.) The believers spoke highly of Timothy, and Paul and Silas needed a younger man as helper on the team; so it was decided that he should join and travel with them. As noted, Timothy came from a mixed Jew/Greek family. Given the current emotion about Gentiles and the Jewish Law, Paul requested that Timothy be circumcised before joining the team.

The three continued through Asia Minor in the area known as Galatia, carrying the decision of the Jerusalem Council, preaching and seeing more people won to the Lord. Paul wanted to break some new ground, and intended to turn south, but could not feel the Spirit's leading there. So they continued northwesterly to the sea, seeking direction from the Lord as to their next area of ministry. That direction came to Paul in a dream—a vision of a man from Macedonia (northern Greece today) calling to him to come and preach there. Paul believed it to be a message from the Lord, and they at once boarded a ship and set sail for Macedonia.

At this juncture another important person joined the mission team: Luke, a Greek physician. We would love to know his background, how he met the team, and why he joined. Look carefully at Acts 16:10 and note the significant pronoun change. Whereas before it had been *"they"* went, now it became *"we"* sailed. The "We Passages" of the book of Acts tell us two things: first that Luke was the author of the book, and second that Luke joined at that point in the second missionary journey.

Luke became a close friend and personal physician to Paul, and was with him off and on from this point through the rest of his life as we know it. Luke traveled through Macedonia, Greece, Asia Minor, Judea, and to Rome. He was with Paul in good times and bad, even in prison. His travel diaries probably account for the source of this last half of the book of Acts. His Luke/Acts two-volume history comprises about one-fourth of the volume of the New Testament. Thank you, God, for sending Luke to the mission.

Timothy Fulfilling His Promise

Timothy trekked faithfully with Paul and the team across the sea to Macedonia, Greece, and back to Asia Minor. Bible scholars think that he was somewhat timid in disposition, because Paul often reminded him to be strong and bold. It is thought that he was somewhat sickly, causing Paul to suggest that he drink wine for his stomach ailments. But Timothy became a valuable, dependable partner, and later a pastor and leader in his own right. In later chapters he will pop in and out of our stories from the second and third missions, and Paul's imprisonments. No doubt he revisited Lystra between overseas jaunts, to the grateful relief of his mother and grandmother.

Timothy lived with the "Greats." He became like a son to Paul, was close to Luke, Silas, Priscilla and Aquila, Barnabas, and Mark. In Judea he knew the Apostles. Lesser known leaders like Aristarchus and Philemon knew him by name also—we find Paul mentioning them together in his letters. It was an exciting life to live, and it all began with the faith that was first in his grandmother Lois, and in his mother Eunice. What a testimony to the value of Christian faith and training in the home. Timothy not only fulfilled his promise, he left us quite a legacy of his own.

My Jack credits his grandmother and mother with his faith heritage also. His faith was *first in his grandmother Louise, and in his mother Georgie.* Eldest daughter of a German emigrant family, Louise grew into a woman of faith. Leaving her California roots while in her twenties, she migrated east to Nevada. There she met and married a railroad man, George, who did not share her spiritual convictions. Faithfully she reared their four children in the Free Methodist traditions. In time, George also believed. After his death, she took their four young children by train to Kansas, where George's sister held out the promise of a new home. There Georgie finished her growing up, and met and married Arch Burton, and they became the godly parents of Jack and his brother, Jim. The faith of a grandmother, passed on to her daughter, and then to her grandsons, is the story of our family also.

Part IV

Women of Macedonia and Greece

Chapter 8
EARTH-SHAKING EVENTS
Lydia Hosts the Mission Team

Chapter 9
GETTING TO KNOW GOD
Damaris Believes

Chapter 10
PARTNERS IN MINISTRY
Priscilla Joins Paul's Mission

Chapter 11
SISTER, SERVANT, SAINT
Phoebe Carries the Letter to Rome

EARTH-SHAKING EVENTS
Lydia Hosts the Mission Team

Acts 16:11–40

Lydia and Phyllis turned off the pavement and onto a trail which led toward the river. The day was balmy and a little breezy—a pleasant afternoon to walk to the place of prayer with a friend. As the trail turned to follow the river southward, the two stepped off and into a grassy clearing, shaded by tall trees and a rocky bluff.

"I guess we aren't the first ones here," Phyllis noted, pointing toward the riverbank where Lucia was busy filling a basket with wild asparagus. "She makes me feel a little lazy," and the two began spreading a quilt and some pillows in the usual way.

Lucia joined them in just a minute, red-faced from bending and working in the sunshine. "Good afternoon, Ladies," she greeted cheerfully. "It's almost the end of the season, and I thought asparagus would be a nice addition to dinner this evening." Setting her basket aside, she joined them on the quilt.

"It's a lovely day, today," Lydia said. "The market place was very busy all day, up until closing time this afternoon. Lots of shoppers because of the nice weather, I guess. I was almost late getting here for prayer—I couldn't close the booth because of a late customer."

"The river is lazy today," Lucia said, turning back to watch it flow by. "The winter snows are gone, and it won't run hard again until next spring. It makes our place of prayer quiet. I like it here."

"It's almost too quiet," Phyllis observed. "The birds aren't even singing this afternoon. I wonder if a storm is brewing over the hill."

"Paul and Silas and the others are a little late," Lydia noted.

"I guess they found someone to talk to on the way," Phyllis suggested.

"Yesterday," Lydia continued, a little worried, "I came with them to prayers, and we were followed by Tullia—that little, demented, fortune-teller girl. She kept shouting and annoying us. That may have happened again today, but I hope not."

"Shouting? What was she shouting?" Phyllis pursued.

"Something like, 'These men are telling about the Most High God. They know how to be saved,'" Lydia responded, gesturing wildly. "It wasn't very good publicity for us who are believers. Paul tried to talk to her, but she would not stop shouting."

"Well—Paul and Silas *are* telling the truth about how to be saved," Lucia ventured, "but hers is not a very reliable voice."

"It's a bad kind of publicity, both for the Jews and us believers," Lydia agreed. "Neither of us even believes in associating with fortune tellers. It's taught against in the Law."

"She's a sad little thing," Phyllis said, shaking her head. "Her owners are getting rich off of her, but she just doesn't have any kind of a life of her own. They sell her to customers all the time."

A running sound on the path behind them startled all

three to their feet as Timothy ducked in to the clearing between two low branches, out of breath. "Oh, Lydia and Ladies—Paul and Silas are in trouble! That fortune-teller slave girl . . ."

"Timothy, slow down, Son," Lydia cautioned, grasping his arm with both hands. "We were just talking about how annoying she was to Paul yesterday."

"Again today," the young man nodded. "And this time Paul couldn't stand it, and he called the bad spirit to come out of her, and healed her!"

"Oh, good," the three chorused.

"That's good, Timothy," Lydia repeated, "but what is wrong then?"

"The owners," Timothy explained. "They were furious because she can't make money for them any more. They dragged Paul and Silas off to the magistrates to stop them from preaching."

"Oh, no!" Phyllis wailed. "I didn't even think about how the owners would react. I was just thinking how good it was that Paul healed her—how good for the slave girl, I mean."

Lucia sank back onto the quilt slowly, her hands over her cheeks. "Now we *really* have something to pray about," she said. "What if they arrest Paul and Silas? They are foreigners, and probably don't have proper papers to be here yet."

"Where is Luke, Timothy?" Lydia queried. "Did they take him, too?"

"Luke told me to come and tell you, because he was going to follow and see if he could help them. He's a Macedonian, so maybe they will release the men to him if he intercedes. Being a doctor and all . . ." Timothy's voice trailed off uncertainly. "Luke said he would come to Lydia's house when he knows something."

"Lucia is right—we need to pray," Lydia agreed. "We are in a good place here to do that. Let's pray, and then we will go to my house and wait for them."

The four friends stood together in the clearing, hands uplifted, for several minutes, all praying aloud at the same time, pleading for the safety of their friends. Then they gathered the quilt and pillows and started for the path toward Lydia's place.

"I'm going first to my own home," Lucia explained. "I'll drop off this basket, and let my family know where we are. They may be able to get word to other God-fearing people who will come and pray with us." At the first paved street she said her good-byes and hurried off into the neighborhood.

On reaching Lydia's home the other two women and Timothy entered at the front door where Erastus was guarding. "Welcome, Miss Lydia," he said respectfully.

"Erastus, we have a problem," Lydia began. "Paul and Silas have been taken before the magistrates. I have no idea how many believers will be coming to pray and wait here. Watch the door carefully while I speak to the kitchen servants about the meal." Getting his solemn nod, she turned to her two guests. "Please make yourselves at home in the courtyard while I take care of a little business here. Then we will continue with our prayers as we wait for word from Luke."

Lydia moved toward the kitchen at the back of the house, and Timothy and Phyllis waited together. "Lydia's courtyard is always lovely and well-kept," Phyllis said quietly. She moved toward the cistern pool to scoop up a drink.

Timothy stepped back to where the faithful guard stood by the entry door. "Erastus, is there a quiet room where we can pray without bothering the servants?"

"Oh, yes, Mr. Timothy, right over here in this family dining room would be good," the servant answered, showing the way. They walked past a cage of brightly-feathered birds beside a vine which trailed above them and up the stairway trellis. Erastus opened the door and they entered the small room. Lydia followed them in just a minute.

"This is a lovely space," Phyllis commented. "Your home is always so well appointed, Lydia."

Timothy was studying the tile floor, and a tapestry which hung on one wall over a low couch. Lydia hurried to explain. "That tapestry has to go," she apologized. "It's one of those Greek mythology scenes of the gods on Mt. Olympus, and I've always rather liked it. But now that I am a believer, I think I'll sell it to someone, and find some art that is more in keeping with my new faith." She began lighting the two hanging lamps as she spoke.

The three stood together in the middle of the floor, and Timothy voiced another prayer, pleading tearfully for the safety of his friend and mentor, Paul. Lydia was about to follow with a plea of her own when the bell rang at her front door. The three stopped to listen. They could hear Erastus as he greeted Luke and some others, and the three rushed back out into the courtyard, hoping for good news.

"Oh, Luke, at least you are here!" Lydia began. "But where are Paul and Silas?

Luke's face was somber, his shoulders stooped, and the friends feared the worst. "They are in jail for the night," he began, but the bell interrupted again.

Erastus admitted Lucia with two of her family who joined the circle anxiously. "What do we know?" Lucia asked.

"I was just saying, Paul and Silas are in jail for the night," Luke explained. "The magistrates couldn't get a straight story from the crowd, because people were shouting and pushing, so they had Paul and Silas beaten severely with rods by the guards, and put them in jail. It was a really bad scene. I feared for their lives, but they seem to have survived it. Their backs were a mess, though, and there was no one to doctor them. They are going to have a very painful night."

Silence betrayed the confusion and fear of his friends. *"Beaten?"* Lydia questioned. "They *beat* them—and aren't they Roman citizens? That's against the law," and she shook her head angrily. "How could they have done such a thing?"

"Paul and Silas didn't get a chance to tell them they were Roman citizens, Lydia. It was a real mob scene, and the guards would not let them talk."

"So they are going to spend the night in the *jail?*" Timothy asked. "In a *rat-infested, filthy jail?* I can't *believe* it! They have not done *anything* wrong! All they did was help that poor slave girl. How can men be jailed for *helping* someone?"

"Will they even have any food?" Lucia worried. "I don't think the guards provide meals in that jail."

"I heard the magistrate tell the guards to keep them in a secure cell," Luke added. "They may even be in leg irons or chains."

"Erastus!" Lydia called to her faithful servant. "Send two slaves with some food to the jail, and see if the jailer

will take it to Paul and Silas. Take my signature—the jailer knows me. And *hurry!*" Then, turning to her friends she explained, "The jailer's family has bought tunics from me for their juvenile sons, and his cousin worked as a seamstress for me last year. Maybe he will treat them more kindly if he knows I know them."

"Have you all had time to pray, yet?" Luke asked, searching the group.

"Yes—at the river when we heard," Lucia assured him.

"And again here—we were praying when you came in," Timothy added. "But I think we must keep praying until they are released—if it takes all night."

Prayers went on in the small room until nearly midnight. Servants would come and go, replenishing the wine bowl, and bringing trays of olives and cheeses and dried fruits which went mostly untouched. Believers came and went, but the prayers were continuous.

A deep rumbling sounded outside the house. "Is that a merchant cart bringing in goods for the market?" Lucia asked. But the sound worsened, and the house began to tremble and jerk. A painted vase on the side stand toppled and shattered on the tile below, and the lamps swung wildly. Terrified, the friends ran from the room into the courtyard.

"Careful! Careful!" Erastus warned frantically, pulling them to the center by the cistern. "It's an earthquake! Roof tiles may fall and hit you on the head. Stand clear of the walls!" He bent protectively over Lydia as he spoke.

A kitchen girl came through carrying a water jar, and barely got it set down before losing her balance on the shifting floor. The jar toppled and sloshed as she grabbed to steady it against the tremors.

"An *earthquake!*" Luke said, dazed. "I haven't felt one of these in several years. What a night for *this* to happen!"

"What will Paul and Silas *do?*" Timothy wailed. "In that stinking jail, chained up—a block could fall on them! Oh, God! Protect them!" he cried, falling to his knees in fear.

Lydia moved to embrace the frightened young man, Erastus by her side. "Just wait and pray," she said. "Our God can protect them." And they huddled together as the last tremors shuddered. Then everything grew very still.

BEHIND THE SCENES
A Study of Acts 16:11–40

"How the West Was Won"

Seeking the guidance and blessing of God's Spirit, Paul and his team had turned west from Galatia, trekking through Asia Minor to the port of Troas. There Paul's vision of a Macedonian man caused the four travelers to board a ship headed for Neapolis. The hundred-mile journey wound through the northern isles of the Aegean Sea for probably two days. Neapolis was the port city on the north shore, about ten miles from Philippi, which was their first destination. (This part of the story is in Acts 16:11–15.)

Luke must have had connections in Philippi. There was a school of Greek medicine there, and it has been conjectured that Luke may have trained in that place. Paul, Silas, Luke and Timothy spent several days in Philippi before week's end. No synagogue is mentioned, but they learned of a place of prayer where some God-fearing Gentiles and Jews gathered to pray on the Jewish Sabbath. In cities which had a small Jewish population, a synagogue could not be supported, and a place of prayer substituted.

The gathering happened to be all female that day. Paul's team of four sat down to join them, and began to share about Jesus. God's Spirit had been at work among these worshipers, and some immediately responded to the message, and opened their hearts to Christ. One was Lydia, a business woman who was a *metic:* a legal foreigner doing business in Macedonia. Lydia and some of her household (possibly family and servants) believed and were baptized by Paul and Silas. She immediately invited the missionaries to live at her home for the remainder of their stay in Philippi, and they accepted.

Much interest has centered on Lydia's unique business. Her family dealt in the purple fabrics produced in their home at Thyatira in Asia Minor. The cloth was expensive because the process of extracting the purple dye from a certain type of mollusk was very labor-intensive. Wools, linens, cottons, and silks, were all used in the business, the wools being dyed while still in the fleece, and the other fabrics dyed as spools of thread. Weaving was done by some of the many guilds in Thyatira. The goods probably came to Lydia by ship or Roman trade route, perhaps as uncut cloth, or in garments, or both.

Her clientele would have been among the wealthy—only officials and royalty could afford the cloth. While Lydia was probably a woman of some means, described as having a house and servants, she would not have been a part of the aristocracy herself. The Greeks valued the arts and philosophy, and looked down on common labor. Merchants, especially foreigners, would not have been part of the higher class of social life.

The Real Significance of Lydia's Story

Much has been said about Paul's entering into Europe at Neapolis and Philippi, bringing the Gospel to the western world. Actually, from the view of those travelers, their passage to the west came much earlier, as they crossed through the mountain pass in the Taurus Range in Asia Minor. "Europe" was not a term they used, and their designation of the continents in that time was not as clear as ours. Paul and Company crossed into Macedonia, a province north of Greece and south of the Balkans, and into a different culture, government, and society.

The important part of the story for us, though, is how Lydia and her household received Christ as Messiah and Lord, and were baptized. The pattern in the book of Acts shows that new believers very quickly followed Jesus' command to be baptized. Often today believers wait a considerable time, perhaps going through classes, waiting for a convenient occasion, before completing this step of obedience. And there is much discussion over modes and significance of the ordinance, so we might talk here a little more about what the Bible teaches us.

Baptism was not a new concept when Jesus submitted to John the Baptist in the Judean desert. Jews had long used it as a symbol of purification, washing, and cleansing. For

John and his followers, baptism took on the extra importance of a change of heart—a repenting of sin, and pledging to live an ethical lifestyle. Jesus, of course, had not yet died, so the Christian meaning was not present in John's baptism. We do value it very highly, though, because Jesus himself went down into the water and came up out of the water (see Mark 1:9–11), and God the Father affirmed his action by sending the Holy Spirit in the form of a dove upon him. The dove was a significant symbol of God's filling and empowering Jesus for his ministry to come. That alone is reason enough for believers in Jesus to follow him into the waters of Baptism.

After the death, burial, and resurrection of Christ, baptism took on an even more important symbolism for believers. Paul expressed it well several years later in his ministry as he told the Romans,

> "We died to sin; how can we live in it any longer? Or don't you know that all of us who were baptized into Christ Jesus were baptized into his death? We were therefore buried with him through baptism into death in order that, just as Christ was raised from the dead through the glory of the Father, we too may live a new life." (Romans 6:2–4)

As today's believers follow Christ in baptism, we announce to the world that we have believed his sacrificial death on our behalf, and are now committing ourselves to walk in a new lifestyle in him. When a believer is baptized she is then part of the Body of Christ—the church—and joins the mission of the Kingdom of God. That mission is to take the Good News of Jesus to the world. We do well to follow Jesus and submit to baptism. We do well to receive *the empowering presence of the Holy Spirit,* and become part of the mission of the Body of Christ. Lydia and her household members became part of that mission in the days ahead.

The Cost of the Mission

It was just a few days later that an incident happened which greatly threatened the new believers in their faith. The healing of the slave girl, as told in Acts 16:16–24, is a story of freedom for her, but of great cost for Paul and Silas. As foreigners they had little voice in Macedonia. As Roman citizens, they should have been spared the terrible beating sentenced by the magistrates. For some reason they were not able to speak up or be heard on this occasion and suffered greatly for it.

It is ironic that the owners of the poor, possessed girl could not see any value to her being freed and healed. Their total concern was for their disreputable way of making a living at her expense. It was another day and time, and we would like to think that we enlightened Americans would have viewed the situation differently. Sadly, many moral compromises are made when easy money can be had at the expense of the vulnerable. Furious that their income was now threatened, they had Paul and Silas hauled in to the authorities. Anti-Semitic barbs, and accusations of unpatriotic behavior, riled the crowds in the marketplace. The result was a beating by rods, overnight imprisonment in a secure cell, and the imposing of very uncomfortable leg stocks on Silas and Paul.

What would you or I have done? The next verses amaze us. (Read Paul and Silas's reaction in Acts 16:25–28.) Unable to sleep, stinging from open wounds, miserable in leg stocks, they began to loudly sing hymns and praise God. What a witness to the listening prisoners! The jailer, meanwhile, bored with it all and feeling that they were safely locked up, went to sleep. An earthquake—not unknown in that part of Macedonia—shook him awake about midnight. Thinking the prisoners had escaped through the opened doors as he slept, he started to take his own life before retribution could come down on his head. Paul intervened, and he came to his senses.

A Clear Statement of Faith

What follows next is one of the most thrilling passages in the book of Acts: the salvation of the Philippian jailer and his family. The question in Acts 16:30, and Paul's answer in verse 31, are among the most valued and quoted in our churches. *"What must I do to be saved?"* he asked. Did he want to be saved from retribution of the authorities, or from the earthquake, or had he understood enough of Paul's message to know that he needed redemption because he was a sinner—as we all are? Whatever his intent, Paul seized the opportunity to present Jesus. *"Believe in the Lord Jesus, and you will be saved—you and your household."* In the terror of the moment the eternal truth penetrated the jailer's mind clearly, and he accepted Christ as Lord and Savior. Then he and his family, like Lydia and hers a few days before, were baptized as an outward testimony to what had happened in their hearts and lives.

What must I do to be saved? Probably the most important question a person can ask in this life. We don't use the term "saved" much in our sophisticated world. Yet Luke used it twice in this chapter—from the mouth of the slave girl (verse 17) and again from the mouth of the jailer (verse 30). A good word, *"saved."* Saved from the power and penalty of sin. Saved from eternity without God and loved ones. Saved from a life outside of the will of God. And *saved to* some things also. Saved to live a new life in Christ. Saved to belong to the Body of Christ and be part of God's purpose in the world. Saved and *empowered* to become our best selves with the help of God's Spirit within. Yes! *Saved* is a very good word indeed! *"Believe on the Lord Jesus, and you will be saved"* today! You can do it right now!

The Beginnings of the Philippian Church

A somewhat curious scene follows. The magistrates decided to release Silas and Paul, whether because they realized there was no just charge to be brought, or because the earthquake roused a superstitious thought that God was on their side. But Paul was not to be appeased so easily. His response (Acts 16:37) must be understood in the larger context. The mission in Philippi was to win converts and establish a church. With the strange testimony of a demented slave girl, the false accusations of her masters, and the wrongful incarceration of the missionaries, things were not off to a shining start. The publicity surrounding the new group of believers was not conducive to bringing in more seekers and building a healthy church. Paul knew he had to clear the believers of any bad reputation, and so he demanded an apology from those who had mistreated him—and got it!

On their release, Paul and Silas went straight to Lydia's house to make contact with the believers. They probably reunited with Timothy there, and perhaps said a temporary good-bye to Luke. The famous "We" Passages are discontinued here until Acts 20, so Luke must have remained in Philippi a while. The team had been asked to leave the city, and Paul turned them southward toward the Macedonian capital of Thessalonica.

In years to come, the Philippian church would become one of Paul's favorites. His letter to them is filled with loving memories. The Bible record tells us that they supported him financially, prayed for him, and befriended him on his later visits to Macedonia. When we read the letter to the Philippians, I like to imagine the slave girl, and the jailer and his family, and Lydia and her household, sitting together and listening to the words of their friend, Paul. Listen to what he told them:

> "I thank my God every time I remember you. In all my prayers for all of you, I always pray with joy because of your partnership in the gospel from the first day until now, being confident of this, that he who began a good work in you will carry it on to completion until the day of Christ Jesus." (Philippians 1:3–6)

So often studying a Bible personality calls someone to mind that we have known in our church ministry. Lydia reminds me of a friend we call "Miss Bea." We met her in Buda Baptist Church where Jack served as interim pastor in retirement. We enjoyed the church—and still do. It's not a very big church, and it hasn't kept up with the times like the city churches do, but it is probably the most loving church we ever served. To walk into the church is to be hugged. It is a warm and welcoming place.

We hadn't been there long when we figured out the source. Miss Bea's unconditional love permeates the congregation. She is tireless in reaching out to newcomers, the lost, the forgotten, the elderly. She lives by the "Three Cs:" cards, calls and casseroles. Every morning she begins her day with the Lord, seeking his face and his will. Nearly every day she finds time to touch lives in some loving way. She values everyone, regardless of the situation. To know her is to wish to be like her.

The Philippian church must have had someone like Miss Bea to show them how to love. Maybe it was Lydia. And what was Lydia's role in all of this? She willingly opened her heart and her home to the mission team. Many churches have been born and nurtured out of the hospitality of a godly woman. The Philippian church was one of them.

GETTING TO KNOW GOD
Damaris Believes

Acts 17:1–33

Damaris eyed her nearly-grown son across the family dining table with a mixture of compassion and annoyance. More and more these days, it seemed, he challenged her wisdom and judgment in matters that governed his life.

"Mother, *why* can't I go to Apollo's feast tomorrow? *All* the boys on our team are going. And the meat offered to Ares will be good for me. I *never* get to go to the fun stuff."

"Son," she answered quietly, "you *know* why. We've had this conversation several times before. Our family worships Jehovah God, and we do not participate in the pagan temple rites. Those gods are not gods at all—they are ancient myths. We do not believe that way."

"But, *Mother*," the youth persisted angrily, "*I do believe* in Jehovah God. *I know* Ares and Zeus and all those are not real gods. So *why does it matter* if I eat perfectly good meat that has been offered to them? I'm old enough to know the difference."

Damaris studied her hands and shook her head with resolve. "The answer is *No,* Jason! We just do not go to the pagan temples or festivals. It disrespects Jehovah. The Law commands us not to participate in the worship of other gods in any way."

"But, *Mother*," the youth could not give up hope, "*all* the other boys on our team will be there. It's a prayer for victory in the games next week. I need to show solidarity with them. They won't understand if I don't show up. It's *important!*"

The door slammed and Uncle Nicolas came into the courtyard, greeting the slave at the door. "What's all the fuss about?" he asked cheerfully, noticing the seriousness of the family conversation.

"Oh, Nicolas," Damaris exclaimed like a prisoner let out of jail, "you have come just at the right time. Jason is asking to go to a festival that his friend, Apollo, is having tomorrow. It's at the temple of Ares. They plan to offer meat offerings for a victory in next week's race. I'm telling him . . ."

"Uncle Nicolas, *listen* to me," the boy interrupted. "I *really* want to go. Father would have let me go—I know he would have." Then, turning to face his mother directly, "And the feast is *not* at the temple, Mother—it will be in Apollo's father's symposium *after* the meat has been offered and roasted. I won't even have to *go* to the pagan temple, if that makes you feel any better."

"We are God-fearers, Jason," his uncle responded firmly but kindly. "We stand apart from those pagan celebrations. And I *know* Apollo's father. He's an Epicurean and he has some pretty wild parties in that symposium. I've heard that his slaves put on some steamy dances and acrobatics at those male gatherings. We just don't hold with that kind of life. I have to agree with your mother on this one, Son."

Jason just could not give it up. "But, Uncle Nicolas, Apollo's family are *good people*—I know them. His grandfather is *on the Areopagus*. I want to be his friend. He's a great athlete—and popular—and he wants me to come to his feast tomorrow. I can take Simeon along to watch over me—I would be safe with him there." The boy clenched his fists defiantly. "I just don't understand you and Mother refusing to let me go."

"Son," Damaris countered gently, "*please*—you are still under age. Uncle Nicolas is our legal guardian. You must abide by his judgment. He has your best interests at heart. Please stop this arguing. It just upsets everyone."

Jason scuffed his feet and looked angrily at the wall. "I just don't know why we have to go to the synagogue and live by these Jewish Laws. We aren't *Jews!* We are *Greeks!* Father's people did not go to the synagogue. I *hate* living differently than my friends at school." He was fighting tears, determined not to give in, knowing that he must.

Uncle Nicolas pulled back a chair and sat down beside the boy, placing his hand on his arm. "Jason, let me tell you my story. When I was your age our family really didn't have a faith at all. Oh, there were gods all around us—goodness knows Athens has more gods and more temples than all the rest of Achaia put together. We went to all the pagan feasts by the calendar. We made the offerings to gods we knew were not real. It was all very meaningless. But three years ago—about the time your father died, and I became legal guardian to you, and your mother's estate, and Joanna—we met some Jews. David and Leah rented the shop next to mine at the market place. Their family had a true faith, based on the Law of Moses. They knew a True God—Jehovah—in a way your mother and I admired."

"We watched their lives," Nicolas continued earnestly. "David is an honest man who treats his family well. He doesn't go to the symposium parties or sleep with temple prostitutes. And he doesn't allow his boys, Jude and James, to do those things, either. And Jude and James are on a team for next week's race—so a pagan party is not necessary to win at the games."

Damaris took advantage of Jason's quiet thoughtfulness. "Your Uncle Nicolas and I talked about it—what we want for you and Joanna—the kind of people we hope you will become. We decided to explore David and Leah's God, so we began to attend the synagogue each week and tried to learn and live by those Laws. It's a better way of life than the Epicureans live, Son."

"They really don't believe much of anything," Nicolas agreed. "They just live for their parties and sensual pleasures. If there is a True God—and I have come to believe that there is—He is not pleased with that kind of living. Can you understand some of that, Son?" the uncle asked quietly.

"Jude and James—they come to the gymnasium, all right," Jason conceded. "They are on a race team, and I know them at the synagogue, too. But they attend synagogue school, and they have . . . well . . . funny customs. They don't even look like us. Apollo makes fun of them at exercise. They cut their bodies!" Jason was embarrassed and confused by what he was trying to express.

Uncle Nicolas tried to rescue him. "The Jewish families circumcise their baby boys on the eighth day. It's a sign of their Covenant with the True God. They believe they are his Chosen People. We don't carry our belief that far."

"Thank the heavens!" the youth exclaimed with disapproval.

"But we do benefit by the good morals and values they

stand for. Apollo should not make fun of those Jewish boys."

"He didn't even invite Jude and James to his feast. He knew they wouldn't be able to come," Jason added.

"What about James and Jude?" Joanna asked, flouncing into the dining room with freshly coiffed hair and nails shining. "We know them from synagogue, don't we?"

Uncle Nicolas smiled admiringly at his lovely niece, and Damaris patted her daughter as she joined them at the table. "Oh, Joanna, we were just talking about why we don't want your little brother to go to a pagan feast with his team tomorrow. I'm sorry he'll have to miss the fun, but we just can't be part of those pagan events any more. Uncle Nicolas backs me up in this."

Jason stood to be dismissed. "Well—I'm off to exercise with the team. We only have three more days to get in shape before the games." Turning towards the courtyard he called for his personal slave. "Simeon! Are you ready to go to the gymnasium with me?"

The tall Egyptian came around the corner, athletic satchel in hand. "Ready when you are, Master Jason," he said obediently.

"Simeon," Damaris addressed her servant, "we have a problem about a pagan feast. Apollo wants Jason to attend tomorrow, but our family does not participate in those events any more. Please make some excuse for Jason, so they will not expect him to attend."

The slave nodded, but Uncle Nicolas interrupted. "Wait a minute, Simeon. Sister, can't we just say, 'Thank you, but we attend synagogue and cannot attend festivals for other gods?' I think it's important for the boy to be honest and forthright. We don't have to be ashamed before these Epicureans."

Turning to the youth he said, "Jason, Son—be a *man!* Stand up for what we believe. Just tell them, 'Thank you for the invitation, but my family does not allow me to participate in offerings and feasts to the gods. But I'll pray to *my* God for victory.'"

Jason eyed his uncle, unconvinced. "Oh, great! Now I don't just have to *live* differently, I have to take up *preaching!*"

The slave tactfully rescued the situation. "It's all right, Master Nicolas, we will take care of it and work it out. Don't worry about this boy—I'll be keeping a watchful eye on him all the way." With that the two fell into step and were across the courtyard and out the door.

Joanna leaned over to her favorite uncle coyly. "And, about my husband, Uncle Nicolas—I mean—what is the news? It's important, you know. My whole life depends on it."

Her uncle cut a quick glance at his sister for assurance before beginning. "Yes, Joanna, it *is* important, and I *am* working on it. Your mother and I are getting together a good dowry for you. We have put back some of you father's gold and art, and . . ."

" . . . and we are considering giving a part of your grandfather's vineyard and a field slave or two," Damaris finished. "The size of the dowry will determine what kind of man we can find for you."

Joanna looked carefully at both her mother and her uncle.

"*But will he be kind,* Uncle Nicolas?" she pleaded. "Father was always kind to me, and to Mother, and to the servants. I could not *bear* being married to a man who treated me badly. It would be a miserable life. I would rather be dead."

"That's another reason we are God-fearers, Joanna," Nicolas explained. "We plan to find you a husband from those men: one who believes in the Jewish values of fidelity and respect. The God-fearers seem to honor the marriage agreement. They don't cavort with slave girls and temple prostitutes. They don't attend the symposium parties or practice homosexuality. It's forbidden in their Law."

Damaris squeezed Joanna's arm and smiled understandingly. "So be patient, Girl. We are working on it. Next summer will be time enough to sign a betrothal, and then you will know who the lucky man will be."

"Well, that gives me a year," the girl responded. "Mother, can we go shopping for some fabrics for my dress? And some jewelry? I would like some jewelry of my own when I marry. And maybe some perfume. I want my husband to treat me like a lady."

Damaris and Nicolas shared a knowing laugh. "Soon, Dear, we will do just that. And we will try out some new hairstyles for you, and eye make up. But we will do it tastefully. I don't want you looking like some dance girl!"

"Mother!" Joanna protested, embarrassed, but pleased.

"You will be even more beautiful than you are today," her mother assured her, standing. "But right now we must prepare for Sabbath."

"Remember what the synagogue reader said last week, Joanna," her uncle chided playfully. "True beauty comes from within—from a pure heart. I think whoever is fortunate enough to marry you will care more for your virtue than for your eye make up."

"Well said, my wise brother," Damaris agreed. "Joanna, in the meantime you might ask Leah to show you some of the fine embroidery she sells at her market. That would be a good skill for you to know as a wife, and you can spend some of this year making household linens for your hope chest. Your husband-to-be would be impressed with that."

Nicolas was on his feet also, pushing the chairs back to the table. "Well, Sister, I'm off to the Agora. I need to hear the news of the day, and learn what is happening in the world of Athenian men folk. I'll check on you all in the morning—unless something comes up and you need me before that."

BEHIND THE SCENE
A Study of Acts 17:1–33

Sharing Jesus Down the Highway

Paul's burning desire was to carry the Good News about Jesus down the Egnatian Way from Macedonia in the north, into Achaia in the south of what we call Greece today. Backs still stinging from the Roman beating in Philippi, Paul and Silas took premature leave of the new believers there and started southward to the capital city of Thessalonica. (Find this story in Acts 17:1–9.) They followed their usual pattern, going first to the Jewish synagogues to explain to the Jews that their Messiah had come in Jesus Christ. For three Sabbaths—two weeks or more—Paul reasoned with the Jews from the Scriptures. It was a hard sell. Jews could not understand a Messiah who was executed as a common criminal. The doctrine of the resurrection was crucial, because it proved that the authorities had been wrong in their judgment of Jesus, and that he was, in fact, the Son of God.

Luke reports that some Thessalonican Jews did believe: *"a large number of God-fearing Greeks and not a few prominent women."* It is of interest to us women readers that Luke singled out the response of women in three different verses of this seventeenth chapter. (Note verses 4, 12, and 34.) In Thessalonica, Berea, and again at Athens, women responded, making their own choices, not bound by the decisions of the men of their households. There was arising in Roman culture greater independence for women, and while Greece was slower to allow it, changes were happening in the First Century world of women.

As had happened before in Philippi, and earlier in Asia Minor, opposition arose in Thessalonica out of the ranks of Jewish leaders. For generations the Jews had held that, to become part of their community of faith—to convert to Judaism—it was necessary to adopt the Laws of Moses and the Covenant sign of circumcision. Paul and Silas came preaching a Gospel of faith—that believing in Jesus was the only criterion. It was unacceptable to the Jews of the synagogues to hear that the God-fearing Gentiles could become Christians without first becoming Jews. To accept the Jewish Messiah would be to accept all of historic Judaism. Allowing full status to uncircumcised Gentiles within the synagogue would have threatened the Jewish control of their faith. This was the basis of their continual opposition to Paul and his message.

The easy answer for these jealous Jews was to rile up the riff-raff of society and create a mob scene. Greeks were paranoid about riots, because it signaled to the Roman occupiers that the Greeks could not control their own territory. When the crowd could not locate Paul and Silas to drag them out, they instead grabbed their host, a man named Jason, and made him post a peace bond. But do not miss the great compliment paid to Paul and Silas and their work in Acts 17:6: *"These men who have caused trouble all over the world have now come here."* The old King James Version is more colorful: *"These that have turned the world upside down . . ."* What a striking statement about the influence the Gospel of Jesus was having on the world. By night the believers secretly sent Paul, Silas, and Timothy away, to continue their journey southward to the next town, which was Berea.

The Bereans responded well (see Acts 17:10–15), and Paul could probably have had a very fruitful ministry there. But the Thessalonican Jews heard that they were again preaching Jesus, followed them to Berea, and caused another scene. This time the believers left Silas and Timothy behind as decoys, but spirited Paul away alone to the coastal highway and accompanied him safely on to Athens.

Scoping Out the Glorious Lady

Athens was long past her glory days of 500–200 B.C. but was still a university city, and a center of art, culture, literature, and philosophy. Where did Paul live as he awaited Silas and

Timothy? Who fed him? Luke spends no words on such mundane things but tells us that Paul's concern was for the overwhelming paganism of the city. Wasting no time, Paul immediately began a double-thrust program of evangelism. He reasoned in the synagogue on Sabbaths, and preached in the marketplace other days. (Find this in Acts 17:16–21.) In the synagogue he worked out of the Old Testament Scriptures, showing how Jesus was the Messiah. But the marketplace was different. Those people had no Jewish background, and the Old Scriptures had little or no meaning for them. He needed a different approach.

Always a man for all seasons, Paul began debating with any who would listen. Athens was deeply into modern philosophies, mainly those of the Epicureans and the Stoics. The Athenians valued the arts and literature, and were obsessed with physical education and the games. We all know about the Olympic Games, named for Mt. Olympus where Zeus and the ten major Greek gods were purported to reside. Boys, age seven and older, went to school to learn the sophisticated subjects mentioned, and to the gymnasiums to exercise and prepare for competition, usually under the watchful eye of a personal slave. Subjects of mathematics and science were less valued and left to the working classes—the freedmen and slaves—who carried on the business of the country. Greek families of any status distained work, leaving it to the slaves and lower echelons of society.

The two main schools of philosophy being debated in Athens in Paul's day probably conjure up memories of your ancient history class in school. Everyday in the Agora, or market, which was the center of both commerce and civil activity, the Epicureans argued their beliefs. **Epicureans** were pleasure lovers. They did not believe in an afterlife, or in consequences for their actions. Although the philosophy had been more noble in its beginning, by the First Century Epicureans lived for sensual pleasure. The gods to them existed but were impersonal, not involved in the lives or morality of men. Their resulting lifestyle was one of drinking, entertainment, prostitution, homosexuality, and other such "pleasures." Much of this activity took place in the symposiums of Greek homes—the men's chambers—where parties were hosted in the evenings. Women and girls were sent upstairs to their quarters. The slaves served and entertained.

The **Stoics,** by contrast, held emotions in contempt. They were pantheists, believing not in the mythological gods, but in a "universal reason." God, they argued, permeated the cosmos, and was not a personal being, but rather a force. Their goal was to live in harmony with the natural world, and they placed a high value on the natural order of things. Their concept of afterlife had to do with being re-absorbed into the divine spirit. Their stoical attitude of self-denial prevented them from identifying with a suffering Savior. Neither philosophy came close to the teachings Paul espoused, so his work was cut out for him in the daily debates.

Revealing the Unknown God

Paul, an educated and brilliant man, waded right in. He took on both philosophies, refuting them from the Old Testament and the teachings of Jesus, and very soon people took notice of him. *"What is this babbler trying to say?"* they were asking.

Athens, while self-governing, was different than Philippi and Thessalonica. The former were true democracies, where the populous made the decisions. Athens had been set up with a ruling council of about thirty men, called the Areopagus. The title, *Areopagus,* referred both to the council itself and also to the rise called Mars Hill, just off the upper city or Acropolis, where the council met. (The Areopagus met in the Areopagus, so to speak.) This council was charged with hearing all new religions, and deciding whether they could be taught in the city. Any new gods had to be passed on by them as a safeguard, to keep insurrections from growing against the Empire.

Before long Paul was asked to go before the Areopagus and set forth his "foreign religion." That challenge is the reason we now have in our Bibles one of the most wonderful descriptions of God ever penned. Study Acts 17:22–31 with awe. It is brilliant in the way it answers the charges and refutes the philosophies of Athens. Every sentence is packed with significance. It is worthy of memorization. And it is a wonderful fulfillment of Jesus' promise in Matthew 10:19: *"But when they arrest you, do not worry about what to say or how to say it. At that time you will be given what to say, for it will not be you speaking, but the Spirit of your Father speaking through you."* Look at Paul's outline.

The Introduction: Acts 17:22–23. Beginning with a compliment to their spirituality, Paul deflected any accusations that he was preaching a foreign god. Paul's God already had a legitimate shrine in the city: *"I even found an altar with* *this inscription: TO AN UNKNOWN GOD. Now what you worship as something unknown I am going to proclaim to you."* There went the civil charges.

God as Creator and Sustainer: Acts 17:24–26. To the Epicureans, who believed in many gods, Paul avowed that there was just one True God, the Creator of the Universe. *"The God who made the world and everything in it is the Lord of heaven and earth."* To the Stoics, who believed in a god-force which permeated the universe, he stated that God was greater than, and outside of, creation. To all who believed the gods were impersonal and not concerned with the morality of mortals, he explained that God is the sustainer of all creation, and the determiner of history. And to all who trusted in idols, he confirmed that the True God was not one made with hands. Looking out from his vantage point on Mars Hill, across all the temples and shrines of Athens, Paul declared that God *"does not live in temples built by hands."*

God as a Seeking, Personal God: Acts 17:27–28. The concept of a personal God, wanting relationship with humans, was strange to the ears of Athenians. *"God did this so that men would seek him and perhaps reach out for him and find him, though he is not far from each one of us."* And then comes my favorite verse about God: *"For in him we live and move and have our being."* God is not an impersonal force in the universe. He did not just create us and leave us to our own devices. He wants to live within us, to *empower* us, to be life itself to us! Surely the minds of the Greek philosophers were challenged by this wonderful concept of "the God who is there."

God Expects a Response: Acts 17:29–31. Then Paul drove home his purpose: God wants each person to repent, turn to him, and get into a relationship with him. *"But now he commands all people everywhere to repent . . ."* Further, judgment is coming. For those who believed there was no afterlife, no consequence for their immoral activities, Paul clarified the situation. God will return to judge the actions of men. Now is the time for all men to repent. And—always the main point of his messages—there will be a resurrection.

As the Council mulled and mumbled over these astounding truths, Paul strode out confidently. Reactions were mixed, but some did believe. Among them was a man named Dionysius, one of the Areopagites. Another was Damaris, a woman with a Greek name. And that is the only statement we have about the heroine of this chapter. She was an Athenian woman who chose to believe in Jesus Christ.

A Persona for Damaris

Where did we get all the ideas that are built into the fiction vignette of Damaris at the beginning of this chapter? Much of it comes from what we read about the women of Athens in that day. Both *The Cambridge Illustrated History of Ancient Greece* and *The Oxford Illustrated History of Greece and the Ancient Hellenistic World,* and other such reference books, are rich with detail. But first, that Luke singled her out for mention indicates she was somewhat known or prominent. She could have been the wife of a well-known man; but, that not being said in the Bible, she could have been widowed or divorced.

Women in Athens were always under the authority of a

man, either a husband or a guardian who was a family member. That would have been a father, older son, or brother. They did not own real property or conduct business on their own. Their only possessions were their clothing, jewelry, and slaves. When divorced or widowed, their dowry and property reverted to their families, under legal guardianship of a male. In our story we chose to show Damaris as a young widow with two teenagers because it opens for us more interesting customs of her day.

Women lived pretty much in their homes. They were, in fact, guarded. Slaves usually kept the front entry. Women's quarters were upstairs or in the back of the house. Men did most of the shopping at the Agora. Women's activities were restricted, so as to guard from the possibility of illegitimate children. Rules of inheritance were very important. An Athenian adult could not marry a foreigner, because the property could not pass out of the hands of the Greeks. Mixed race children were not allowed. Men married for the purpose of having legitimate heirs and having a wife to guard their possessions. For pleasure they had mistresses and prostitutes. Fidelity was not valued in the Greek culture.

So while we know almost nothing of Damaris, we do know some about Greek women, and what her life would have been like. But the truly unsolved mystery is: where did she come into contact with Paul, and hear the message of Christ? Since women did not attend the Areopagus, she must have encountered him either at the synagogue as a Greek-speaking God-fearer or in the market place. Because women did not often go to the market, we chose to place her in the community of God-fearers. Now, you will forgive the conjecture but have some understanding of how we arrived at it.

Why did the Greeks go to the synagogues? What appealed to them about the Jewish concept of God? Many found emptiness in the philosophies of their day. The mythical gods were less believed, less a reality, than in centuries past. The Greeks were seeking other belief systems. The higher morality and values of the Jews, the concept of One True God, this made sense to them. Although they attended the synagogues to learn and practice this Jewish religion, many did not convert. Especially the men were unwilling to submit to the rite of circumcision, so they came only as seekers, not as converts. But these seekers were a ripe field for Paul to harvest for Christ. Faith in Jesus was open to people of all genders and races, and there was no requirement except genuine belief and baptism. Many converts found in Christianity what they had been missing in Greek philosophy, or seeking in the Jewish synagogues.

On Knowing God

"That I may know Him . . ." was a lifelong goal of the Apostle Paul. *"I want to know Christ and the power of his resurrection, and the fellowship of his sufferings, becoming like him in his death, and so, somehow, to attain to the resurrection from the dead."* These were his later words to his Philippian friends (see Philippians 3:10–11). Paul discounted all his other credentials, all his achievements, and cared only for the relationship that he had with his precious Savior, Lord, and Friend, Jesus. At the end of his life he was still *pressing on* toward this goal of becoming all that Jesus wanted him to be.

Damaris came to know God in Athens, and we have no further word on how her new relationship with Christ developed. Paul did not tarry long in Athens, and we have no record of a church forming there. He apparently wrote no letter there. So what became of Dionysius and Damaris and the others who believed? For us, we know that coming to know Jesus as Savior is only the beginning of a lifelong pursuit of intimacy with a God who wishes for us to seek Him. We wonder if Damaris continued in her new faith in months and years to come.

Paul wanted to know Jesus' *power*, so that he might be effective for his Lord. He wanted to understand Jesus better through sharing in *suffering*—something he certainly did through beatings, imprisonments, stoning, and even shipwreck. He was *willing to die* for him. Whatever it took to find the intimacy and perfection of the Christ-life, Paul was willing to endure. His intensity amazes and challenges us in our own Christian walk with the Lord.

In his wonderful book, *So You Want To Be Like Christ?*, Charles Swindoll explores what is necessary for developing the intimate walk with Christ. He warns that it does not come easily or automatically, but must be sought at a price. *"Seeking intimacy with the Almighty requires focused determination, demands specific changes in attitude and behavior, and will come with a number of heartbreak[s] and setbacks."*[3] His careful, insightful, book-length development of Philippians 3:10 is worth your thoughtful and prayerful study. Do you want to be like Christ? To know him intimately? It will cost you, as it cost Paul. Be brave—begin the journey!

PARTNERS IN MINISTRY
Priscilla Joins Paul's Mission

Acts 18 and 19

The house was still almost dark as Priscilla came downstairs and into the kitchen. Her faithful servant, Keila, was tending the baking, and Naphtali stirred a wheat porridge simmering on the fire. For a few minutes the three went over plans for the day. With three men as houseguests, Priscilla could not leave for the shop until meals were planned, marketing directed, and hospitality assured.

Hearing a stirring, she quickly gathered some porcelain cups on a tray, added a decanter of juice and a pitcher of goat's milk, and headed for the courtyard. Silas and Timothy had found seats by the fountain, where the morning sunrise was beginning to touch the upper walls and kiss the top of the climbing rose which trellised almost to the second story. Priscilla and Aquila had left much of what they loved behind when forced to flee from Rome, but her love of flowers had prompted her to plant the rose and several other blooming plants in the courtyard of their rented home. "It helps us live with the ugliness of Corinthian life," she often explained to guests. Corinth was a very hard place to live, but it afforded opportunities to sell tents and tapestries, and that is how they survived in the chaotic world into which they were born.

"Look what we have here! Thank you!" Silas greeted her with enthusiasm. "You and Aquila are so kind to let us take rooms with you here. I guess we are all Jewish refugees in Greek exile, so to speak, but it is a little like home, having a place with our own kind of folks. We thank you for that." He was pouring juice into a cup as he spoke.

"I'll just have a little of the milk, if I may," Timothy chimed in. "All the travel and excitement has my stomach a little on edge today." And he poured himself a cup full of the fresh, warm stuff.

"Are you both sleeping well?" Priscilla asked her guests. "I hope the servants are taking good care of you." And both men nodded gratefully.

"I think Paul is sleeping *too* well," Timothy quipped. "He was still dead to the world when we left the guest room."

"He was up late writing a letter to the believers in Thessalonica by lamplight," Silas explained. "You know that he just didn't get to stay with the Thessalonican church as long as he wanted to. He really fell in love with those people and continues to be concerned for their growth and safety. Finally he just had to write them and encourage them before he could get to sleep last night."

"Oh, oh!" Timothy responded. "Now he'll want me to pack up and take the letter up north for him and bring him back word again about how they are doing. And I just got back last week!" He spoke with a mixture of laughter and resignation. "I probably told him too much about their struggles, and he will have to give them advice and counsel. He's just like a father, always instructing, always guiding, always worrying."

Silas nodded and laughed with him. "He would go himself, but things here are just too fragile for him to leave. Unless he can find another trustworthy messenger, you probably will be the one, Son. I think I need to stay here and help him with this new group at Titus Justice's house."

"We are doing well, though, don't you think?" Priscilla asked. "I was surprised when Paul decided to leave the synagogue, but it has worked out well to be next door at Titus' house. And with Crispus and his family joining us, others felt free to come with them. We have quite a nice group of believers now, and worship is so much calmer without all the debating and arguing with the Jewish traditionalists."

"It's better than I had feared," Timothy ventured. "I thought we were in for another uproar like we had in the Macedonian towns, but things have calmed down quite well. I hope it stays that way."

Silas took a long drink, drained his cup, and balanced it on his knee. "I also questioned Paul's judgment about leaving the synagogue," he admitted, "but I think he was just sick and tired of being badgered by the Jews day in and day out. This has been dogging us since Philippi—these Jewish legalists who keep insisting on observing all the Jewish rites and refusing to believe that Jesus is the true Messiah of God. Paul has talked until he is blue in the face, and they just won't believe. So I think the move was a good one . . . but . . ." Silas left the thought unfinished as he saw a somber Paul coming out of the guest room. All turned to look in the direction of his stare. Setting down his empty cup, he moved toward Paul with concern. "Are you feeling well, Friend?" he asked, putting a supporting arm around the smaller man.

"Yes, Silas," Paul responded quietly, "I am well. But I have just had a very strange dream—or maybe it was a vision—and I am trying to process it—to know what it means."

Silas walked beside Paul toward the fountain area where the group had gathered, and helped him find a seat at the low table. The morning sunlight was brightening that corner, and Paul shaded his eyes from the glare as he gathered his words. "I had a vision—God spoke to me last night. I think we are doing the right thing."

"What is that, Paul?" Priscilla questioned gently. "Tell us about the vision, if you can." Everyone was leaning close, sensing that the moment was important.

"The Lord told me, *Do not be afraid, Paul. Keep on speaking, and do not be silent. For I am with you, and no one is going to attack and harm you, because I have many people in this city.*' So I think we are doing the right thing by leaving the synagogue and establishing a separate place for the believers to meet and worship."

"Well, I think so, too," Timothy agreed. "If God is promising protection, then we did the right thing to get away from the Jews before they took in after you again, like they did in Thessalonica and Berea. It makes me feel better to hear that God has affirmed your decision so clearly."

"I think that makes us all feel better," Priscilla agreed. "You all have been through so much in Macedonia—it's good to know that God is watching and caring, and that he plans to protect you here." Paul smiled at her, grateful for her understanding.

"I guess the Lord knew how much I needed that assurance," he admitted.

"Would you like a cup of milk or juice, Paul?" And she reached for the decanter and a clean cup.

Keila and Naphtali came in with a pot of hot porridge and a tray of cheese and bread. "Where you would like for us to serve breakfast, Miss Priscilla?" Keila asked. "Here, or in the dining room?"

"I think we will just stay out here in the courtyard this morning, Keila," Priscilla answered, taking the tray from her and placing it on the table between the cups. "We're all enjoying talking, and this is a sunny, warm place. Thank you, and would you bring us a new decanter of juice, please?"

Keila gathered the empty vessels onto the serving tray and started back to the kitchen for refills. "She is a good helper," Timothy observed. "I think you treat her well, and she appreciates it."

Priscilla smiled and began to ladle porridge into available cups. "All the servants are very helpful when Aquila is away on business like this," she explained. "Meshach and Obed really look after the house and go to the docks for imports. And old Menahem stays faithfully by the door. I don't know what I would do without them. And it has helped so much to have both you and Silas working at the shops, especially with Aquila gone. Business has been good, and there is so much to be done to keep up with the orders."

"Well, it has certainly freed me to stay with the witnessing," Paul added thankfully. "So it looks like everything has fallen into place, and God is continuing his work."

"If the Jews will just leave us in peace, we will probably see many more come to faith in Jesus in the weeks ahead," Silas predicted. "Corinth is a miserable, wicked city, but God is doing the best work here we've seen since we left Philippi. It's just that . . ." and he hesitated, leaving the thought dangling.

"It's just what, Silas?" Priscilla pursued. "What is troubling you? We thought everything was going well."

"Oh, he's just a worrier," Timothy said, giving the older

man a playful shove. "He'll find something to worry over when all is going well."

"What, Friend?" Paul asked, ignoring Timothy's light-heartedness. Experience had taught him that Silas' intuition was usually worth noting. "What is troubling you?"

"At the shops yesterday I heard some chatter about troublemakers in the synagogue who won't let the believers rest. It seems they are angry that we left them without settling the question about the Gentile converts, and the stronger we grow the more threatened they feel." Silas looked around the group with worried eyes. "I had hoped they were going to let it go now that we have moved out, but I'm afraid some of them are not. They have threatened Crispus, and I fear they may come after you, Paul. We just may not have seen the end of it yet."

"Oh, no—I hate to hear that." Timothy turned toward Paul, waiting for him to respond to this new and troubling information.

"I didn't want to mention it last night, Paul," Silas continued. "I knew you had that letter on your mind, and I didn't think you would sleep at all if you knew. But I had to tell you now so you will be watchful."

There were what seemed like several minutes of silence as Paul sat thoughtfully sipping his juice, shaking his head. When he responded he was resolute. "No, we aren't going to let this stop us," he answered. "Last night's vision was just what we needed. We are on the right track. God is going to protect us—we have that promise now. So we are going to move straight ahead, and let the chips fall where they will. Some day—I don't know when—the Jews are going to understand that they cannot stop us, either by arguing or threatening or rioting. I wish it were not this way—I want them to believe in Jesus so much—but we will move ahead, whether we have their consent or not. We have our mission. We dare not disappoint God."

Heads nodded. It was the right thing, and they all knew it. And everyone moved to begin another day.

BEHIND THE SCENE
A Study of Acts 18

Tentmakers on the Move

Priscilla and Aquila are an exciting couple, and their story takes us from one end of the Empire almost to the other. Aquila, we are told, was from Pontus, a province in the north of Asia Minor up by the Black Sea. Priscilla may have been from that area also, but we are not told of her beginnings. Their trade, tent making, could involve many things. Usually tents were either of a tough fabric or of skins. Those who worked with skins were actually leatherworkers, and their trade branched off into other leather products. Those who worked with fabric generally made not only tents, but also draperies and upholstery materials. The Bible does not specify which kind of work Aquila and his wife were engaged in, but the guess is the fabrics. Leatherwork involved handling and tanning hides, and the Jews were not drawn to that work because it was unclean.

Acts 18:1–4 tells us that Paul also was a tentmaker, and that was how he and Aquila became acquainted. Paul was from Tarsus in Cilicia, another province of Asia Minor, located 200 to 300 miles south of Pontus. Cilicia was goat country, and the strong fabric used to make tents and draperies was produced in that region from goats' hair. This all lends to our thinking that, when Paul found these news friends in Corinth, they shared the skills and knowledge of the trade of making things from Cilician cloth.

Somehow Aquila and Priscilla had been following their trade in Rome, but were forced to leave when Emperor Claudius ejected all the Jews from that imperial city. Historians tell us that Claudius was a weak emperor, but had generally favored the Jews. He assured freedom of worship to the large Jewish settlement in Alexandria, Egypt, and had promised them similar freedoms throughout the empire. However, troubles in the Jewish communities of Rome angered him. A Roman historian, Suetonius, is frequently quoted as saying it was *"because of their continual tumults instituted by Chrestus"* that this edict for expulsion was passed in 49 a.d. Many think that the Greek, *"Chrestus"* is a misspelling of the Greek, *"Christus,"* which referred to Messiah or perhaps Christians. So it is possible that it was one of several times when the Christians were driven from Rome.

We note that there is no mention that Aquila and Priscilla were converted through Paul's ministry, which leads to the assumption that they came from Rome already believing in Christ. Recall that there were some from both Pontus and Rome present at Pentecost (see Acts 2:9–10), so the Gospel had been taken there twenty years prior to Paul's visit to Corinth. Now driven from Rome, this Jewish refugee couple had taken up residence in another town on the trade route, Corinth, located on the isthmus between Macedonia (northern Greece) and Achaia (southern Greece).

Corinth, a city of commerce, wealth, and immorality, boasted a population of about 200,000 free men and 500,000 slaves in Paul's day. It was the Roman capital of Achaia, situated on a large hill overlooking three harbors, two of which were active. It was common for trading ships, wishing to avoid the dangerous travel around the southern coast of Greece, to come into the safer harbor at Cenchrea, east of Corinth. There they would offload cargo, transport it across the land bridge (isthmus) and load it onto other vessels at Lechaem, west of Corinth. It was a shortcut to Rome and the west beyond. Nero tried, just after the time of Paul's visit, to cut a canal across the isthmus, but was unsuccessful. (That was not achieved until 1893.)

In Corinth one would find temples to many Greek gods, including Poseidon, Apollo, and Aphrodite, goddess of love. The Temple of Aphrodite was known for its one-thousand temple prostitutes. The comings and goings of sailors and tradesmen of many nations fed the wide-open immorality of the area. It no doubt afforded Aquila and his wife good opportunities to serve both the military and civilian travelers with tents. And the wealth of Corinth brought a market for household draperies, wall hangings, and upholstery. It seems likely that they imported the cloth and then manufactured by hand the items requested. Paul attached to them for his eighteen months there and was probably an employee, helping to make such items. We can even imagine that Priscilla may have had skills in interior design, making them popular vendors for Greek homemakers. But much of this is educated guessing.

Rebuilding a Confident Ministry

We learn, by reading the letter Paul wrote to the Corinthian Christians a few years later, that he had come to Corinth from the north somewhat broken. (Check 1 Corinthians 2:1–5.) In Philippi he and Silas were beaten and jailed, and then asked to leave town. In Thessalonica they were run out by jealous Jews, who objected to Gentiles being given status as believers in the synagogue without circumcision. In Berea that scene was repeated. Sent away secretly and alone to Athens, Paul went up against the Epicurean and Stoic philosophers in the Areopagus. He was brilliant, but results were minimal. Discouraged, not knowing why Silas and Timothy delayed coming to find him, Paul moved on to Corinth. There, instead of going immediately to a synagogue, he found a tentmaker (Aquila) and began working at his secular trade. Through Aquila and Priscilla he was introduced to the Jewish synagogue and began again trying to persuade Jews and Greek God-fearers that Jesus was Messiah.

When Jewish opposition again arose, Paul backed off. He did not wait to be run out of the synagogue as in other towns. This time he left willingly, with Silas and Timothy now beside him. Probably Aquila and Priscilla, in whose home he and the team were living, went with him. And on their heels came the ruler of the synagogue, one Crispus, and his family and household slaves—all believers in Jesus! To lose members is one thing, but to lose the ruler—the top official of the synagogue—is something else! Others, encouraged by Crispus' brave stand, came with him. A God-fearer named Titus Justus opened his home to them as a gathering place, and it was conveniently located right next door to the synagogue. What a slap in the face of the Jews! Every time they looked over, there were Paul and his followers believing in Jesus as Messiah. It was more than they could allow.

The Lord knew the trouble that was brewing, and prepared Paul through a vision. *"Do not be afraid; keep on speaking, do not be silent. For I am with you, and no one is going to attack and harm you, because I have many people in this city."* What an encouragement to Paul to know that God had built a protection about him. He could confidently continue to preach and debate in the marketplace, and in Titus' home, knowing he would not be physically harmed. What an affirmation of his decision to break with the troublesome synagogue leaders.

Still the Opposition Came

As the story continues in Acts 18:12–17, the Jews came at Paul through the courts, but God intervened. The new proconsul was Gallio who served in Corinth 51–52 A.D. He was a fair man, and seeing that the accusations were trumped up religious charges, he refused to hear the case. He even ran Paul's accusers out of his courtroom! In anger the Jews turned on their new synagogue ruler, Sosthenes (what had he done or not done?) but Paul and his group were spared. Interestingly, Sosthenes, who took the brunt of the mob's anger, may be the one who was later a co-worker with Paul, mentioned in 1 Corinthians 1:1. God works in mysterious ways.

Paul continued his work in Corinth for eighteen months before moving on. We get a better picture of that work by looking at the two letters he later wrote back to the Corinthian church. They give us clues to the problems faced by new believers living in a very wicked city. In the first letter Paul advised them about their internal bickering over leadership, their sexual misconduct, marital problems, meat offered to idols, misuse of the Lord's Supper, and improper use of their spiritual gifts. It is hard to come out of a life style as pagan as Corinth's. Paul's work there was cut out for him.

After a year and a half of teaching and winning people to Christ, it was time for Paul to make a quick trip home to Syria, to report back to the church which had commissioned him. Priscilla and Aquila took the opportunity to sail east with him, but only as far as Ephesus, across the Aegean Sea, on the west coast of Asia Minor. Ephesus was another trade center, and for the next few years, this wandering couple of tentmakers pursued their trade in that new location. As we shall see, they carried their faith with them there. For when Paul came back to Ephesus a few months later, he wrote back to the Corinthian church these words: *"Aquila and Priscilla greet you warmly in the Lord, and so does the church that meets at their house."* (See 1 Cor. 16:19.) So the exciting story continues, but now in Ephesus.

PARTNERS IN MINISTRY, PART 2

Friends were gathering for the evening prayer and worship service. Priscilla, always the gracious hostess, moved among them, greeting each one warmly. A servant kept the entry, taking wraps as new guests came in. The late fall evening being quite cool, Aquila had lighted lamps and a brazier in the great room to take off the chill. Couches provided close seating for about three dozen, and younger believers found places on the floor. Fellowship was warm among these who shared a common faith in Jesus as Lord.

Teresa caught Priscilla's robe as she passed and whispered, "It is so good of you and Aquila to let us meet in your home each week. We feel so comfortable here."

"We are just grateful to have our own home again," Priscilla responded. "Corinth was very foreign to us. *Metics* were not allowed to own land, and good rentals were hard to find. And I had to be so careful there. Women are watched closely and seldom go out. I did most of my work from our courtyard at home. We are glad to be away from there. We find life in Ephesus much more to our liking."

"Do you plan to stay on here permanently?" Teresa asked. "We certainly hope that you will."

"Well, our plans are not definite," Priscilla began. "Of course, we loved Rome, and would go back if we could. But as long as Claudius is in power, that is not likely. So we may be here a while—we just don't know."

Antony was listening in from the next couch and spoke up quickly. "But, Priscilla, did you not hear the latest on that?"

"I guess not," she responded, moving closer. "What is the news?"

"Word in the Agora late today was that Claudius has died. The rumor is that his second wife poisoned him—but I don't know if that is true."

Gasps came from several who had not heard that news yet. The loss of an emperor would bring uncertainty in many segments of life.

"Aquila!" Priscilla called to her husband, who was across the room. "Aquila, did you hear that?"

Hurrying across to where she stood, Aquila asked, "Hear what? Am I missing something important?"

Priscilla nodded toward Antony who spoke so all could hear. "Word at the Agora, for those who have not heard, is that Claudius has died—poisoned by his wife."

Murmurs spread throughout the gathering, and the room was buzzing by the time Paul came in from his quarters across the courtyard a few minutes later. Several were quick to fill him in on the news.

"Have they said who the next emperor will be?" Paul asked the group. "It will have strong implications for how openly we can spread the Gospel. Who is expected to take his place?"

"I'm guessing it will be his adopted son, Nero," Aquila ventured. "He is probably not a bad choice for us—a pretty rational man—though certainly not a believer."

After several more minutes of conjecture and concern, Paul summoned the group for prayers. One major request was for the future of the empire and the outlook for the spread of Christianity. The other main concern of the evening was for those who had recently come into faith from the world of sorcery. Paul called on one of them, a former diviner of spirits, to share a testimony of his new faith. The believers were amazed at his telling of how the Gospel was catching fire among that group.

"Two nights ago, in a location outside the Magnesian Gate, we had a gathering," he told the wide-eyed group. "Many sorcerers and magicians brought their secret formulas, and their scrolls, and we had a bonfire and burned them. These people are serious about turning from their magic and professing Jesus as Lord," he said earnestly. "The value of those scrolls exceeded fifty thousand drachmas." The sum astounded hearers all over the room. "Please, I implore you, accept them when they come into the gathering. They are risking much to begin a new life in Christ."

The meeting lasted late into the night. There was excitement in knowing that the story of Jesus was being told and believed, that the people of Ephesus were beginning to hear and understand. But there was also danger.

"We heard rumblings in the market that the craftsmen who make the images of Diana for tourists are upset because their trade is falling off," Erastus told Paul. "I don't know if anything will come of it, but it could bode trouble."

"Paul, do you think Christianity is having *that much* impact?" Priscilla asked. "Could the influence of the Gospel be the reason their sales are falling off?"

"The silversmiths are a very strong guild, Paul," Antony warned. "You must be careful not to go into the part of the city where they are until we know if this is going to turn into anything. If their purses are hurting, they are sure to be looking for someone to blame."

The evening ended after midnight, and everyone left reluctantly, with much on their minds. A new emperor, a revival among the sorcerers, trouble with the silversmiths—more excitement than most folks wanted in one evening. Paul, Timothy, and Erastus stood a while longer with Aquila and Priscilla in the courtyard before retiring for the night. Priscilla dismissed the servants for bed, but still the five friends stayed to talk.

"Paul, will this news about Claudius change your plans for the future?" Timothy asked. Timothy's own future was so much bound up in Paul's that he could not help wondering.

Paul looked at his young friend with great fondness. "Son, it may just do that. I have been wanting to plan a trip to Rome—and maybe on to Spain—but the time did not seem right so long as Claudius was on the throne. Now, it may become a possibility."

Timothy's eyes were shining. "How soon might that happen?" he pursued.

"Oh, not for a while. I am just finishing this second letter to the believers at Corinth. I will need for someone . . ." and he eyed the young man knowingly " . . . to carry that across the sea to them before winter sets in."

"Oh, oh! I think I hear my name," Timothy answered.

"I think you do," Paul agreed. "Maybe you and Erastus together. And after that, we have the offering for the needy in Jerusalem area to collect and deliver. So it will be another year or so, but it is definitely in the future."

Priscilla and Aquila eyed each other and smiled.

"What are you two thinking?" Timothy asked playfully.

"We just might be seeing all of you in Rome one day," Priscilla ventured. "Our dream has always been to return. With Claudius gone, Jews may again be allowed to do business there, and that would be our choice, I think." She looked to Aquila for affirmation.

"That would be our choice," he agreed. And on that note the friends embraced and turned for their quarters to rest for what was left of the night.

Janet Burton

BEHIND THE SCENE AGAIN
A Study of Acts 19

Returning to Ephesus

Paul had left Priscilla and Aquila in Ephesus and made a quick trip home to Syria, but was soon *en route* back through Asia Minor to his friends in Ephesus. It was a thriving trade center, ripe for the Gospel, and he could not wait to begin working there. As always, Paul began his witnessing among the Jews and God-fearers at the synagogue. But after three months, opposition began again. (See the story in Acts 19:1–10.) Now having determined to minimize the struggle between the Jewish traditionalists and the new believers, Paul made a decision to take the believers and leave the synagogue.

The significance of his renting the lecture hall of Tyrannus in the off hours is this: it is the first time we know of a Christian church gathering on a regular basis in a free-standing, rented location. Other mentions are of synagogue gatherings, or meetings in private homes. And, while the church at Ephesus did meet in the home of Priscilla and Aquila (see 1 Cor. 16:8–9 and 19), Paul met daily at the *siesta* time (from about 11:00 a.m. until 4:00 p.m.) in this rented public facility, to draw more seekers into the fellowship.

Wonderful things began to happen, not the least of which was a major revival among the sorcerers and diviners of the area. (Read that exciting story in Acts 19:11–20.) Luke does not tell us that Emperor Claudius died about this time. Paul's two years in Ephesus are thought to have been 53–55 A.D. Claudius reigned in Rome from 41–54 A.D. Paul's plans to include a fourth mission trip, this time to Rome, probably coincided with this change in the climate of things in Italy. (Note his words in Acts 19:21–22.) This event also probably accounts for why we find Priscilla and Aquila in Rome a few years later, when Paul writes the church there to advise them that he will be soon coming to visit. (Find that in Romans 16:3–4.)

Risking Their Lives for Paul and the Gospel
Paul's memory of Aquila and Priscilla was, *"They risked their lives for me."* Many Bible scholars tie that phrase to the story in Acts 19:23–41. The silversmiths did indeed cause trouble. Nothing upsets merchants more than taking a hit in the pocketbook. As the influence of Christianity pervaded Ephesus, the silversmiths feared that their lucrative tourism trade—the sale of silver images of the goddess Artemis (Diana)—would be damaged. Calling a meeting of the guild, Demetrius riled the group with these warnings, and laid the blame squarely on Paul: *"And you see and hear how this fellow Paul has convinced and led astray large numbers of people here in Ephesus and in practically the whole province of Asia."* What a compliment to the work of Paul and his team!

A terrifying riot ensued, and Paul's friends, seeing that he wanted to intervene, prevented him from going into the twenty-four-thousand-seat theater where the tradesmen were meeting. Surely Aquila and Priscilla were among those who held him back. The bedlam continued for about two hours, until a city official was able to talk some sense into the crazed mob. (Visualize trying to restore order with no public address system!) Paul and his friends were protected by God, but the damage was done. Paul knew it was time to move on. Shortly, the winter being past and the weather accommodating, he set out for Greece to collect an offering for the needy saints of the Jerusalem area. That trip took him north through Macedonia, and back to Corinth, where he stayed long enough to write the letter to the Romans. But that is a story for the next chapter.

A Strong Woman in Ministry

Isn't Priscilla an interesting woman to study? Her life inspired us to write *two* stories—one in Corinth and another in Ephesus—instead of the usual one. And, even with that, we did not get to the part where she and Aquila instructed the great teacher, Apollos, and brought him to faith in Jesus. (That part of the story is in Acts 18:24–28.) What a lady! Wife, business partner, tentmaker/seamstress, church planter, risk-taker, teacher, gracious hostess, friend—she was all of that and more! We only hope we have done justice to her in our fictionalizing of her life.

"Tentmakers" have made it into our own era. Patterning after Priscilla and Aquila, who made their own living but traveled to distant places starting churches, even today groups of lay-missionaries are proudly called by that term. There is such a need in our world for Christians who can remain self-supporting but have the freedom to travel and serve Christ in far away places. It is a venture of faith.

We cannot study Priscilla and Aquila without remembering our good friends Dorothy and George Hayner, who serve in much that same way with the International Baptist Convention. Every year—sometimes oftener—they leave their home in Central Texas, and go to some European location. There they serve an English-language church while the pastor goes home to America for a month or maybe three. Their travels have taken them to Germany, Bulgaria, the Ukraine, Rumania—some of those places several times. To support their work they have an antique importing business. Funds raised in the sale of antique furniture and other items pay the costs of their travel.

On these overseas jaunts, George preaches and pastors, and Dorothy helps him and uses her wonderful gifts of hospitality and administration. Both are retired from the military, so globe-trotting is in their blood. We held our breath one year as Dorothy took a supply of medicines and cash (strapped beneath her clothing!) on a plane/train venture deep into the Ukraine because a missionary family was in need. And she went alone! Both are amazing, but when we talk about them (just as with Priscilla and Aquila) we often mention Dorothy first. George is such a strong, steady, stalwart guy—the Rock of Gibraltar type, and rather quiet. But Dorothy is the effervescent, bubbly conversationalist. He the solid gold setting; she the sparkling jewel he holds tightly. Together they are quite a pair! Tentmakers extraordinaire!

No wonder we think of them when we read the stories of Priscilla and Aquila. Their lives say to us: *There is always a place for a strong woman to partner with others in the work of the Lord.* Surely the ministry of Paul on his second and third journeys was made easier, safer, and more joyful, by his partnership with this wonderful couple.

SISTER, SERVANT, SAINT
Phoebe Carries the Letter to Rome

Acts 20:1–6 and Romans 16:1–2

Smells of changing tides permeated the damp dawn air as Phoebe came downstairs to begin another busy day. A merchant ship from Cilicia and Asia was due in by early morning—as soon as it was light enough for the sailors to navigate the channel safely. Dock hands would be off-loading cargo by mid morning, and she hoped her shipment of Cilician cloth would be aboard.

Quickly she checked with her house servants as she sipped a cup of broth and nibbled some fresh bread. Satisfied that the chores were underway, Phoebe tossed her wool shawl over her shoulders, grabbed her satchel of papers, and tucked in some cheese and bread for midday. Checking to be sure her purse was safely in it, she started for the courtyard door.

"Neco!" she called, looking for her faithful right-hand-man. "Let's be on our way! The ship will be here in just a couple of hours."

Shamgar unlatched the door and held it for her as she rushed past, with Neco close behind, reaching to take the heavy satchel for her.

"Careful, Miss Phoebe," he chided with a laugh. "You'll run into somebody in the darkness going at such a pace."

"Too much to do today," she called over her shoulder. Handing the bag to her long-time worker she explained, "If we wait until the sun is up any higher, the ship will be in and unloading, and the captain will be looking for his money. If this is the same ship that came in last month, that captain doesn't like to be kept waiting. He'll be pacing the dock until all the cargo is claimed and paid for."

Neco nodded his understanding. "I remember, Miss Phoebe. He's an impatient one, if I ever saw it. Those Italians are like that."

"And we have customers waiting for this cloth," she continued. "Winter is almost over, and people want to get their shelters and projects finished before travel weather arrives. We'll have customers in all day, and probably some deliveries to make."

They hurried past a row of houses and several tenements, and turned northward to walk the familiar five blocks down hill toward the waterfront. Phoebe's import shop was near the docks, and while she did not handle the incoming cargo herself, she liked to be near to check the merchandise when it arrived. Cool, damp breezes blew up from the water, and Phoebe drew her shawl closer as she hurried to get in from the gray morning cold.

Reaching the shop, she waited as Neco unbolted the door. Both entered and began to light the lamps and organize orders for the new shipment. "I hope the full number arrives, Neco. We are expecting fifteen bolts of tenting—count them carefully. Hire one of the carts to bring it up the hill. Will you bring me word if there is any problem? I only have five days before I leave for Rome, and the orders have to be ready for portage and loading at Lechaem in just three days."

"You do run a tight schedule, Miss Phoebe. I'll do my

best," Neco assured her. She handed him the cargo orders and purse, and he was out the door to see to his chores. The two had worked together so long Neco knew the business as well as she did. But Phoebe always felt better if she kept a close eye on the process, especially on days when cargo was coming in from the docks.

There were always deliveries to get ready, orders to take, and customers to tend to, and so the morning passed quickly. It was nearly noon when Phoebe sat down to open her snack of wheat bread and cheese, and pour a cup of wine from the jug beside her desk. She had just begun eating when Neco startled her, rushing in unexpectedly, closing the door behind him.

"Are you already back?" she asked. "You really worked fast today!"

"Well, I had to," the servant explained fretfully, "because I was hearing things that troubled me, and I needed to get back to you."

"What things? What did you hear?" she asked, putting down her bread to listen. Neco was a man of few words, but she knew him to be trustworthy.

"I was at the docks, waiting my turn to talk with the captain and pay for the order," he began, "and they were just a little way away, sort of behind the pile of cargo; but I could hear them, and I knew you would want to know."

"Know what? Who was behind the cargo? Start at the beginning, Neco."

"Some Jews making their plans to sail in two days to their celebration feast—what do they call it? 'Passing Over' or something?"

"Passover?" she asked. "Some Jews going on the pilgrim ship to Jerusalem? Is that what you mean?"

"I guess so, Miss. I don't know much about their customs. But they were talking, and I heard them mention Paul, and the name caught my ear. So I moved closer—but careful not to let them know I was listening. I pretended to be looking at my papers, but I was listening hard as I could." He paused to see whether she thought his fears were important.

Phoebe stood up and leaned forward, not wanting to miss a word. "Go on," she urged. "What did they say about Paul? Was it our Paul, or someone else?"

"Well, Miss, I think it was our Paul, because they spoke about hearing that Paul and his partners would be on the ship with them, and they would have money, and it would be their best chance."

"Paul and the others *are* planning to sail for Jerusalem in two days, Neco. And they are taking the collection with them. What else did they say?"

"They talked kind of muffled, but I thought they sounded mean. They said it would be their best chance and it would solve the problem for good. What do you think they meant?" he asked. "Are they going to try to hurt Paul on the ship?"

Phoebe stepped back and sat down slowly, trying to process what she was hearing. "I have no idea, Neco," she responded, "but I am *very* glad you came to tell me. What could they have in mind to do to Paul on the ship?" She took another bite or two and tossed the remaining bread aside. "I think we had better let Paul, or Gaius, or someone know that there may be trouble so they can be prepared."

"Would you like for me to go, Miss Phoebe? If I start now, I can be at Gaius' house in two hours' walking—maybe three, because I'm a little tired from the hauling. I remember the way."

"Let's both go, Neco. Step outside and see if the carrier will help you bring the bolts into the shop quickly. Then ask if he will carry us to Corinth immediately. If he doesn't have another order, he may be glad for the work." As he started for the door she added, "Make it a return trip, Neco, so we can be home by nightfall. I have a feeling when Paul hears this news it may change his plans."

They had never worked so fast, but shortly the fourteen bolts—one had been missing at the dock—were safely inside the shop. The carrier was happy to have another half-day's work, and they made the trip into Corinth without incident. Although the channel road west was always a busy one, the weather was pleasant, and they made good time. Gaius' house was just seven blocks from the city gate, but it was an uphill climb, and the animals were breathing hard by the time the cart reached his gate.

It was about the eighth hour when they arrived, and everyone was just finishing the midday meal. Gaius' slave recognized Phoebe when she knocked and let them in at the door. Taking her shawl, he led them to the dining area where Gaius, Paul, Aristarchus, Secundus, and several others were eating. Gaius rose to greet them warmly.

"I need you to hear my man, Neco," Phoebe told the group. "He was at the dock for me this morning and overheard a troubling conversation between some Jews who were buying fares for the pilgrim ship in two days. I think you need to hear what they said." Turning to Neco she urged, "Tell them everything you heard, please" and the servant stepped forward.

The group listened silently while he retold his story. As he finished, Phoebe said, "We thought you should know, Paul. It doesn't sound good to us, and maybe you should wait for a later ship, just in case they have mischief on their minds."

"I should think so," Aristarchus agreed quickly. "We can't risk that kind of trouble. Those Jews have been after you up and down the coast for years, Paul. And—what a *perfect plan!* If they could get you alone at sea on the trip home, they could knock you out and toss you overboard, and we would *never* be able to prove a thing!"

"Or, maybe they are after the *money*," Timothy ventured. "They may have heard through some of the Jewish believers that Paul has been collecting money for the Jerusalem church. *That* could be what it's about."

Everyone began talking at once, upset at the possibilities, trying to figure the alternatives. After a while Timothy and Gaius suggested a new plan. "Let's just not go on the ship, Paul. We don't have to make Passover. It would be better to take a month or so, go north through Macedonia, and sail out of Troas. We could possibly arrive in Jerusalem by Pentecost. At least we would get there alive with the collection intact."

Paul was thoughtful for a few moments, weighing the idea. "I think so," he finally said. "But, Phoebe, since you and Neco are here, would you consider doing another special favor for me? Coming to warn us as you did was a great favor, but I have another one to ask of you."

"Anything, Paul," she assured him. "I owe you *so much*, I'll do anything I can. What do you need?"

"Tertius and I finished the letter we have been writing to the church at Rome, and I know you go there from time to time on business. I'd like to get the letter to Aquila and Priscilla by the safest way. Would you be able to carry it with you next time you go, and deliver it to the Roman believers for us? I had intended to bring it with me and ask you day after tomorrow. But since we will not be sailing out of Cenchrea now, this is the best opportunity for me to get it into your hands."

Priscilla did not hesitate. "Of course I will, Paul," she assured him. "I plan to sail out of Lechaem in just five days, and I would be happy to take it along. In fact, I feel honored that you would trust me with it."

Paul dispatched Tertius to get the scroll. "Wrap it well for travel," he called. "We don't want the sea air to cause the ink to run. Make it tight, so it will not be too bunglesome for her to carry. Oh, and add a note asking the church there to help her on her way." Tertius nodded and disappeared into their guest room to do the chore.

"We were up late last night finishing it," Paul explained. "It was so helpful to have Tertius to write for me as I thought out the message. Writing is getting harder for me these days. I want so much to go to Rome—well actually to Spain, but Rome on the way—but that will be a few more months from now. Meanwhile, it seemed a good time, since we had the winter here in Corinth, to pen my thoughts to them—let them know I plan to come."

"I didn't know you had plans to go to Rome, Paul,"

Phoebe answered. "I think Priscilla and Aquila will be thrilled to know you are coming. I am really looking forward to seeing them again."

"They have known it was on my heart," the Apostle assured her. "We talked about it back in Ephesus some months ago. But this collection came up, and all the trouble in the church here, and I just could not break free to go. Now, after these brothers and I take the money safely to Jerusalem, I hope to sail to Spain, and make Rome a stop on the way."

"Spain!" Phoebe's eyes were shining. "I've never been there, Paul. Why Spain?"

"Spain has not heard the message of the kingdom yet, Phoebe. Rome has heard—they do not need me to evangelize there. Actually, I need them to help me on my way. But Spain . . ." Paul's brows were raised and his face glowed with anticipation at the thought . . ." Spain is new territory—no man has ever taken the Gospel there, so far as I know. I want to be the first to bring the news to them."

Tertius arrived with the bundled scroll and handed it to Neco carefully.

Gaius stepped forward. "Well, Sister Phoebe, I think we will not see you again on this trip, then," he said a little sadly. "If we are not going to sail east out of Cenchrea in two days, and since you are sailing west out of Lechaem in just five days, our paths may not cross again soon. We certainly do thank you and Neco for making the trip to let us know of this danger. It could have been a fateful voyage, had we not known."

Others echoed his gratitude, and Phoebe started for the

door. "Neco and I really must hurry back to Cenchrea. We left a new order of cloth stashed in the shop, and we have to get it processed for portage to Lechaem in just three days. We need to be home by dark. We promised our carrier we would not keep him past sunset." Then turning back, she walked over to embrace Paul warmly. "We will be praying for your safe journey home," she assured him. "For all of you," she added, nodding to the others. "And Neco and I will take the greatest care of this scroll, Paul. It is a special privilege for me to be able to take it to Priscilla and Aquila and the believers in Rome for you."

"God's peace be with you, my sister," he told her, and they parted to prepare for their separate missions.

"Thank you *so much*, Neco," she said as they climbed into the cart for the trip home. "It's just chilling to think what could have happened if God had not put you in the right place at the right time this morning. All the believers will be grateful to you for your quick thinking." And they rode in thoughtful silence the eight miles back to Cenchrea.

BEHIND THE SCENE
A Study of Acts 20:1–6 and Romans 16:1–2

Paul's High View of Women

Romans 16:1–2 is an unusually intimate look at Paul's high regard for Phoebe. It is the only mention of her in the Bible, but it tells us much. Many scholars agree that Phoebe was entrusted with the task of carrying the precious *Epistle to the Romans* across the Adriatic and around to the believers at Rome. Most of Paul's correspondence was hand-carried by trusted friends, and often he gives a clue in the text of the letter that indicates who the messenger was. In this case, it seems to have been a dependable, respected lady named Phoebe from Cenchrea.

Cenchrea was one of the port towns for Corinth. Situated high above the channel which separates northern Greece (then called Macedonia) and the southern peninsula (then known as Achaia), Corinth was a strategic trade center. A narrow tract of land (isthmus) joined Greece's two parts, but prevented merchant ships from sailing all the way from east to west. Ships coming from the eastern Mediterranean, wanting to avoid sailing around the treacherous southern coast of Greece, could come into the eastern port at Cenchrea. There they off-loaded their cargo, sent it by portage across the isthmus, and reloaded it on westbound ships at the port of Lechaem. From there it sailed on to Rome and places west.

We do not know what Phoebe's business was, but, living in the port town of Cenchrea as she did, it is easy to imagine her being involved somehow in importing and exporting. That she knew Priscilla and Aquila (note how they are mentioned together in Romans 16:1–4) makes it possible that they shared an interest in the importing of fabric for tent making and other related projects. Very likely they had met, either through business or church connections, when Priscilla and Aquila lived in Corinth a few years before. We chose to make that connection in our fiction story, but it is not assured from Scripture alone.

What we do know of Phoebe is that Paul referred to her by three terms: *sister, servant, saint*. She was a Christian sister, known to some of the Roman believers. And she was a serving, ministering woman. Paul used the term *deaconess,* which could have meant several different things to him. Interpreters differ and none has the sure answer. It could mean, first, that she held the office or position of deaconess in the Cenchrean church. There is no indication that women of this position were in an official capacity, but rather that they were recognized as serving in the churches. The same term is applied to the women who served Jesus in Luke 8:1–3. It is a term that denotes women whose lifestyle and commitment set them apart as respected servants of the congregation.

Second, it could refer to wives of deacons, who served along with their ordained or appointed husbands. The office of deacon is well known, as described in 1 Timothy 3:8–13. Men chosen for this office were to be living lives of integrity, fully grounded in the Scriptures, mature and tested. Their wives were given special notice in verse 11: *"Their wives [deaconesses] are to be women worthy of respect, not malicious talkers but temperate and trustworthy in everything."* Whichever Paul meant as he called Phoebe *"servant"* would show his high regard for her as a believer and church woman.

And the List Goes On

Paul did not stop in his Roman letter with saluting just Phoebe and Priscilla. This list of his friends in Rome includes at least seven more women. Read through Romans 16:1–16 joyfully, and see how warmly he remembered his female friends and co-workers. We know almost nothing about most of these: *Mary, Junius, Tryphena and Tryphosa* (probably sisters, and likely twins), *Persis, Rufus' mother, Julia,* and *Nereus' sister.* But what comes through is that, as Paul thought forward to the day when he would soon visit the Roman church for the first time, he could call at least thirty of them by name—nine of them women. Since he had not previously been to Rome, he had met and worked with these ladies in other settings. We have already discovered that he had known Priscilla in Corinth and later in Ephesus. All over the Mediterranean world Paul had known, worked with, loved and respected the women of the congregations. Romans 16 reads like a love letter to his friends of both genders.

Sensible Cautions

But what, you ask, of those prohibitions and regulations he wrote regarding women in worship and church leadership? What of 1 Corinthians 11:3–16, and 14:33–38; Ephesians 5:22–24; 1 Timothy 2:9–15; and other such passages? Paul spoke some very hard things in the context of Corinth and Ephesus. (1 Timothy was originally written for the church at Ephesus.) That *he did not say similar things* to the churches of Rome, Thessalonica, and Philippi is also worth our noting. Some interpreters have felt that the situations in Corinth and Ephesus were unique because of the large temples there for Aphrodite and Diana respectively. These fostered fertility cults, and both had hundreds of temple prostitutes. The climate in Corinth was grossly immoral, as we have seen. Paul may have been more strict with the congregations in those two cities because he did not wish the Christian women to be mistakenly thought to have that standard of living.

It is always somewhat risky to assume that scriptural teachings were intended only for a certain location, or for a particular generation, and therefore do not apply to us now. Yet other customs have changed over the generations, and we do not question those changes. We no longer meet on the seventh day for worship (the Sabbath) as is sternly commanded in the Ten Commandments; and that change is widely accepted. We do not hold our worship services in homes, yet that was the habit of the Early Church. We do not live communally, as the early Jerusalem Christians did, holding all assets in common. And we do many new things, which would be foreign to First Century believers. We publish and use curriculum along with our Bibles, and they did not do that. Many of today's churches prohibit their ministers and elders from use of alcohol, but Jesus made and drank wine. (Paul taught moderation in its use.) We participate in many secular, Sunday activities, but our Bible clearly teaches that we are to keep that day separate—a day for rest and worship. We have an annoying tendency to pick and choose which of the First Century teachings we will keep and which we will ignore.

Were we to insist on keeping things just as they were in Paul's day, we women would all be wearing long robes, head squares, and sandals, and cooking on hearth fires. Life moves on, and the church moves on with it; but as we do we must carefully consider what customs we will adopt and what we will refuse to change. Churches today generally prefer to put those restrictive teachings (mentioned two paragraphs above) alongside others which balance them. Look at Galatians 3:28: *"There is neither Jew nor Greek, slave nor free, male nor female, for you are all one in Christ Jesus."* That puts us all on pretty equal ground. Or Paul's other teaching in 1 Corinthians 11:4–5, which allows women to pray or prophecy in public worship, so long as their dress is modest and feminine.

In the matter of women's participation and leadership in the church, it is possible to come down adamantly on one side or the other, to make the point which is most comfortable to us. The truth is, the teachings of Paul are balanced, and each congregation is allowed to decide under God's Spirit what they feel works for them in their neighborhood. Perhaps what worked in Philippi or Rome would not work in Corinth and Ephesus. Fussing about it neither furthers the work of the Kingdom, nor attracts non-believers to our gatherings. We have more important issues on which to focus.

The Importance of Phoebe's Assignment

Romans is often thought to be the most important of all Paul's writings. Rome was the capital of the Gentile world. Paul had not been able to go there in his journeys, because his work in Asia Minor, Macedonia, and Greece had kept him fully occupied. He did not feel the need to go there to evangelize (see Romans 15:23–24) because others had taken the Gospel there, probably twenty years before. But he needed the Christians at Rome to help support him on his further mission to Spain. The Roman letter was written to introduce them to his teachings and ask them for their support. That Paul asked a woman to carry his precious document is testimony to her integrity and his trust in her.

Much of the time when Paul sat down to pen a letter it was for the purpose of settling some problem or quarrel, or correcting a false doctrine or practice in one of "his churches." He spent a lot of homemade ink and imported papyrus on "putting out brush fires," we might say. The Roman letter did not carry that burden. Instead, Paul wrote down in clear order his theology. And in so doing, he left us a treasure of doctrine and teaching to which we turn again and again. Countless decisions for Christ have been made based on the priceless teachings of "The Roman Road:" verses which clearly mark the way to salvation. Those verses (Romans 3:23, 6:23, 5:8, and 10:9–10) are simple enough to explain to most anyone how to become a Christian. For those alone we value the book of Romans. *Salvation by faith* is the theme of the book.

The backdrop of the Roman letter, as with all of Paul's writings, was the ongoing conflict between Jewish believers and Gentile believers. Issues of whether the Jewish Old Testament laws and rituals had to be observed by Gentile believers never were settled during Paul's lifetime. Their problems may seem strange to us, but we can see ourselves in it easily by looking at the issues of control that still divide our churches today. We may not argue over the need for circumcision; but we certainly fuss over whether one must accept the Bible as without error only in the original Hebrew and Greek manuscripts, or also in today's English versions. We do not hear about whether to eat meat offered to idols now, but we certainly disagree over whether we can use alcohol, hold dances in the church, or allow women to teach mixed classes and be ordained. Issues of control are always with us. Whether it is the Jew setting himself up over the Greek, Pharisees imposing laws on the citizenry, men taking authority over women, or fundamentalists arguing against the moderates—control issues divide us today as much as they did in Paul's day.

In writing the book of Romans, Paul attempted to get beyond the petty issues of the day and lay out basic truths. He talked about the lostness of all people: the Gentiles are lost without Christ, and the Jews are lost without Christ. He laid down the theology of salvation through faith in Christ alone. He taught how important it is to walk in the Spirit and be led by the Spirit. And he gave us wonderful guidelines for living together in harmony, and walking as citizens in our secular world. We turn to Romans again and again for help and light, and we thank Paul (and Tertius) for writing it and Phoebe for carrying and protecting it. It is the Constitution of our faith.

Breaking Down the Walls of Prejudice

Acts 20:1–5 is just the barest summary of Paul's struggle with those who opposed him. After the terrible riot in Ephesus, Paul left and planned to sail directly to Corinth. But finding that the church there was still in turmoil over the issues dealt with in his first letter to them (factions, immorality, misuse of spiritual gifts), he decided to change his plans and delay his visit to them (2 Corinthians 2:1–4). Instead he sent Titus to straighten things out—Titus was probably bolder than Timothy, and could handle the conflict. (Check 2 Cor. 8:16–24 on this.) Paul, meanwhile, traveled the northern route to Troas, Macedonia, and finally back to Corinth when conditions there had improved.

Paul's purpose on this third mission, partially, was to take up among the churches a collection for the poorer, persecuted believers in Jerusalem. In his mind he felt that, if the Jewish believers could see that their Gentile brothers cared for them and wanted to reach out to them with gifts, it would bring the two quarreling factions of the Christian community closer. He arrived in Corinth in the winter, along with a delegation of brothers selected by churches from all over Asia Minor and Greece. Their work was to safeguard the offering, and assure that there was no misuse or loss of it as it made its way to Israel. Winter was not travel time in that part of the world—it was too dangerous to sail after the end of October. So Paul spent three months in Corinth and used his time to write the Roman letter.

It was just as he was ready to sail east to Jerusalem for Passover in March (Acts 20:3) that the plot was discovered which threatened his life. We do not know who discovered it or how it was communicated to Paul and his friends. They were apparently living in the home of Gaius (Romans 16:23), and word must have reached him there. Dr. Barclay in his book, *The Acts of the Apostles,* provides the insight about the pilgrim ship which was setting sail for Israel, and on which Paul probably intended to travel.[4] Paul and his friends foiled the plot by changing their plans and going north instead to Macedonia.

On reaching Philippi, the delegation sailed across to Troas. Paul remained behind a few more days in Philippi with friends (remember Lydia and the jailer's family?) In the process he picked up his old friend Dr. Luke, and the familiar "We Passages" resume in Acts 20:6. Luke and Paul sailed to Troas, rejoined the group, and continued on towards Jerusalem. They did not make Passover, but did plan to arrive in time for Pentecost seven weeks later. Phoebe, meanwhile, was carrying his Roman letter west, to a joyful reunion with her friends in Rome.

Phoebe's Sisters among Us

Our churches are full of Phoebe's sisters: trusted, spiritual women who take responsibility, hold leadership, and are worthy of the title "deaconess." Where would the church be without women as teachers, committee chairpersons, project leaders, mission volunteers, mentors, and ministers? Whether or not we are given official status, we do the work happily, capably, *"as unto the Lord."* We do not need an office, a position, a rank, an ordination, to find and do the things God has gifted us to do in his Kingdom. Like Phoebe, we can be *"a great help to many people."* People do not need to authorize, recognize, or applaud. We do our work for God alone. He sees, he knows, he rewards. That is all we need. By her simple act of carrying God's message around the boot of Italy to the saints at Rome, Phoebe became a hero of the faith.

PART V

Women of The Prison Years

Chapter 12
FOUR GIRLS WHO PROPHECIED
Philip's Family Hosts the Travelers

Chapter 13
LOYALTY AND ROYALTY
Philip's Daughters Witness Paul's Courage

Chapter 14
LETTERS FROM PRISON
Apphia, Empowered to Forgive

FOUR GIRLS WHO PROPHECIED
Philip's Family Hosts the Travelers

Acts 21:1–14

"You girls will all be sleeping in the upstairs room tonight, so the men can have your beds," Philip explained to his four daughters.

"Yes, Father," Miriam answered for the group, reaching to clear the dishes from in front of their guests. "We don't mind that at all."

"You have a gracious family, Philip," Sopater responded gratefully, "but we hate to put the girls out that way. Since we will be staying several days, we easily can sleep in the upstairs room and on the rooftop. The weather is good—summer is almost here."

"Yes, definitely," Gaius agreed. "Nine of us men are quite an imposition on your family, and we would be happy to take the upper quarters, Philip. We have slept outside many times before. In fact, it's almost a habit!" His comments prompted a chorus of nods and laughs among the visitors.

"We don't mind, really," Huldah assured them. "The upstairs room is too small for all of you, but we four girls can fit in very nicely. And it will be cool and pleasant. We will be fine, won't we?" she asked, surveying her sisters.

All heads nodded, and Sopater replied, "We do appreciate your hospitality, Philip, and your gracious abandonment of your bedroom, Girls. And the evening meal was very good. We thank you all."

"Let's ask our closing blessing together," Philip suggested, and the group stood to offer the traditional thanks, hearts and hands uplifted.

"Deborah and Anna, help your sisters finish taking the dishes to be cleaned," their mother instructed, "and then you girls retire upstairs so the men can talk freely down here. And make room for me—I will join you later." Quickly the two younger girls moved to clear the remaining cups and spoons from the table and carry the leftovers to the cooking area. The men settled back on their couches, nibbling from trays of fruit which were left on the table.

Upstairs the evening dusk was creeping in over the sea, and night birds were twittering and diving in the twilight. Here and there the neighbors' lighted lamps and braziers shone in the semi-darkness, and the smell of cooking fires lingered in the air. An early star was visible on the eastern horizon as the girls found cushions and benches and gathered to talk about the day. The family frequently hosted company in their house, but nine men were more than the usual crowd.

"Had we met Paul before?" Anna asked her older sisters.

"He was here five years ago on his way home, but only for a night. You were probably too young to remember," Miriam reassured her. "He is usually in a hurry to get somewhere, but this time he seems to want to stay a while. Pentecost is still a few days away."

"Well, he is older, and I think he may be tired," Huldah ventured. "From what I overheard, this has been a difficult couple of years, what with the riot in Ephesus, and the trouble at Corinth; and then this plot to kill him on the way home. I think he feels secure here."

"It's a risky thing," Deborah suggested, "traveling with all that collection money. They have probably been looking over their shoulders all the way. Anyway, I'm glad they are staying over. I like to hear them talk. And . . . I think Timothy is kind of cute."

"Deborah!" It was Huldah correcting her sister with mock disapproval, and they all giggled. "He's much too dedicated to Paul to even think about finding a wife!"

"Well, I can dream, can't I?" Deborah defended. "Who knows but what God might wish for him to find a wife to share his work—right here in Caesarea?" she finished hopefully.

"And it just might be you—right?" Huldah retorted. "What about Miriam—she's first in the marriage order! Or even me! What makes you think he would pick you?"

"Father isn't looking for any husbands for us to marry," Miriam countered rather sternly. "He feels he needs us in the work of sharing God's word here in this Caesarea area. So, for the time being, none of us needs to plan on a betrothal."

"He told Mother that he did not find any available men among the believers," Deborah added with resignation, "and he won't promise us to anyone who is not a Christian. So I guess we can just all count on being old maids for a while."

"There is also the matter of a dowry," Hulda argued in her practical way. "We aren't a family of much means. Being displaced as they were when they were young, Papa and Mama lost everything. It has been hard for him to start over as a Christian in this Jewish and Roman town. I think the dowries are a big reason he will not promise us."

"Maybe so," Miriam insisted in her older-sister voice, "but the matter of telling the Good News of Jesus is the reason Father gives. He feels we are a great help to him in witnessing about the Lord, and he doesn't want to lose us to men who might not value his work."

"Just forget I mentioned it," Deborah defended. "I was just talking silly talk. We don't have a lot of say about husbands anyway," she conceded with resignation.

"Oh, I thought maybe you were giving us a prophecy," Anna teased. "Let me see . . ." and she drew a mocking line on her open hand. "I read the omen in his palm—it said, 'You will marry the eager third daughter of a deacon.'"

Footsteps on the outside stairs hushed the foolishness, as Timothy and Luke appeared. "What's going on up here?" Luke called. "Would you allow a couple of tired men to come up and enjoy the salt air?"

The four girls stood respectfully, smiling. "Of course," they chorused.

"Here—take this bench," Miriam offered. "We girls can sit on the mats and cushions—we usually do anyway." And she eyed her sisters as they stepped away from the benches to make room for their guests. "Anna and Deborah, run downstairs for some cups and a water jar. We might like a cool drink in a few minutes."

"Please tell us about your voyage," Huldah asked as her younger sisters scurried down the stairs. "Did you come all the way from Troas on one merchant ship?"

"No, two—on two ships," Timothy answered. "Paul chartered space on a small, local, coastal ship from Troas.

It brought us through the islands and around to Patara. But the trip to Tyre was on open water, and that first ship was really not large enough or safe enough. So he found room on an Alexandrian grain ship returning home and booked fares on that. It worked out well. We had a good trip." The girls sat entranced as Timothy spoke.

"We haven't been to sea," Huldah admitted, looking out toward the misty horizon. "We watch the ships come and go—Caesarea is always a busy port—and we wonder what it would be like."

"Maybe some day you may go," Luke offered. "Women do travel some, if accompanied by a husband or guardian. Do you think you would get seasick?"

The two girls looked at each other and giggled. "Probably Anna would," they responded. "She can get sick on the backyard swing!" And everyone laughed.

"But—tell us about your time in Greece and Asia," Huldah pursued. "We haven't been there, either, but maybe some day we can do that, too. We heard about the trouble in Ephesus—the awful riot—and about the plot in Corinth last month."

"Do you always have such exciting adventures?" Miriam asked.

"I'm afraid we do!" Timothy answered, shaking his head. "Life with Paul is just one adventure—often one danger—after another."

"And I think we are in for another one in Jerusalem," Luke finished, soberly. "All the signs point to more trouble there. We don't exactly know what, but we do expect trouble for Paul—and maybe for all of us."

"Oh, I hope not," Miriam responded with sympathy. "Surely he has been through enough. And, with taking the collection to the believers there, the Jews should see that he is trying to be friendly and helpful."

"But the warnings have been very strong," Timothy insisted. "He says the Holy Spirit warned him when he started for home that prison and hardships are waiting. We have all tried to dissuade him from going, but he feels so compelled—so driven—to go."

"Couldn't the others take the collection for him and let him stay here with us?" Miriam suggested. "I would hate to think of trouble befalling him, but I don't have a good feeling about what you are saying."

"We could," Luke nodded, smiling at her concern. "And we have suggested that, but Paul feels he must go himself—even after the Ephesian elders begged and pleaded with him in tears not to go."

"And also those at Tyre," Timothy added. "They also feared for him. But he just won't be dissuaded. We have tried." Timothy shook his head sadly, resigned.

For a few minutes they were silent, but soon Anna and Deborah came bounding up the outside stairs with the water jar and cups.

"Be careful with that jug!" Miriam warned.

Safely on the roof, the two offered drinks to the guests. After a little more conversation, Luke got up and walked to the roof wall, and Timothy followed. They stood looking out over the darkened sea thoughtfully. Stars were shining brightly above, and lights twinkled softly in houses all around. A chilly breeze had picked up, bringing the damp sea air with it.

"This is a splendid harbor," Luke remarked. "But we probably need to go downstairs now, and let you girls get on with your bedtime routines. If we don't stop Paul from talking, he'll go on until midnight."

"Like at Troas," Timothy added, laughing. "He preached so long a young man went to asleep and fell out of the upstairs window!"

"Oh, no!" Deborah exclaimed. "Did he die?"

"He should have," Luke responded, "but he didn't. Paul restored him, and he seemed little worse for the wear. The benefits of youth, I guess. If it had been me, I'd have broken my head for sure."

With that, Timothy and Luke headed down the stairs, and the girls retired to their room. Huldah lighted the brazier against the cool evening air, and they spread their sleep mats, each taking her turn at the wash basin. Before long they were settled under their wraps, thinking quiet thoughts.

"I'll bet I know who Deborah dreams about tonight," Anna whispered.

"Hush and go to sleep," Miriam scolded gently.

"Maybe she'll have a prophecy for us in the morning," Anna giggled impishly.

"Anna, *really!*" Miriam fussed. "You must not make fun of prophecy. It's a gift, and something to be carefully guarded and respected. Do not tease about it any more."

"I know," Anna defended. "I was just having fun."

Several days were spent in the busy chores that come with a houseful of company. It takes a lot of grinding and baking, cooking and serving, cleaning and washing, to see to nine extra men. The girls were a great help to their mother, as Jewish girls are trained to be. It was probably a week later when an unexpected knock brought Philip to the front door.

"*Agabus!*" Philip responded joyfully, "Shalom, Friend," and he ushered the old prophet in the door. "*Miriam!*" he called toward the back room. "Have the girls bring water for our guest's feet and a cup of wine to cut the road dust." Gesturing to a couch, he offered the old man a seat. "We have a houseful of guests, my friend," he explained, "but we can always find room for one more. What brings you in from Jerusalem?"

"I've come to see Paul," the old prophet explained. "I just heard he was headed for Jerusalem, and that doesn't bode well. There will surely be trouble if he shows his face there."

Philip frowned, worried. "We are hearing that from everyone, Agabus," he responded. "Paul and the other men are out at the baths right now, but they will be back soon. You will want to talk with him, and see if he will let the others take the collection to the Jerusalem believers for him. He could stay here with us while they do that."

Anna came in with a basin of water and a towel on her arm, and set about removing the sandals and bathing the dusty feet of their latest guest. Miriam followed with a cup of mixed wine and a napkin of bread. "Can we get you anything else, Agabus?" she asked. "Supper will be a couple of hours away—after the men return from town. But we can fix a tray of fruit and cheese, if you are hungry."

"Thank you, girls," the old prophet said gratefully. "Travel is difficult at my age, but I just felt this was so important. I felt compelled to come and warn Paul. And, yes, I'll take a few figs, if you have them. They are good for what ails you."

Miriam nodded to Deborah who was standing in the doorway, and she disappeared to fill the order. "Luke says everyone has tried to warn Paul," Miriam ventured, "but he just will not change his plans. He says he'll be heading to Jerusalem tomorrow or the next day, in time for Pentecost. He doesn't want to miss the feast."

"He had to miss Passover because of a plot among the Jewish pilgrims to kill him on the ship!" Philip's indignation was evident. "So he is determined to make Pentecost, and I doubt if you can change his mind. But you are certainly welcome to try."

"I hope he will listen to you," Miriam added. "It would be such a loss if anything were to befall him."

"I will do my best, Girl," Agabus responded. "I'll do what I can to make him hear me. That's all I can do. If I have to *draw him a picture,* I'll do that, too."

Miriam disappeared into the cooking area to see that extra food was prepared. "The crowd just keeps growing," she told her mother. "I'll go and grind some extra grain. If we don't need it this evening, we surely will in the morning." Miriam started out the courtyard door, but turned back with a request. "And, Mother," she said earnestly, "do pray that Paul will listen to Agabus when he gives him a warning about the Jerusalem trip. It is all sounding very ominous—very frightening." With that, she slipped outside to the mill.

BEHIND THE SCENE
A Study of Acts 21:1–14

Discovering Philip

We have just two verses about the four daughters of Philip in Acts 21:8–9: *"Leaving the next day, we reached Caesarea and stayed at the house of Philip the evangelist, one of the Seven. He had four unmarried daughters who prophesied."* Those two sentences send us racing to find answers to our questions. Which Philip was this? Why were his daughters unmarried? What role did women prophets play in that situation? Research helps us some, but much will be left to intuition and reason.

We are told which Philip: *"one of the Seven."* Recall the story of the choosing of the Seven in Acts 6, which we embellished in Chapter 2 of this book. From that we know that he was *"known to be full of the Spirit and wisdom."* His name betrays that he was from the Greek-speaking, Hellenist community of Jews, and he was respected and trusted to be one who would look after the needs of the growing Christian church in Jerusalem.

We pick Philip's story up again in Acts 8, following the death of Stephen. That story was our introduction to Saul (now Paul), who was assenting to the bloody death by stoning. Soon a great persecution broke out, scattering the believers from Jerusalem into the surrounding territories. *"Those who had been scattered preached the word wherever they went. Philip went down to a city in Samaria and proclaimed the Christ there."* (See Acts 8:4–5 and following.) His preaching was so powerful that crowds listened and believed. One thrilling incident from Philip's mission concerns an evil sorcerer named

Simon, who had claimed to have divine powers. When the town folk turned away from him to believe in Jesus, Simon also pretended to believe—but with wrong motives. Hoping to regain his popularity and following, he tried to buy the power of the Holy Spirit with money. The Apostles soundly reprimanded him, and he came to true repentance. (Find this in Acts 8:9–24.)

Probably a better known incident from Philip's work at that time was his encounter with the Ethiopian God-fearer on the Gaza Road. The man was in the service of the queen of Ethiopia and was returning home from worshiping at the Temple in Jerusalem. Philip engaged him in conversation about the scroll of Isaiah, which he was reading, explained Jesus to him, and led him to faith. When they came to a desert watering stop, the Ethiopian asked Philip to baptize him. Joyfully the man went on his way as a believer, and *"Philip . . . appeared at Azotus and traveled about, preaching the gospel in all the towns until he reached Caesarea."* (See that wonderful story in Acts 8:26–40.) It was one of the first instances of the Gospel being carried into Africa by a new believer.

Now we find Philip, about twenty years later, still in Caesarea, married, and with four daughters. In this instance Philip is hosting Paul and his friends on their journey to take the collection to Jerusalem in time for Pentecost. Does it strike you as interesting that Philip's first experience with Paul had been when his close friend Stephen met death by stoning at the hands of Paul's friends and with Paul's blessing; but now, twenty years later, he gladly opens his home to this former adversary? Can you visualize Paul—the former Saul who had run Philip and all the Christians out of Jerusalem, costing them their homes and all they had—now being welcomed into Philip's home for a lengthy stay? It is a shining story of forgiveness and second chances, adding further to our admiration of this deacon and man of God.

About Those Daughters . . .

Why were Philip's girls unmarried in a culture which betrothed their daughters at age fourteen or before? Someday we will ask them, but several possibilities occur. They were involved with their father in the work of preaching, and perhaps he had dedicated them to that work and to the single life. In 1 Corinthians 7 Paul gives teachings about single living. (See verses 25–35.) Because of his sense of urgency about sharing the gospel, Paul suggests that the unmarried stay that way and give themselves to the work of the church instead. *"An unmarried woman or virgin is concerned about the Lord's affairs. Her aim is to be devoted to the Lord in both body and spirit."* Paul contrasts this to married women who must also be concerned for the needs of their husbands and families. This thinking may have come into play in Philip's house.

Another possibility is the dowry problem. Families were expected to provide handsome gifts of property to the prospective groom. It could be possible that Philip, having given himself to ministry all those years, was not a man of means. Recall that he was part of the dispersion following the death of Stephen, and very likely left behind all that he had begun to own in Jerusalem. His material situation may not have allowed him to bargain for husbands he felt worthy of his very special girls.

Lastly, as we suggested in the fiction vignette, he may not

have found suitable men to whom to promise his daughters within the community of believers in Caesarea. Paul was teaching that a believer should never marry an unbeliever. Certainly, if the girls were engaged in sharing the Good News, Philip would have to find Christian husbands for them. Maybe, at this point, he was still looking. We have no clue as to their ages, but have guessed, from the time frame of Philip's life, that they may have been between twelve and eighteen years old.

Even more intriguing than the unmarried state is their ability to prophecy. We are always curious about how that role played out in the Early Church. You probably noticed that, in the fiction story, we assigned each of the four girls a name, and the names were borrowed from women whom the Bible calls prophetesses. *Miriam* is described in Exodus 15:20. She was the sister of Aaron and Moses, who led the Israelite women in singing and dancing to celebrate their crossing over the Red Sea. *Deborah* was a judge of Israel (Judges 4:4), who held court and also led the troops to victory in battle! *Huldah* was the prophetess to whom the priests went for counsel during the days of Josiah, when the lost scroll of the Law was found in the temple (2 Kings 22:14). *Anna,* of course, is the old prophetess who met Mary and Joseph in the Temple and blessed the infant Jesus (Luke 2:36). We have no idea what Philip and his wife named their daughters, but these seemed suitable for our fiction vignette.

On the Business of Prophesying . . .

In Old Testament times prophets were sometimes called *"seers,"* because they had visions and dreams and interpreted

God's message from them. At times they were called *"diviners,"* because they were able to understand and explain the mysteries of God. In New Testament times, prophesying was not just a phenomenon of the Christian church. Greek prophets read oracles and omens. Sorcerers used magic to divine. But it was different in the Christian community.

The New Testament definition of prophet is this: *a spokesperson for God, who receives God's message and gives it to the people.* The message did not always involve a future mystery: often it was simply a message for that day and situation. Prophecy differed from teaching in that it did not interpret the message, but just spoke it in total truth. Prophets were brave people, because the word of the Lord was not always popular. Sometimes we compare this concept of prophesying with preaching—telling the word in truth. Philip was engaged in the Acts 1:8 concept of witnessing *"in Jerusalem and Samaria."* His daughters were doing that with him.

Are women given the gift of prophecy? We have just discovered four who were so designated in the earlier Scriptures, and four more here who had that gift. At Pentecost, Peter quoted the prophet Joel in saying, *"I will pour out my Spirit on all people. Your sons and daughters will prophecy. . . . Even on my servants, both men and women, I will pour out my Spirit in those days, and they will prophecy"* (Acts 2:17–18). There is no gender prohibition in Scripture against women speaking for God. To be gifted for that task and to be called to do so, but to refuse, would be a sin. *To prevent a gifted and called woman from speaking God's message would be to run counter to the work of the Holy Spirit.* That is a warning some churches need to heed today.

Understanding Paul's Desire to Go to Jerusalem

In Acts 20:16 we catch the urgency of Paul's trip home to Syria and Jerusalem. He had missed Passover, the most sacred of Jewish feasts, because of the discovered plot against his life in Corinth. Now, hoping to reach Jerusalem in time for Pentecost, he set out to take the northern, overland route. He and his seven traveling companions went instead through Macedonia, staying in Philippi on the way. Their mission was to collect a benevolence offering from the Greek and Macedonian believers for the poorer saints at Jerusalem, caught in famine and persecution. To safeguard the venture, Paul had requested a delegation of trusted men from the contributing churches to accompany him to Jerusalem. In this way he could assure that no funds would be lost, and there could be no suspicion cast on the mission. Paul was always a person of integrity and accountability. (Check this out in 2 Corinthians 8:16–21.)

Look at those outstanding delegates listed in Acts 20:4. Take special note of the names, for they are heroes of the church, but not often mentioned or familiar to us: *"Sopater son of Pyrrhus from Berea, Aristarchus and Secundus from Thessalonica, Gaius from Derbe, Timothy also [from Lystra], and Tychicus and Trophimus from the province of Asia [Minor]."* In Philippi Paul added Luke, so with those two, the party numbered nine trusted men. Finally, after getting together at Troas, they began the journey eastward, first by coastal ship, sailing through the islands off the shore of Asia Minor. Because of the hurry, Paul did not make a stop with friends in Ephesus, but rather sent for the elders of the church to come to him at the coast, thirty miles distant. The Apostle's emotional charge to them is recorded in Acts 20:17–38. Paul felt this would be his last meeting with them, and his words were full of love, deep concern, and warnings to *guard the flock*. Fearing for his life, and sensing the dangers ahead, the Ephesian elders begged Paul not to go up to Jerusalem. It was the first of many recorded warnings he received.

Reaching Patara, they would have transferred to an ocean-worthy vessel, and crossed the open sea to Tyre. The ship stayed there seven days, and again the local believers begged Paul not to go on to Jerusalem (Acts 21:3–4). The sailing leg of the journey ended at Ptolemais, where the party spent one day with those believers; and then continued overland on their way. Caesarea was a major stopping place. There are fifty days between Passover and Pentecost, and by the time they reached Caesarea at least thirty-eight of them had passed. Paul had a few more days to rest before the feast, and chose to spend those in the home of Philip and his four daughters. It was while he was there that he received the third and fourth warnings against going to Jerusalem.

A curious incident happened when the old prophet Agabus came from Jerusalem. Knowing the situation in the city and hearing of Paul's plans, he spoke frightening words to the Apostle. (Find this story in Acts 21:10–11.) In the manner of Old Testament prophets, Agabus used an object lesson to try to dissuade Paul. He took Paul's leather belt and tied himself with it, hands and feet. *"The Holy Spirit says, 'In this way the Jews of Jerusalem will bind the owner of this belt and will hand him over to the Gentiles.'"* On hearing this, Paul's friends did not just *ask* him not to continue the journey, they *pleaded with him* to remain in Caesarea. They could take the collection for the saints to the city without him. Surely it was not worth the risk for him to go. Why would Paul not heed these many warnings? We find the answer back in Acts 20:22–24.

> "And now, compelled by the Spirit, I am going to Jerusalem, not knowing what will happen to me there. I only know that in every city the Holy Spirit warns me that prison and hardships are facing me. However, I consider my life worth nothing to me, if only I may finish the race and complete the task the Lord Jesus has given me—the task of testifying to the gospel of God's grace."

Walking in the Spirit

It may not even be possible for us to understand that level of commitment. Paul, knowing his life was in danger, understanding clearly that prison and hardship lay ahead, was willing to risk all that he had in order to further preach the Gospel in every possible place. Paul was living out his own advice from the eighth chapter of Romans, the letter he had written just a few months before. Hear these selections:

> "The Spirit himself testifies with our spirit that we are God's children. Now if we are God's children, then we are heirs—heirs of God and co-heirs with Christ, if indeed we share in his sufferings in order that we may also share in his glory . . . if God is for us, who can be against us? . . . Who will bring any charge against those whom God has chosen? . . . We are more than conquerors through him who loved us."

Paul's faith was amazing! A few years later, after the worst prophecies had proven true, having spent several years already in prison, Paul wrote his Philippian friends from

Roman house arrest. Listen closely for whether he regretted his decision to go on from Caesarea to Jerusalem.

> *"I eagerly expect and hope that I will in no way be ashamed, but will have sufficient courage so that now as always Christ will be exalted in my body, whether by life or by death. For me, to live is Christ and to die is gain."* (Philippians 1:20–21)

The entire first chapter of Philippians is worthy of reading at this very point in the story, for it shows the heart of a man we cannot begin to match. Life to Paul *was* Christ. Safety, comfort, status, being exonerated—these had little value for him. He cared only that his life glorify his Lord, and that the Good News be preached. Suffering brought him deeper in his knowledge of Christ. It opened doors for him to testify. He welcomed it, at whatever cost. Is it any wonder that those who traveled with him, those who loved him, those who housed him in Caesarea, held him in highest regard? He bade them goodbye, and the party was on their way.

That is the last Bible mention of Philip's four daughters in whose home Paul and company sojourned. We have to wonder at the impact that week had on their lives. We common mortals grow mightily when we rub elbows with great men (and women) of God. The example they set, the words they speak—these stay with us beyond anything we may read in a book. Surely, in years to come, the girls would look back on the week Paul visited in their home, and measure their own actions and decisions by what they had experienced. But, do not tell the girls good-bye just yet. We will meet them again in the next chapter.

LOYALTY AND ROYALTY
Philip's Daughters Witness Paul's Courage

Acts 21–26

"Philip! Come quickly!" Charisa called to her husband through the courtyard door. "I hear people outside, and the dogs are having a fit."

Closing the goats up quickly, Philip left his late evening chores and hurried into the house and toward the front door.

"Who could be at the door at this late hour?" Charisa worried, close on his heels. "We were not expecting guests, were we? The girls have already started for bed."

"I guess we'll see," Philip answered as he made his way to the door and slid back the bolt. "Who is there?" he called, opening the door just a crack. "Oh!" he said, startled at what he saw.

"Shalom, Brother—we apologize for coming so late at night," Gaius responded. "But we have been traveling three days, and just arrived from Jerusalem. It is Aristarchus, Timothy, and I. Could you put us up for the night?"

The door was open wide by now. Philip embraced the three warmly and showed them into the house. Miriam came in from the girls' room and greeted the guests with surprise.

"Mother, shall I get Deborah to help me with a wash basin and some wine?" she asked. "Our guests are surely tired and thirsty." Getting a nod, she disappeared into the next room.

"Here, let me help with your travel bags," Philip offered. "And please make yourselves comfortable. We would be happy to have you all stay here. What brings you back to

Caesarea so soon?" he asked, as they settled onto couches. "It's been hardly two weeks since you left for Pentecost in the city. We expected that you would remain longer before returning."

"We have very bad news," Timothy answered anxiously. "Paul has been arrested on false charges. There was a hearing, but the Jews were potting to kill him; and so the commander has brought him here for safety."

"Here to Caesarea?!" Philip questioned as he sank onto a couch. "Why here? Could they not handle it in Jerusalem where he has friends and family?"

"You cannot imagine the danger—the rioting—the hysteria—over this," Aristarchus explained. "The whole thing is a terrible misunderstanding, but Paul was almost killed twice, and the commander had to get him out of the city."

"They sent him with four hundred foot soldiers and seventy cavalry, and traveled by night to protect him," Timothy added. "We didn't even know about it until the next morning. Paul's nephew came and found us to let us know. The three of us just grabbed up our belongings and headed out immediately. We had to follow and find out how Paul is doing."

"Four hundred foot soldiers?!" Philip echoed, questioning.

"And *seventy mounted soldiers*," Gaius affirmed. "Unbelievable, isn't it? Enough to guard a king." And they all shook their heads.

Miriam came in with a jar of mixed wine and cups. The travelers took the offering gratefully as she poured for each of them. "Deborah will be here in a minute to cool your dusty feet from the road," she told them. "But, please tell us more. I just don't understand how all this came about."

"Neither do I!" Charisa agreed. "Why did Paul get arrested in the first place? What did they accuse him of?"

"Well, it's something of a long story," Aristarchus began. "But I'll shorten it because the hour is late, and we need to let you people get to bed. When we first got to Jerusalem, everything went well. The church received us gladly—"

"—and received our offering gladly, I might add," Gaius said a little wryly.

"They asked about Paul's work, and he made a report," Aristarchus continued. "Everything seemed to be fine. But then James and the elders brought up some problems, and made some suggestions, and it all went sour very quickly."

"What were the problems?" Philip prompted.

"And what were the suggestions?" Charisa pursued. "We can't imagine."

"The problems had to do with false rumors circulating about Paul's teaching," Aristarchus explained. "The Jerusalem believers—those of Jewish heritage, at least—are very much tied to keeping the Law, and apparently some people had told them that Paul was teaching the new Christians to disregard the Law—which he has never done."

"In fact, Paul has always had utmost respect for the Law," Timothy defended. "He even required that I be circumcised before he would let me join his mission."

"But he did not ask that of Titus," Gaius reminded him. "That may be where the rumors began. At any rate," he continued, "James and the elders thought it would put the rumors to rest if Paul sponsored some men who were taking the Nazirite vow—to demonstrate his respect for the Law."

"So, he did that," Aristarchus continued, "at great expense to himself. He paid for their offerings—"

"There were four of them," Timothy interrupted, "—four men—so he had to buy four lambs and four rams, and the other offerings, and pay for the burning of their hair, and all of that."

"He paid for them, and was at the Temple with them each day," Aristarchus continued, "but some visiting Jews from Ephesus area saw him in town, and recognized Trophimus and Tychicus who are also from that province. They accused Paul of bringing Greeks into the Temple. And they started a mob scene—right there in the Court of the Gentiles."

"Paul had not done that," Timothy defended. "He had not taken Greeks into the sanctuary, but they would not listen to his defense. They would have beaten him to death if the soldiers had not arrived quickly to stop them."

"So," Miriam asked, "is that why they brought him here to Caesarea? I should think the cohort in Jerusalem could have settled that."

Deborah came in with water and towels and began washing the guest's feet. The cool water helped soothe the agitation aroused by the retelling of unsettling events.

After a few moments, Gaius continued. "Actually, the Jews were so incensed that the commander could not get a straight story, so he locked Paul up, and was going to have him flogged, but—"

"Flogged?!" Philip interrupted. "He is a Roman citizen—they cannot *flog* him!"

"They didn't," Timothy assured him, "but they had every intention of it. They even had him stretched out and tied up when he asked them if they could flog a Roman who had not even had a trial. The commander, Lysius, came personally and had him untied but held him in jail overnight for safety."

"They had a hearing before the Sanhedrin the next day," Aristarchus continued, "but it did not resolve anything. It just turned into a big argument when Paul told them he believed in the resurrection. You can imagine how that set the Sadducees against the Pharisees! The commander thought Paul was going to be torn into pieces, so he took him back to jail."

"That was the last time we saw him," Timothy said sadly. "Then his nephew came and told us about the plot and Lysias having him brought here by night. We had thought it would all blow over and he would be released, but now he is here under Felix's jurisdiction, and we don't know what will happen. Felix can't afford any more conflict with the Jews—he is in trouble with them already."

"They are holding him in Herod's Palace, I guess," Philip surmised. "That is where they take people like Paul. But what was this plot? Who was behind that?"

"The Jews—we think the Zealots," Gaius answered. "You know how the Jews had been after Paul in all the cities of Asia and Macedonia and Achaia. Paul's nephew was in the Temple and happened to overhear some of them talking secretly about killing Paul. They were going to ask the Sanhedrin to call him in again for further questioning, and then forty of them were going to lay in wait and kill him as he was brought from the fortress to the hearing room." Gaius stopped to take another drink before continuing. "The nephew went to the prison and told Paul, and Paul sent him to Lysias."

"And did Lysias listen and believe him?" Charisa asked skeptically. "That would surprise me."

"Actually, God was with him, and Lysias *did* listen and told him not to let anyone know he had revealed the plot," Gaius responded. "Then Lysias got together the four hundred footmen and seventy cavalry, and mounts for Paul to ride also, and made the trip by night to Antipatris, and then on to Cesarea. We think they arrived late yesterday or early today."

"But the foot soldiers only went as far as Antipatris," Timothy clarified. "We met them coming back as we were setting out on the way day before yesterday. We heard part of this story from them, so we know it is true."

"So now Paul is back *here?*" Deborah asked, trying to pick up the story, having missed the first part. "Then, where are the others—Sopater, and Secundus, and Luke, and the others? Are they also coming back? Because we girls can move upstairs again, if that is true."

"Not tonight, Deborah," Timothy assured her. "They will be here in a day or two. I think they will want to stay until after Paul's trial under Felix, and then sail back home as soon as they know he is free. We can stay up in the upstairs room tonight, so you won't have to waken your sisters and move."

"That sounds like a good plan," Philip agreed. Then, turning to his wife, "Charisa, we will need to take food and drink to Paul in the morning and see if they will let us care for him while he is incarcerated."

"Yes, of course," she responded. "But, it sounds to me as if that plan of James to pacify the Jews really backfired."

"Yes, it did," Timothy quickly affirmed. "And James and the elders were nowhere to be found when the trouble happened."

"Didn't they try to see him, or intervene with the Jewish leaders?" Miriam asked, surprised. "I would have expected them to come to his defense."

"Well, no—but then they hardly had time before the trouble began," Aristarchus hedged.

"I think they are so fearful of another persecution breaking out that they just want to keep their heads low and keep peace with the Sanhedrin," Gaius ventured. "I had expected more courage from them, but—"

"—but it didn't happen," Timothy finished. "I guess we expected more than they felt they could give."

"That disappoints me," Philip responded thoughtfully. "I knew them to be braver than that twenty years ago when Stephen was killed. I hope they are not losing their fire for witnessing. We all need them to be strong."

"Well, I hope this trial gets over soon, and Paul gets released," Timothy said solemnly. "We have plans to go to Spain by way of Rome, and Paul had hoped to sail before winter. He has already written the church at Rome of his plans, asking them to send him on his way. And Luke and I plan to sail with him."

"He *will* be going to Rome," Miriam spoke with conviction. "But maybe not as soon as he planned. These trials can sometimes drag on and on."

" . . . Like this conversation," Gaius countered with a smile. "We have kept you all up long enough. Thank you for the drink and the thoughtful hospitality, Girls. We men can see ourselves upstairs, and let you all get some rest. In the morning we will rise early and go to check on Paul."

The three men shouldered their duffle and started for the door. "Here," Miriam said, handing a lighted lamp to Timothy. "Take this to light the upstairs lamps. It's warm, and I doubt you will use the brazier, but there are several blankets in that chest in the corner of the room if you need them."

"I'll follow you up and bring some water for the night," Philip offered. "And in the morning, I'll go with you to Herod's Palace. I know some of the guards and perhaps can get permission for us to visit Paul. We will all rest better after we have seen and talked with him."

"Meanwhile, let's all be praying for his quick release," Timothy pleaded. "God has much more work for him to do." And with that they started for their beds.

BEHIND THE SCENE
A Study of Acts 21–26

A Study in Loyalty

My husband is often heard to say, "God is infinitely resourceful." We never know from where he will provide resources to meet our needs—his options are endless. He can work good out of the worst events of our lives. Who was this nephew who came to Paul's rescue when the Jews hatched their ugly plot to kill him? We have no previous mention in the Bible of Paul's family. We know him to be from Tarsus in Cilicia, and Luke has given no earlier clue that he even had a sister, let alone a nephew in Jerusalem. There is no explanation for how or why the young man was in position to overhear the plot. But we can be thankful that God put him in the right place at the right time and that he had the sense to go immediately to his uncle and reveal what he had heard. His loyalty illustrates the old adage, *"blood is thicker than water."* Seemingly out of the blue he acted to save Paul's life.

Did you pick up on the absence of James and the elders when Paul was up against the wall? We cannot be certain that they kept silence and distance. Dr. Stagg and others feel that Luke's omission of their involvement shows they did nothing to defend Paul after his arrest.[5] He relies on the historian Josephus, who indicated that James and the other elders had taken the path of appeasement or compromise with the Jewish leaders, keeping the Law along with them, to avoid further persecution. Stagg equates this stance with the loss of power in the Jerusalem church. We have to wish this is not the true interpretation, but it could be. If so, it sheds light on why God arranged for the nephew to be available for the crisis.

Certainly no loyalty was to be found among Paul's former colleagues, the Jewish leaders. Paul's conversion to Christianity had turned him from an ally to a formidable adversary about twenty years before, and they had been laying traps for him every day and in many cities across the Mediterranean since. So deep was their grudge, and so bitter their hatred, that they tried to kill him on at least four occasions during this episode. The first time occurred in the Temple, when the Roman soldiers intervened. It happened again in the court of the Sanhedrin, when the commander took Paul away to the barracks; and again with a plot to ambush him as he was brought back for a second hearing. (Find these in Acts 21:27–36, 22:22–25, and 23:12–22.) The fourth incident happened about two years later, when the Jews appealed to Festus to return Paul to Jerusalem for trial, again plotting to ambush him on the road. (See Acts 25:3 for this last plan.) God protected Paul on each occasion. It may have been partly for Paul's protection that God allowed this Caesarean imprisonment to last over two years.

The Prison Years in Caesarea

Caesarea was the Roman capital of Judea: a port city, and headquarters for the Roman army stationed in that area. The Roman governor, Felix, probably held Paul in the Palace of Herod, which had been converted to the Roman praetorium. After five days the high priest, Jewish leaders, and their esteemed lawyer came from Jerusalem to Caesarea to bring charges against Paul personally. Their accusations actually seem to us to compliment Paul's success: *"We have found this man to be a troublemaker, stirring up riots among the Jews all over the world. He is a ringleader of the Nazarene sect and even tried to desecrate the Temple."* (See Acts 24:5.) Paul's influence, and the success of his preaching, was surely being felt by his adversaries.

Paul made a good and reasonable defense. An educated, brilliant, and experienced lawyer himself, Paul explained that none of the above could be proven. He also stated the true purpose of his visit to Jerusalem: *"After and absence of several years, I came to Jerusalem to bring my people gifts for the poor and to present offerings."* (See Acts 24:17.) Felix could see that this was a matter of Jewish in-fighting, so he determined to hear an objective view from the Roman commander, Lysias, who had witnessed the riots.

Meanwhile, we find a very significant statement in Acts 24:23: *"He ordered the centurion to keep Paul under guard but to give him some freedom and permit his friends to take care of his needs."* In the strength of this statement, we have chosen to re-involve Philip's wife and four daughters with Paul's plight. Surely they were among his friends in Caesarea, and would have seen to him and his companions again. Less than two weeks had elapsed since Paul had left them to go to Pentecost.

In the long interval as they awaited Lysias' coming (there is no word that he did come), Governor Felix and his wife, Drusilla, sent for Paul and listened to him discuss the Christian faith. We would feel better about Felix's interest if the text did not disclose that he was actually hoping Paul would offer him a bribe for his release. It is further testimony to Paul's integrity that he did not take the offer. Felix was an unpopular ruler, and the Jews had already protested to Rome about him. After two years, he was recalled to Rome, and replaced by Festus. Unwilling to further anger the Jews, against whom he would have to defend his governorship to Roman authorities, Felix did not release Paul, and the incarceration extended beyond the two years.

Were Paul and his friends discouraged? Humanly speaking, we would think so.

Paul had his mind set on sailing as a free man to Spain, by way of Rome. This was an unwelcome delay, and we do not know how he spent the time. Perhaps he wrote letters, similar to those which are credited to the Roman imprisonment which followed. Knowing Paul, we can be certain that he witnessed at every opportunity. It is likely that the delegates who had traveled with him eventually returned home, but some may have stayed. Their stories are another study in loyalty.

What Became of Paul's Traveling Companions?

Three of the eight are not mentioned again after this trip to Jerusalem to bring the collection to the poor. *Gaius,* originally from Derbe (see Acts 20:4), may or may not have been the same Gaius who was with Paul in the Ephesus riots (Acts 19:29). Gaius was not an uncommon name. There was also a Gaius who had hosted Paul as he lived in Corinth the second time while writing the letter to the Romans (find this in Romans 16:23). *Sopater,* also called *Sosipater* in Romans 16:21, had been with Paul earlier in Corinth, but is not mentioned again in the Scripture. *Secundus* of Thessalonica also fades from the picture at this point. It is likely these three returned home as the imprisonment dragged on.

The other five continue to surface in Paul's later writings. We know that *Aristarchus,* also from Thessalonica, was present with Paul in the Roman imprisonment (see Colossians 4:10 and Philemon 1:24). Paul actually refers to him as his *"fellow prisoner." Trophimus* and *Tychicus* who were the Asians (probably Ephesians) sighted with Paul in Jerusalem—the immediate cause of the Jews' Temple riot—both have later mention. In his Roman prison letters, Paul credits Tychicus with carrying the letters to Colosse, Ephesus, and Philemon for him. (Refer to Col. 4:7–9 and Eph. 6:21–22.) Writing to Timothy during what is believed to be his second Roman imprisonment shortly before he was executed, Paul mentioned that Trophimus had been left in Miletus because he was ill (see 2 Timothy 4:20). We will meet some of these again in the last chapter of this book.

Timothy, of course, remained close to Paul much of the remainder of his life, and was like a son to him. (We looked at Timothy closely in Chapter 7 of this book.) We have to think that these two years in Caesarea were significant ones in Timothy's life, as he visited Paul in prison often to comfort his "father in the faith." Perhaps he brought him food and clean clothing. Paul must have used the visits to instruct Timothy more deeply in the faith and share his heart with him. Realizing that his own days of active ministry were growing short, Paul began to rely on Timothy to take up his work and extend his witness. Just a few years later he sent Timothy to Ephesus as pastor. These two years in Caesarea could have been part of Timothy's training—his "seminary education," so to speak.

Finally, *Luke,* Paul's trusted friend and physician from Philippi (whom we also met more fully in Chapter 7), and the only one still with him in the second Roman imprisonment ten years after Caesarea (2 Timothy 4:11). How did Luke spend these two years? We can envision him visiting with Mark and Matthew in Jerusalem, talking with them about the Gospels they had written, finding out their sources. Luke had not been present in Israel during Jesus' life, and we know he structured his Gospel on research and interviews (Luke 1:1–3). Luke's gospel is very like Mark's and Matthew's—we call them *the Synoptics* for this reason—but it contains material not found in those two. He must have talked with Jesus' brothers to learn the birth narratives and family stories, which are in his Gospel alone. From Peter and the other Apostles he heard and included stories that had been omitted from the writings of Mark and Matthew: treasures like *the Good Samaritan* and *the Prodigal Son* are found in Luke's writings alone. We think he also may have talked to Cleopas or his wife and learned about the Emmaus Road experience.

In addition, Luke likely used the time to research for the early chapters of Acts—also events which took place before he became part of Paul's work. He must have talked with Peter about the Pentecost miracle, and his early missions to heal Tabitha and preach to Cornelius. Mark may have told him about the night the angel freed Peter and sent him to his mother's house. Philip could have revealed the story of the choosing of the Seven, and the Ethiopian's conversion on the road to Gaza. When else would Luke have had time for all that research? The Caesarea years were significant to Luke—and so to us, as we benefit greatly by the two books he left us: Luke and Acts.

Witnessing to Royalty

The strongest truth of Acts 21–26 is how Paul took every opportunity to witness about Jesus, regardless of personal risk. In these six chapters of Acts, which relate to his arrest in Jerusalem and the two years in Caesarea, Paul witnessed fearlessly on at least five occasions.

- Standing under Roman guard on the steps leading up to the Fortress of Antonia, Paul asked permission to address the angry mob which had just nearly beaten him to death. He them told clearly, in their preferred Aramaic, of his conversion on the Damascus Road, and his call to take the Gospel to the Gentiles (Acts 22:6–16).

- Before the Sanhedrin, highest court of the Jews, on the very next day Paul again testified to his belief in the resurrection of Christ. That night, God encouraged Paul through a vision of the Lord himself saying, *"Take courage! As you have testified about me in Jerusalem, so you must also testify in Rome."* (See Acts 23:11.)

- At his first hearing before Governor Felix, and with his accusers present, Paul again stated his belief in the Way of Jesus and his resurrection (Acts 24:14–15).

- In his private talks with the governor and his wife, Drusilla, Paul discussed his faith again (Acts 24:24–26). The topics he bravely chose stood in stark contrast to the sinful lives of this Roman authority and his wife.

- Two years later, before Governor Festus and the King and Queen of Judea, Agrippa II and Bernice, Paul again told his conversion story (Acts 26:18). Follow that story on to see how he confronted the King with an invitation to believe in Jesus.

Drusilla, Bernice, and Agrippa II are a study in themselves. All were children of Herod Agrippa I and grandchildren of Herod the Great. They lived soap-opera lives of multiple marriages, affairs, and incest. Their personal disgraces were not what Paul saw when he witnessed before them however, but rather their need for the Lord. Such was the courage, the single-mindedness, of Paul's mission. He shared Jesus with everyone and in every circumstance. No wonder that his friends returned such admiration and dedication to him. (We considered making Drusilla and Bernice the focus of this chapter, but concluded that their lives were not worthy of that much attention. They were empowered women, to be sure—empowered by their royal positions—but that is not the *spiritual empowerment* which is the focus of this book.)

Faithful and fearless would describe Paul. How his friends must have watched in awe as he spoke out time and again in front of the high priest and Jewish leaders, the Roman commander and governors, the king and queen—and now was on his way to testify before Caesar Nero himself!

The Ministry of His Friends

Two years is a long time to wait in a Caesarean prison. How did his friends minister to his needs? (Recall here Acts 24:23.) We can easily imagine Philip's wife and daughters praying for his release through all the ups and downs of the trial processes. Generally prisoners had to provide for their own food and clothing while incarcerated, so they probably helped him in that way, too. Visits and encouragement would have been welcomed. Perhaps they housed some of Paul's friends during all or part of that time.

Paul was God's man for the hour—the Billy Graham of that day! Though he would have preferred to sail to Rome as a free citizen, he followed the wisdom of God and made the most of every opportunity. He was living out his own advice to *redeem the time* and be an *ambassador for Christ*. And all over the empire Christians and adversaries were watching to see if his life would ring true under these adverse conditions and unexpected setbacks. We have one more chapter to go, and it is a thrilling (and unexpected) ending to our known-story of the *Empowered Women* of the Early Church.

LETTERS FROM PRISON
Apphia, Empowered to Forgive

Acts 28:11–31 and Philemon

Epaphras and Aristarchus were up before the others, preparing the usual breakfast. Wheat porridge bubbled softly in an earthenware pot over the charcoal fire, and the smoke curled lazily upward, seeking a vent hole in the wall above the hearth. The two friends set out ten stoneware cups and a bowl of mixed wine. Breakfast would be ready when the others awoke. It wasn't fancy fare, but it would see them into the day.

Below on the street heavy carts rumbled by, finishing their night's work of carrying limestone and mortar supplies to the construction site down the way. The man in the apartment beneath them was stirring—they could hear him calling to his sons who worked with him on the river barges. It was time to head for the docks. Rome was rising to another summer day.

Looking out their small window, Aristarchus could not see the river. Rows of apartments blocked that view. Only the drab gray of stone tenements was visible in either direction down the narrow street. A lonely window box of flowers here and there was all that colored the view. "Where do all these people come from?" he wondered aloud to his friend. "I always thought Thessalonica was a big city, but I never knew what 'big' was until we came to Rome! There must be a million people here—and they all speak a different language."

"Colosse was never like this, either," Epaphras concurred. We had a lot of people, but not nearly so many slaves and foreigners. This is really a strange place to live. I not only *am* a foreigner, I *feel like* a foreigner—every time I set foot on the street. I get homesick each time Tychicus and Onesimus talk about going home to Colosse. My heart would really like to go with them, but I just can't leave Paul yet. Maybe when his trial is over we can all go home."

"Maybe so," Aristarchus agreed. "I guess we are all hoping that will be soon."

"Did I hear my name?" It was Onesimus, tying a belt over his tunic and running his fingers through his hair. "Did you decide to go with Tychicus and me, Epaphras? We'd be glad for the company." Aristarchus ladled a cup of wheat porridge for him and handed him a spoon.

Ephaphras filled a cup of porridge for himself and turned to his young friend, shaking his head sadly. "I was just saying that I get homesick every time I hear you and Tychicus talking about going home, but I want to stay here until Paul's hearing is over. When will you leave?"

"Paul said he would write a letter for me to take home to my master," Onesimus answered. "When he and Tychicus finish the letter to the church in Colosse, and he adds that note to my master, Philemon, I guess we can be on our way. Tychicus is to carry the letters for him—and smooth the way for me. Wish me luck," he finished with a fearful look.

"We will do more than that," Aristarchus assured the young slave. "We will pray that your master will be gentle with you and receive you as a brother now that you believe in Jesus."

"Yes, we will," Epaphras agreed. "I know Philemon and Apphia well, and they are good people. I think they will be lenient with you—especially if Paul asks them to."

The runaway dropped his eyes and studied his bare feet before answering. "I don't deserve their kindness. I stole some pieces of their family silver when I left, to buy my fare across the sea, and I have no way to repay them. I may be in for a sound thrashing. Or they could even *sell me* to get their money back. I don't know what to expect—I just know Paul says I have to go home and try to make things right."

"Maybe God will smooth the way for you," Epaphras said hopefully, putting an arm around the young man's shoulders. "Pray and believe, Brother."

The others were beginning to stir, and Aristarchus ladled more cups of porridge for the crowd as they came into the kitchen one by one. Luke took his gratefully and started back toward his room, cup in hand.

"How is the book coming?" Aristarchus asked him. "Have you filled up that scroll yet? At the rate you are going, you'll be out of papyrus soon—or out of ink!" The group laughed as Aristarchus poked a little fun at their doctor friend.

"This is his *second* full scroll," Timothy added playfully. "He's already filled up the one about Jesus, and now this one is looking pretty fat to me. I hope he finishes soon, or he'll want me to tote it around for him, and I'll need a goat cart!"

Luke turned back and smiled at their good-natured fun. "Well, I'm getting pretty near to the end of the story. I've finished all the part about Peter and Philip, and most of the story of Paul's first missions. Paul has been so busy with the letters he is writing, I can hardly get him to sit still and talk with me about it. The good thing about the part I am writing now is, I lived through a lot of it with him, and so did Timothy and Aristarchus. Between the three of us we can reconstruct most of the story pretty well, and we don't have to bother Paul for details often." Looking at Timothy across the room he added, "I was hoping you and Epaphras could run down to the shops and buy us some more papyrus with part of that Philippian love offering. We really are about out."

"Sure, Luke—when we come back from the baths we will do that—if it is all right with Paul to spend the money. Have you gotten to the part about our shipwreck yet?" Timothy asked, his face lighting up at the memories. "That could take a whole scroll by itself! What a *trip* that was! What a *winter!* I hope never to live through something like that again!"

"Nor me!" Aristarchus agreed. "One shipwreck in a lifetime is enough for any sane man! We were blessed to get through it alive."

"We got through it because God wants Paul to testify before Nero," Luke said firmly. "Probably we would all have been lost had not God promised to get Paul to Rome safely. I think Paul has a special connection to God—his prayers get heard more than mine do—though not always in the way he expected! It's an adventure to be his friend."

"Paul is chosen," Epaphroditis chimed in from the doorway. "That's why God looks out for him. His work is important to the Kingdom. We are *all* blessed to be his friends."

"So, you are up, Epaphroditus," Epaphras noted. "When

do you and Timothy leave for Philippi? Paul has finished that letter, hasn't he?"

"Yes, he has," Timothy and Epaphroditis answered almost in unison.

"We're just hanging around a while to see how the trial comes out," Epaphroditis explained. "But if Burrus keeps delaying the date, we may have to leave without hearing the outcome. Paul wants us to get his message to Philippi before the sailing season is over—so that just leaves us less than two months, and we don't have a date for the hearing yet."

"You may as well begin packing," Aristarchus said drearily. "It doesn't look like this trial is going to get on Nero's docket for a while. It just isn't that important to him, and the Jews won't come from Jerusalem to press charges. They are just happy to have Paul here under guard and out of their hair."

"Paul just sent another inquiry to Burrus' office last week," Luke countered. "He hopes to hear something today or tomorrow about a trial date."

"Oh!" Epaphras interrupted—"we should offer a cup of porridge to Philo—we should not forget him. He's been on duty all night and is probably starving. It's about time for his replacement to show up." He ladled a cup of wheat broth for the guard and held it out expectantly.

Timothy took it and started out the door. "It's time for the old man to get up anyway," he said. "I'll wake Paul and see if he is ready to eat," and he disappeared down the hallway toward Paul's sleeping quarters. Luke took the opportunity to slip quietly back to his room and resume his writing. Epaphras followed Timothy with a cup of broth for Paul.

Right on time there came a sharp knock at the door, and a voice announced, "Roman guard!" Epaphroditis moved to unbar the apartment door and stood aside as Hermes entered in full uniform. Months into the routine, Paul's friends knew most of the guards by name and welcomed them warmly.

"Philo and Paul have not come out yet," Epaphroditis explained. "You can knock on his door—I think he is up. Timothy and Epaphras just took them some breakfast."

The guard moved toward Paul's room with a nod, removing his cape and helmet as he walked. The apartment was almost a second home to him, he had drawn this duty so often. His knock brought Philo to the door. The two exchanged a few words, Philo came out and Hermes went in, and another day had officially begun.

Before Philo could take his leave and start down the stairs, another knock sounded, and a woman's voice called out, "There are three of us here with your breakfast. May we come in?"

Silence hung heavy as the group waited for Philo to approach. "State your business," he said with some authority, opening the door wide.

Startled at the sight of the uniformed soldier at the door, the ladies stepped back against the stairwell wall. "We are from Paul's church," Julia began, somewhat intimidated, "and we have come to tend the house and bring food— that's all." The three ladies waited for permission to enter.

"Very well," Philo consented, and he bolted past them and down the stairwell, happy that his watch had ended.

Epaphroditis, still near the door, welcomed the women and showed them into the crowded kitchen. "We've had porridge, but I think we would not turn down something more interesting. What did you ladies bring?"

"We stopped at the Greek bakery down the way for hot bread," Julia began, setting a basket down on the small table. "We know how Paul loves the Greek pastries, and we thought it would cheer him."

"And Andronicus sent this large cheese to go with it," Junias added, lifting a cloth heavy with the stuff from her shoulder. "Where is a knife, so we can cut this?" she asked, rummaging in a crock of utensils.

Aristarchus reached up over the hearth, took one from a hook, and began slicing generous chunks for everyone. Those who had finished their porridge refilled their cups from the wine bowl and began to devour the treats.

Persis had straggled in the door last, broom and bucket in hand. "Would one of you men mind terribly going down to fetch water from the pipe to fill this bucket, so I can begin the cleaning? We came to do the slave's work, since none of your wives is here to tidy up the place, but I can hardly manage a full bucket up three flights of stairs."

Embarrassed appreciation spread over the men. "We thank you ladies for tending to us," Aristarchus answered. "We're too poor to hire servants, too far from home to have slaves, and too clumsy to keep the house very well. Eight men can really mess the place up," he apologized.

"Here—I'll haul it for you," Onesimus said, reaching for the empty vessel. "I'm good at this kind of thing, and I may as well get back in practice. I'll be doing it for my mistress when I get home—if they will have me back." And he was out the door and down the steps tending his chore.

"Shalom, Brothers and Sisters," came a voice from down

the hallway. Paul and Hermes had emerged from his quarters and were settling on couches in the main room. At his voice the others began to drift down the hall and find seats about the room and on the floor. It was time for morning prayers, and they had much on their hearts. Sunlight filtered dimly through the small window as the group gathered. The women left their chores, Luke came out of his room, and Onesimus arrived and set down his bucket. Paul's guard took a respectful position by the entry door. Prayer time with Paul was the high point of their day. It was a touch of heaven in a strange and pagan world—a touch that eased their anxious minds. Quiet settled over them as Paul began the day with a blessing.

Requests and prayers followed, with special earnestness concerning a date for Paul's trial. Almost a year had passed since their arrival, and they were all ready to get on with their lives, yet reluctant to leave without knowing Paul's fate.

"How is the Colossian letter coming?" Luke asked Paul. "We are almost out of papyrus and ink."

"We are well into it," Paul began. "Should finish it . . ."

"I want you to hear what Paul wrote them yesterday about Jesus," Tychicus interrupted. "It's really beautiful—I think inspired. Let me get it for you," and he moved to retrieve the scroll from Paul's room.

"I'll get a light," Timothy offered. "It would be hard to read in this room the way it is." He hurried to the kitchen to light a candle from the cooking hearth and returned just as Tychicus was unrolling the scroll to read.

"Here it is," Tychicus said. "Listen to this little part, and you will see what I mean."

"He [Jesus] is the image of the invisible God, the firstborn over all creation. For by him all things were created: things in heaven and on earth, visible and invisible, whether thrones or powers or rulers or authorities; all things were created by him and for him. He is before all things, and in him all things hold together."

"And it goes on, but I just wanted you to hear Paul's wonderful description of Jesus."

The group nodded agreement, and Paul began to explain. "The Colossians are having such a struggle with the Jewish heresies, and the influence of Greek thinking, and they are confused. I think the best remedy for that is to give them a high view of Jesus. When they understand who he is, they will not need the other ways of thinking."

"Well, I agree the words are inspired and beautiful, Paul. Thank you..." Aristarchus broke off his thought as another sharp knock sounded at the door.

"State your business," Hermes called, and a voice answered.

"I bring a message from Burrus."

Hermes opened to the currier, took the parchment with a nod, and closed the door. The group waited anxiously as he handed the sealed paper to Tychicus to read.

Breaking the seal, Tychicus glanced over the notice and looked at Paul soberly. "It isn't good news," he said, shaking his head. "They have postponed the hearing again, until next month."

Paul sighed and took a deep breath. Then looking at Timothy he said, "Son, I think you and Epaphroditus need to pack and leave for Philippi tomorrow. If we wait, you will miss the sailing season." Turning to Tychicus he continued. "And Tychicus, it is time for you to take Onesimus and head home to Colosse. If you will help me pen that letter to Philemon today, we can send you on your way with our blessings. I think this is the best way."

The group was silent a few moments, processing the disappointing turn of events. Finally Timothy stood and moved to where Paul was sitting. Kneeling beside him he pled, "But Paul, we do not want to leave you now—not until we know. We could stay a few more weeks."

Paul's eyes were earnest as he answered. Putting one hand on Timothy's shoulder and the other on Tychicus' knee, he tried to reassure them both. "I will be just fine here. Luke and Aristarchus and Epaphras will stay with me." Looking across to where the women sat weeping he continued, "and Priscilla and Aquila are here—and these fine ladies from the church. I will be in good hands here. I want you to go. Book your fares at the docks today, and try to be on a ship in a day or two."

"But—what if—" Timothy could not bring himself to finish the thought.

Paul reached out to embrace his young companion for a minute, and then released him. Taking Timothy's shoulders in both hands he said softly, "Remember what I told the Philippian church in my letter, Son:

> 'For me to live is Christ and to die is gain. If I am to go on living in the body this will mean fruitful labor for me. Yet what shall I choose? I do not know! I am torn between two: I desire to depart and be with Christ, which is better by far; but it is more necessary for

you that I remain in the body . . . Whatever happens, conduct yourselves in a manner worthy of the gospel of Christ.'"

With that he squeezed Timothy's shoulders, stood and motioned to Tychicus. "We have work to do, Friend. Let's get that letter to Philemon and Apphia written so these men can be on their way."

"The papyrus is low, Paul," Luke reminded him. "Shall we go and buy another few leaves at the shop today? We both still have writing to do."

"How much is left?" Paul inquired.

Luke and Tychicus eyed each other, and Tychicus ventured a guess. "I think only about three or four pieces," he said.

"Then I would rather save our money for the ship fares of these men," the old Apostle decided, "and we will just use fewer words and make do with what we have."

Luke and Tychicus nodded their understanding. It was time to begin the work of the day.

BEHIND THE SCENE
A Study of Acts 28:11–31

The Trip to Rome

It took three ships and a near-fatal shipwreck, but Paul and his three friends finally arrived in Rome, probably in the spring of 60 a.d. Luke gave many precious sections of his

Acts scroll to the harrowing trip, and we wonder if he was still working through the trauma as he remembered and wrote about it. Don't miss his amazing retelling in Acts 27 and 28. Historians credit Luke with one of the best accounts that has come down to us of sea travel in that day.

Paul must have had some trepidation about arriving in the magnificent capital city of the empire. Here he was, one small Jewish tentmaker, standing against the powers of the world of his day. His countrymen were against him, the government was indifferent to him, and the city overwhelmed him. How relieved he must have been when two Christian welcoming parties met him on the road between the port of Puteoli and the city of Rome—a journey of about 140 miles. To feel the warm embrace of brothers, and know some were concerned about his plight and would look after him, must have set his heart at ease (Acts 28:11–16).

In Rome Paul was held under house arrest, not in the infamous prison dungeons. (See Acts 28:16 for this. He would experience the dungeons several years later when he was re-arrested.) The leniency probably resulted from Festus' letter to Burrus, who was in charge of Nero's affairs of state (Acts 25:25–27). A good recommendation from Julius, the centurion who had seen him safely through the seas to Rome, may also have helped. We know that Luke was with him because he included himself in the famous "We Passages" regarding the trip recorded in Acts 27–28. Timothy was there, as noted in Paul's salutations to the churches at Colosse and Philippi (see Phil. 1:1, and Col. 1:1). And Aristarchus must have come along from Caesarea also, because Paul includes him in Colossians 4:10, along with Mark and Demas, whom we did not mention in the fiction story.

Life in the Imperial City

Rome was a crowded metropolis of about one million when Paul arrived. It is estimated that about a third or more were slaves, and thousands were foreigners who lived and worked there in various capacities. Paul and his friends and guards would have entered through the Appian Way, under the large Appian Aqueduct, and proceeded past the Circus Maximus northward to the imperial palace and official government buildings. It must have been a daunting entry. Assigned to live on his own, and at his own expense, until the trial, Paul and his friends must have been at a loss to find housing. Only the rich could afford individual houses in Rome by that time. The precincts around the central city had been converted to tenements and apartments many years before, and rents were high. It was said that a flat in the city cost as much as a house in the country.

The magnificence of the city was somewhat tarnished by the stench of sewage and decay. So many residents in so small a space presented great dangers. Heating, cooking, and lighting were by open flame, and apartment fires were frequent. Caesar's fire brigades could not usually contain them before great damage had occurred. Although there was an abundance of fresh water for all, sanitation was primitive, and disease rampant. Crime forced residents to bar their doors and windows. Ventilation was poor, so living was stuffy and dreary. After weeks on the open seas, Paul and his friends must have felt very closed in by life in Rome.

In his book, *Life in Ancient Rome,* F. R. Cowell enlightens us about the society of the First Century.[6] The cities were crowded, and the land outside had been gobbled up by personal estates and villas of the rich. Common folks had no land on which to raise their food, so the Roman government had developed a plan to provide free grain to its citizens. Rich from taxation of its outlying provinces, Rome imported millions of bushels of wheat from North Africa, Egypt and Sicily. This was stored at the port of Ostia in huge warehouses, and barged into the city daily up the Tiber River, where it was distributed. Large mills processed the flour. Olive oil was imported through the same route. The Roman men, with slaves to do their menial work, spent their days at the baths, the Forum shops, and the gymnasiums. Women stayed mostly at home, while the men did the marketing for them. It was a far different life than most of Paul's companions had known.

Searching for the Women in Paul's Life

Paul's Roman apartment was a formidable male domain! We know from Philippians 2:19–30 that Timothy and Epaphroditus were there, preparing to carry Paul's thank-you-letter back to that church. Epaphroditus is one of the heroes of whom we hear little, but he meant much to Paul's work. Colossians 4:7–14 explains that Tychicus had been busy helping Paul write his letters (compare to Ephesians 6:21–22) and was about to be trusted to take the Colossian letter home. In tow he would have the now-repentant, run-away-slave Onesimus, returning to his master Philemon to make amends for his crime of desertion. Epaphras, another Colossian, had chosen not to go with them but would stay behind with Paul. Add Luke, Aristarchus, Mark, and Demas to that, and we have an apartment full of Christian brothers. But where are the women?

Reaching back to the letter Paul wrote to Rome from Corinth about two or three years earlier, we found them in Romans 16:3–16. Believing that several of them were still there, we borrowed them for our fiction story. It was the pattern that Paul's friends looked after him during his times of incarceration. Luke affirms in Acts 28:30–31 that Paul had the freedom while in Rome to have his friends in and out of the house, but with a guard always present (see 28:16). From the list of Paul's Roman friends we chose three to represent the women in his life: *Junias,* who was his relative, *"Persis, another woman who has worked very hard in the Lord,"* and *Julia,* another of the saints.

Priscilla and Aquila may also have still been there. It is thought that they had re-established their tent-making business in Rome after Nero came into power in 54 A.D. (check Rom. 16:3–4); and remained there until the great Rome fire of 64 A.D. made it imperative that the Christians again flee. Much later we find them back in Ephesus (see 2 Timothy 4:19).

There is another woman who fits into this era with Paul, and we will meet her shortly. But before we sail across the sea to Colosse, let's take a few minutes to look at one of the letters Paul wrote from his Roman house arrest. It will help us give *Philippians* greater value as we read and study it in the future.

Paul's Prison Letter Examined

Ephesians, Philippians, Colossians, and Philemon are the letters credited to Paul's first Roman imprisonment. In each of these Paul references his chains, but in Philippians he says much more. The Philippian church, always dear to Paul's heart, had sent him a love offering to help defray his living costs in Rome. It was not the first offering they had sent him (see Phil. 1:3–5, and 4:10–19), and it came at a very critical time. The offering was brought personally by Epaphroditus (Phil. 2:25–30) who had fallen quite ill during his stay in Rome. Now that he was better, Paul was sending him back with Timothy (Phil. 2:19–24), who was his right-hand man.

Sharing his heart in an unusual way with these Macedonian friends, Paul wrote to them of his incarceration and the concern that he might not be exonerated at the trial. His thoughts were not for his own well-being, but for the furtherance of the Gospel to which he had given his life. *"Now I want you to know, brothers, that what has happened to me has really served to advance the gospel"* (Phil. 1:12ff). He goes on to explain how his confinement had emboldened the Roman Christians to speak out for the Lord. Further, through Paul's faithful witness, even the palace guards and officials had heard the gospel and some had believed (see Phil. 4:22).

The concern for his safety was not idle worry. Nero was an unpredictable and cruel tyrant. In the earlier years of his reign he was less violent toward Christians, and the climate for them improved. But as his madness consumed him, the outlook began to change. Facing the uncertainty, Paul counted his life expendable. He prayed for courage to stand strong whatever the circumstances should bring. And he kept hope that he would be released to return to his original plan: a fourth mission to Spain, where the Gospel had not yet been proclaimed. He instructed his friends to do the same:

> "Whatever happens, conduct yourselves in a manner worthy of the gospel of Christ... I know that you will stand firm in one spirit, contending as one man for the faith of the gospel without being frightened in any way by those who oppose you... For it has been granted to you on behalf of Christ not only to believe on him, but also to suffer for him..." (Phil. 1:27–29).

Then he went on to instruct them in love and warn them of false teachers.

Paul truly believed that through suffering he could better know Jesus, and that was his ultimate goal. He served because he loved. Christ was his whole life! Probably the most challenging verse of the book is found in Philippians 3:10: *"I want to know Christ and the power of his resurrection and the fellowship of sharing his sufferings, becoming like him in his death* . . ." It was his passion, his obsession, the goal for which he let go of all else and moved forward with a single purpose. Is it any wonder his life had such power and integrity before his friends? He was an incredible man!

The Rest of the Story

Luke cuts the story off abruptly at the end of Acts 28. Many historians believe that Paul was released about 62 A.D., and had possibly three-to-five years to preach and travel before his second arrest and martyrdom. If so, what did he do during that time? His life pattern was to travel, preach, establish churches, and write letters; and we have to believe that he continued that until the end.

The New International Version Study Bible expounds this view eloquently in the article, "Paul's Fourth Missionary Journey," giving references and maps to illustrate.[7] (See the map and notes in 1 Timothy.) Based on Paul's hopes in Romans 15:23–29, and his admonitions to friends to prepare his guest room, they suggest that he and his team probably visited Spain, Crete, Miletus, the towns of Asia Minor; and then Philippi and Nicopolis in Macedonia. The Early Church father, Eusebius, is quoted as implying that all this took place.

Two of Paul's pastoral letters, 1 Timothy and Titus, are dated to these last few years of freedom. Second Timothy is the last known writing that we have, and it was written during his second imprisonment, just before Paul's death. Paul had sent Timothy to be pastor in Ephesus and had left Titus for the work in Crete. Others had gone elsewhere on missions. *"Do your best to come to me quickly . . . Only Luke is with me. Get Mark and bring him with you . . . Do your best to get here before winter."* (Read his last, poignant written words in 2 Timothy 4:9–22.)

The question remains, why did Luke discontinue the book so abruptly? Where is the rest of the story? Let this humble writer suggest a reason or two. The length of the book of Acts is telling. It was a long volume by First Century standards. The scroll was probably very full—twenty-five feet long or longer. (Refer to the article on "Papyrus," in *The Zondervan Pictorial Dictionary*.) Luke had reached a natural stopping place. He had accomplished his purpose: that of tracing the movement of the Gospel from *"Jerusalem, and all Judea and Samaria, and to the ends of the earth."* If there were more story to come, he could write a third volume later. For the time being, he had no more to tell, and the book was full.

Since Luke was with Paul when his final letter to Timothy was written (see above) any further travels by Paul probably included him. Why did he not write that third scroll? We can only speculate. Perhaps his friend's death at the hands of Nero's executioners traumatized him seriously. Could it be that Luke, too, met death at that time? For some reason not only Luke, but also Timothy, Titus, Aristarchus, Mark, and the others chose not to chronicle the closing years of Paul's life. We shall have to wait to ask them about it when we see them in heaven. But we do have one more tale to tell!

ONESIMUS ARRIVES HOME

Onesimus and Tychicus had been most of two weeks on the water, and another week trekking overland, by the time they reached the outskirts of Colosse. The rugged climb up from the port below Ephesus, through the mountains and the highland pastures, had caught them unprepared. Months of living in the smoggy city of Rome, followed by time confined shipboard, left them unfit for mountain foot travel. By the time they caught sight of the city, both were spent and anxious to find a place to rest.

"We are not far from Philemon's place now," Tychicus called over his shoulder. "How do you want to handle this delicate situation? Would you like to go first and make your peace with your master, and then I'll follow?"

"I've been thinking about that for miles—for days, really," the runaway slave began. "No, I think I would rather you go first and make peace for me, and then I will follow. If you could talk with my master, and show him Paul's letter, maybe he will not be so angry when he sees me."

"I'll do that, if you think it best," Tychicus assured his companion. "But I have a pretty good feeling about this, Onesimus. I think he will hear Paul's request and take you back. We have all been praying for that."

The two walked in silence as Onesimus thought about his answer. "I don't know, Tychicus. A slave can be beaten, or flogged, or even crucified for stealing from his master and running away. I lay awake at night thinking about those things. I only hope you are right."

So it was that, when Philemon's front door slave responded to the knock, he found only Tychicus standing at the entry. "Please tell your master that Tychicus of Ephesus is here to speak with him," he said quietly.

"My master is busy, but I will call his wife, Sir," the slave replied, closing the door gently.

Tychicus spent a few thoughtful moments rehearsing his speech as he waited for them to return. Shortly the slave reopened the door, and Tychicus was face to face with a matronly lady, almost old enough to be his mother.

"I bring you tidings from the Apostle Paul, Ma'am," he began, handing her the parchment. "He sent a special message to you and Philemon from Rome."

Apphia took the letter and stepped back to invite the stranger in. "If you are Paul's friend, then you are welcome here," she said. "Please tell me your name and how Paul is doing. We heard that he had been sent to Rome for trial about a year ago, but we have had no word recently." Unrolling the letter, she glanced at it as Tychicus answered her questions; but rolled it up again, unable to read its words. "Let me call my son, Archippus," she suggested. "He can read the letter to me. My husband is gone for a few hours on business."

As she left, she spoke to the front door slave about water for their guest's feet and wine to cool his thirst. Tychicus settled onto a couch near the door, waiting.

It was not long before Apphia returned with her handsome son and introduced him to Tychicus. Archippus was reading Paul's letter as he came into the room behind his mother. He stopped to properly greet the guest before asking, "Where is he? Where is Onesimus? Has he come home?"

Apphia caught her breath at his words. *"Onesimus?!* Is *that* what this letter is all about?" she demanded, looking at Tychicus. "How do you know about Onesimus?"

It took Tychicus several minutes to relate the story of how they had found Onesimus homeless at the Roman baths and had invited him to Paul's apartment where he could find food and a bed and get in out of the cold. It was Epaphras who had recognized the slave and confronted him, causing his secret to come out. In the days to follow, Paul had allowed the runaway to stay with them and had shared Jesus with him. "Onesimus is now a believer," Tychicus finished hopefully, "and he wanted to come home and set things right with you. He knows he wronged you when he left."

"Where is he now?" Archippus asked again.

"I believe he is around back at the slave quarters," Tychicus answered. "He wanted you to know the whole story before he came to ask your forgiveness. Perhaps we should call for him, so he can tell you himself." Tychicus was carefully studying the faces of Apphia and Archippus as they pondered these truths.

"We never expected to see the man again," Apphia said softly, sinking onto a couch across from Tychicus. "He stole some silver when he left—I guess that is how he bought his way to Rome. *Rome?!*" she repeated, shaking her head. "He's been in *Rome* all these months? No wonder we could not find him, Archippus! We never would have dreamed that he would be in *Rome!*"

"I wonder what Father will say," Archippus responded.

"Paul hoped he would be understanding and lenient," Tychicus said quietly. "Onesimus has changed—he is a believer now. Paul really loved him, and wanted to keep him, but he felt he could not do that without your father's permission. He hoped your father would take the slave back, or . . ."

"But what of the *silver?*" Apphia asked. "He should at least have to be punished for taking the silver."

"Paul is offering to pay for that himself," Tychicus hastened to explain. "I think he said that in the letter, Ma'am."

A slave came in with water for Tychicus' feet, followed by a second one carrying a bowl of wine and some cups. "Let's just take a few minutes to think about this before we call Onesimus in, Mother," Archippus suggested. "I know he has wronged us, but if he has repented and is asking our forgiveness, there would be nothing gained by punishing him. I think Father may see it that way."

The slave served a cup of wine to each one and returned to the kitchen for a tray of cheeses and olives. Tychicus received the gracious hospitality gratefully and made light conversation. "You have a lovely home here," he commented. "We have been in Paul's cramped and crowded apartment for a year, and it feels luxurious to be in a real house."

"The church meets here," Apphia responded. "In fact, they will come this evening. We have a strong church here. Epaphras was our first leader—he brought the Gospel to us—but now that he has gone to Rome, my son Archippus leads us." She smiled at her son proudly as she spoke. "He knows Paul well."

"You know, Mother," Archipppus said quietly. "This situation with Onesimus is very like our own."

"Whatever do you mean, Son?" his mother asked. "We are not slaves—we have never been. We were born free citizens."

"Yes, that's true, Mother. But we were slaves to sin, and Jesus redeemed us." Then, turning to Tychicus, he asked, "Do I read between the lines here that Paul would like to have Onesimus back—a free man?"

Tychicus' eyes were shining. "Yes, Archippus, that would be Paul's heart in this. He would not ask your father for that, but it would be his dream. He has really come to love and depend on Onesimus over these past months."

Archippus turned to his mother again. "Do you see it, Mother?" he asked. "Jesus has redeemed us from our sins and set us free. Now we have an opportunity to do that same thing for our brother, Onesimus. We can make a gift of him to Paul. How can we do less?"

"Talk with your father when he returns," Apphia answered quietly. "Perhaps he will see it in that light and give Onesimus his freedom. Now," she addressed her guest brightly, "will you honor our home by spending the night with us before you go on your way?"

"I would like that very much," Tychicus answered. "I am carrying a second letter from Paul to the churches here in Colosse and Laodicia, and would like to have opportunity to present it at tonight's gathering."

"Wonderful!" Archippus responded enthusiastically. "We will want to hear and study carefully everything he says. And all the believers will want to hear the news about Paul. We pray for him every time we gather, you know—and also for Epaphras, who is one of us."

"I will tell the servants to prepare the guest room. The believers will bring food for a supper after the gathering. It will be a joyful evening, Tychicus—a very special evening indeed!"

POSTSCRIPT
Philemon

How we wish we knew the ending of this story! The Bible leaves to our imagination how Philemon received Paul's request to deal gently with his repentant slave. For us who have never lived in a slave society, the entire situation is difficult to comprehend. But we are indebted to Dr. William Barclay, the famous English theologian, for a tantalizing historical footnote to Onesimus' story.[8]

Dr. Barclay tells us that, about fifty years after Tychicus and Onesimus brought Paul's plea to Philemon in the

Colosse area, the venerable church father, Ignatius, was being taken to Rome to die as a martyr. As he traveled he wrote letters, some of which still survive. One was to the church at Ephesus, extolling their wonderful bishop. And what was the name of that bishop of Ephesus about 110 A.D.? He was Onesimus! Could he have been "our" Onesimus, the converted, runaway slave? We can never know this side of heaven. But if there is a chance that he is—and we have to love that possibility—it is a great testimony to the saving grace of Jesus in the lives of a slave and his master.

Over the centuries scholars have pondered why this one little piece of personal correspondence from Paul survived to be included in the Bible. Surely he wrote many personal letters on papyrus, but in time they were destroyed or decayed. Paul's letters to the churches, on the other hand were copied over and over, and preserved carefully for us. And along with them this little piece of writing to his friend, Philemon, also survived. It is known that Paul's letters were officially collected together in Ephesus long after his death, probably—you have already made the connection—by the bishop at Ephesus. So, could it be that Bishop Onesimus added his personal letter to the collection as a witness to the power of Jesus in the life of a believer? That would make the story even dearer.

We are indebted to Apphia, who is thought to have been the wife of Philemon (see Philemon 1:1–2), for giving us reason to end our book with this heart-warming story. With her we conclude our study of *Empowered Women* in the Early Church. We have traveled from Israel to Asia Minor, trekked through Macedonia and Greece, sailed to Rome in stormy seas, and now we leave the story in the highlands of Phrgyia. All along the way we have pushed back the curtains of the stage where men had the leading roles, to find the women behind the scenes. They, too, were *empowered* by the Holy Spirit to share in the work of carrying the Gospel to *the ends of the earth*. We are proud to call them our foremothers and mentors in the faith. Proud indeed!

Endnotes

1. Wyatt, Kenneth. *The Apostles*. Tulia, Texas: Y-8 Publishing Company, 1989.

2. Stagg, Frank. *The Book of Acts: The Early Struggle for an Unhindered Gospel*. Nashville: Broadman Press, 1955. Page 140.

3. Swindoll, Charles. *So You Want to Be Like Christ? Eight Essentials to Get You There*. Nashville: Thomas Nelson, 2005. Page xiii.

4. Barclay, William. *The Acts of the Apostles*. Louisville: Westminster John Knox Press, 2003. Page 161.

5. Stagg, Frank. *The Book of Acts: The Early Struggle for an Unhindered Gospel*. Nashville: Broadman Press, 1955. Page 222.

6. Cowell, F. R. *Life in Ancient Rome*. New York: Berkley Publishing Group, 1980.

7. *The NIV Study Bible*. Grand Rapids, Michigan: Zondervan, 1985. Pages 1836–1837.

8. Barclay, William. *The Letters to Timothy, Titus and Philemon,* Philadelphia: Westminster Press, 1960. Pages 315–316.